When Giants Fall

When Giants Fall

An Economic Roadmap for the End of the American Era

Michael J. Panzner

WILEY

John Wiley & Sons, Inc.

Published by John Wiley & Sons, Inc., Hoboken, New Jersey.
Published simultaneously in Canada.

For general information on our other products and services or for technical support, please
contact our Customer Care Department within the United States at (800) 762-2974,
outside the United States at (317) 572-3993 or fax (317) 572-4002.

Wiley also publishes its books in a variety of electronic formats. Some content that appears
in print may not be available in electronic books. For more information about Wiley
products, visit our web site at www.wiley.com.

Library of Congress Cataloging-in-Publication Data:
Panzner, Michael J.

   When giants fall : an economic roadmap for the end of the American era/
   Michael J. Panzner.
      p.   cm.
   Includes bibliographical references and index.
   ISBN 978-0-470-31043-4 (cloth)
      1. United States—Economic conditions—21st century.   2. International
economic relations—21st century.   3. Natural resources.   4. Geopolitics—21st
century.   5. Balance of power.   I. Title. II. Title: End of the American era.
   HC106.83.P36   2009
   330.973—dc22

                                                                2008040635

Printed in the United States of America
10   9   8   7   6   5   4   3   2   1

To Catherine,
A light that is always there, warming my soul

Contents

Preface

Most people accept change as a constant in their lives. They are born, grow old, and die. Their lifestyles, relationships, and perspectives fluctuate and evolve. They interact with others in a variety of settings, deal with new and unusual circumstances on a regular basis, and add to a burgeoning catalog of unique experiences without necessarily trying too hard. Meanwhile, the march of progress and an array of natural and man-made cycles constantly interject themselves, forcing everyone to adjust and adapt along the way.

Still, acceptance goes only so far. If, for example, you ask Americans how their lives might change when the United States is no longer the world's military, political, economic, and cultural leader—or even a superpower at all—many will look at you strangely, as if you had two heads. Yet history teaches us that empires always come and go. Before the United States, there were Great Britain, Spain, and the Netherlands. Further back, there was Rome. Why should this time be different? Could the American era really turn out to be the one and only exception to a recurring pattern of geopolitical birth and death that has spanned thousands of years? Frankly, the odds are against it. In fact, there is plenty of evidence to suggest that the United States' days as hegemonic leader are already numbered.

Once the embodiment of prosperity, the United States now finds that its finances are in shambles, utterly dependent on borrowed money and the kindness of foreigners. The dollar is no longer an undisputed store of value or a universally accepted medium of exchange. For decades, the United States was an economic, social, and cultural beacon, shining brightly around the world; in recent years, the foundations that made it so have gradually been worn away. At the same time, emerging powers like China, Russia, and India are increasingly unwilling to toe the U.S. line. Despotic regimes in North Korea, Iran, and Venezuela repeatedly challenge the nation's authority. Even its long-vaunted military supremacy is called into question amid the debacles in Iraq and Afghanistan.

Adding insult to injury, numerous polls reveal that the longtime leader of the free world is no longer respected or admired as it once was. Many of those who live in places such as the Middle East, Asia, South America, and even Western Europe are rejecting U.S. standards, rules, political goals, and cultural norms in favor of their own. They are becoming more self-confident and assertive, believing their approaches to living, working, governing, and realizing their full potentials as individuals and as nations are as good as—or better than—the American way of doing things. More and more, they question whether the United States is even relevant to their lives. In sum, foreigners are acknowledging a tectonic shift in the global order that most Americans don't even know is taking place.

But it seems that even those who accept that the world is changing haven't fully thought things through. Typically nowadays, many believe that no matter what happens more broadly speaking, it won't have much impact on *their* lives. Others suppose that while things could get a bit dicey, we live in a sophisticated age. In their view, it is not in anyone's interest to make too much fuss or to meddle with a system— regardless of its origins—that seems to work. The upshot: a belief that any troubles that flare up will blow over quickly. And finally, more than a few people have some vague notion that whatever transition does occur will be benign or maybe even positive—akin, perhaps, to what took place many decades ago, when the United States grabbed the leadership baton from its English-speaking predecessor, Great Britain.

But circumstances are different now than they were back then. The stakes are also higher. Nuclear proliferation, breathtaking technological advances, and a decades-long economic boom have increasingly leveled the global playing field. Myriad financial and structural imbalances; competition for energy, food, water, and other resources; and growing social and political divides have fostered a divergence of interests and a hardening of differences. Taken together, these factors suggest that the world will be a vastly more dangerous and unsettled place in the years ahead. It will be a time of vulnerability, disorder, and divisiveness, where individuals, groups, and nations will discover that they are locked in a relentless, often desperate struggle with others—occasionally out of choice, more often out of necessity.

Businesses will find it hard to survive, let alone thrive, amid increasing violence and conflict, shortages and logistical disruptions, and a breakdown of markets and financial mechanisms. Individuals will be forced to rethink livelihoods, lifestyles, living arrangements, and locales. Political structures will be in flux, as local and regional leaders gain influence at the expense of national authorities. Around the globe, gangsters, maniacs, and mobs will compete with established regimes for the reins of power. Nuclear attacks, domestic terrorism, and other threats that once seemed remote to most Americans will become an all-too-frequent reality. So, too, will breakdowns, epidemics, and other fallout stemming from economic deterioration, growing social unrest and criminality, and a forced shift toward greater self-sufficiency.

For many Americans, the years ahead will be nothing short of a modern Dark Ages, where each day brings forth fresh anxieties, unfamiliar risks, and a deep sense of foreboding. However, for an enlightened few who grasp the full extent of what is going on and who take the steps necessary to steel themselves for whatever happens next, the post–American era may well prove to be a unique moment, when they can achieve the financial goals they never thought possible. Those who pay close attention, plan carefully, and act accordingly may even realize a degree of wealth, security, and inner peace that leaves them head and shoulders above everyone else.

To do this, of course, people will have to understand how things got to where they are now. More important, they will need to know how things will all play out in future. *When Giants Fall: An Economic Roadmap for the End of the American Era* answers those questions—and more. From an examination of key economic, political, geopolitical, and social issues to the practical realities of earning a living, protecting and preserving wealth, running a business, and looking after loved ones, the pages ahead provide a straightforward and comprehensive overview for making the most in uniquely unsettled times. For those who can't afford to get it wrong, *When Giants Fall* is a clear, no-holds-barred guide that will help ensure they get it right.

Acknowledgments

I would like to thank my agent, John Willig, for his persistent belief in my writing and my vision; Debra Englander, Kelly O'Connor, Kevin Holm, and Adrianna Johnson, whose efforts have been more than enough to convince me why John Wiley & Sons is among the best in its industry; my extended family of enthusiastic supporters, including Mom, Dad, Irene, Elsie, Bernie, Dwayne, Jennifer, Andrew, Teresa, Max, Linda, Rachel, Paige, Edward, Mary, and Anne; and, of course, my wife, Catherine, and my daughters, Sophie, Emily, Mollie, and Nellie, without whom I would have been lost a long, long time ago.

Introduction

I n late 2007, a Chinese submarine suddenly "popped up" in the middle of U.S. military exercises taking place in the Pacific Ocean. According to Matthew Hickley of the United Kingdom's *Daily Mail*, the 160-foot Song class diesel-electric attack submarine "sailed within viable range for launching torpedoes or missiles" at the USS *Kitty Hawk*, a 1,000-foot aircraft carrier with 4,500 personnel on board that was being guarded by a dozen warships and at least two submarines. The newspaper added—in a report that received scant U.S. media attention—that American military chiefs "were left dumbstruck." One North Atlantic Treaty Organization (NATO) official said that "the effect was 'as big a shock as the Russians launching Sputnik'—a reference to the Soviet Union's first orbiting satellite in 1957 which marked the start of the space age."

But it isn't only in the military arena where there are signs that the United States is not quite in a league of its own. An August 2007 *New York Times* editorial, "World's Best Medical Care?" highlighted two studies that revealed the U.S. health care system, contrary to popular belief, had fallen significantly behind those of other nations. The first, published by the World Health Organization seven years earlier, ranked the United States 37th out of 191 countries worldwide. The second, detailed in May by the well-regarded Commonwealth Fund, rated the United States "last or next-to-last compared with five other nations—Australia, Canada, Germany, New Zealand, and the United Kingdom—on most measures of performance, including quality of care and access to it."

For a nation that has long viewed itself as the leader of the pack, the results were curiously incongruent. Yet so is the gap between the apparent economic standing of the United States and its long-term financial health. Such could be seen in an eye-opening commentary published in the July/August 2006 issue of the Federal Reserve Bank of St. Louis *Review*. Written by Laurence J. Kotlikoff, a Boston University economics professor, the essay posed a provocative question: "Is the United States Bankrupt?" Citing a $65.9 "fiscal gap" stemming from unaccounted-for pension and health care benefits that 77 million baby boomers are expecting to receive in their golden years, Kotlikoff argued that "unless the United States moves quickly to fundamentally change and restrain its fiscal behavior, its bankruptcy will become a foregone conclusion."

Many, if not most, Americans believe that their country's place in the world is not much different than it was two decades ago, when the collapse of the Berlin Wall left the United States as the last superpower standing. Some memories go back even further, to a time when the United States was a beneficent bulwark, helping allies and rivals alike to recover from the ravages of World War II. Yet vignettes like those—along with other evidence—point to the fact that, as music legend Bob Dylan once wrote, "The times they are a-changin'." Indeed, not only is the United States losing its grip on the reins of global leadership, but other nations, including China, Russia, India, Iran, and Venezuela, are asserting their right to set the international agenda.

For those with some sense of history, the prospect of a new world order should not be all that surprising. Indeed, when it comes to the relative fortunes of countries and empires, the only thing you can be sure of is that tomorrow's winners will be different from today's. Advantages that might once have pushed a nation to the top of the heap can become untenable burdens. Technological advances can level the playing field, sometimes abruptly. Those who have lagged try harder, in the hope they can lead. Sometimes, people simply tire of the old and seek out the new. Whatever the reasons, the United States' loss of status and the prospect of intense jockeying for power by individuals, groups, and nations around the globe will have far-reaching consequences for economies and markets.

There's more to it, however. As unsettling as a seismic geopolitical shift might be, it is not the only major challenge the world will face in the years ahead. Developments that have played a role in fostering geopolitical upheaval will also heighten other strains. Among the most daunting is the issue of resource constraints. For any American who has experienced the painful consequences of sharply higher prices at the gas pump, it is apparent that circumstances are different than they were only a few years ago. The same holds true in regard to the price and availability of other important resources and the vast array of globally traded commodities. All of a sudden, the promise of a land of plenty has been found wanting.

Thanks to years of booming economic growth in countries around the globe, more people now have the opportunity—as well as the desire—to enjoy what Americans and others in economically advanced nations have long taken for granted. In places like China, for example, with its population of 1.3 billion people, there has been a clamor for automobiles, air conditioners and heating systems, and an agricultural product that many once viewed as a luxury item, served only on special occasions—that is, meat. Meanwhile, the rest of the world has not stood still. Hundreds of millions of people have bought homes, cars, flat-screen televisions, and computers; have increased the miles they drive and the vacations they take; and have kept on consuming as if the horn of plenty could only grow larger.

Coming Home to Roost

Now, though, circumstances are changing. The mistakes and excesses of the past are coming home to roost. It is much more costly and difficult, for example, to obtain the fuel needed to power the spending and consumption habits of an increasingly energy-dependent world. Burgeoning appetites for food have stressed the global ecosystem, undermining the availability of resources that mankind has depended on from time immemorial. Water supplies and sanitation facilities not only have failed to keep pace with the population growth of the past century, they have lagged behind the increases in developing-country per-capita consumption levels that have occurred during the past decade.

Around the world, these concerns have spawned restiveness, protests, and riots. Evidence suggests, however, that the roots of heightened social instability are broad-based. After years of pressure and propaganda from businesses and policy makers for greater integration, people are challenging the utopian promise of globalization and unfettered cross-border commerce. Emboldened by the self-confidence that comes with improving fortunes, the Chinese, the Indians, the Russians, and other up-and-comers are no longer willing to kowtow to the wishes of the West or to suppress the resentments of the past. Many are feeling the powerful tug of tribal roots. All of a sudden, there is much less impetus to keep primal urges under wraps.

The blistering economic successes of the emerging powers, aided by mercantilistic trading strategies, the luck of geography, and a powerful marriage of economics and politics, have also fostered other developments that will destabilize the economic and financial landscape ahead. Around the world, numerous imbalances have sprung up, many unprecedented. Export-driven powerhouses and commodity-rich nations like China, Japan, Russia, Brazil, and oil producers in the Middle East have accumulated outsized foreign currency reserves, with much of their holdings, until recently at least, kept in U.S. dollars. Large chunks have, in turn, been plowed into U.S. stocks, real estate, and bonds, especially government and agency-issued securities.

For a while, this recycling process seemed almost symbiotic, a kind of perpetual-motion machine. The United States—its government and its citizens—would spend more than it could afford on a wide range of goods and services produced elsewhere. Foreign vendors—or, more likely, their public-sector overseers—would redirect the proceeds back into U.S. assets, helping to keep liquidity abundant, market conditions stable, and the cost of borrowing low. This combination would foster the illusion of never-ending nirvana, encouraging everyone to continue carrying on as before. Spend. Borrow. Repeat. It was seemingly a golden age of peace and prosperity for all.

In the end, though, things didn't quite work out as many had hoped. U.S. public and private sector debt levels soared to all-time highs. Wages stagnated, domestic opportunities disappeared, and the costs of living suddenly rose beyond the reach of ordinary working-class Americans. The allure of buying cheap products from foreign-based manufacturers, together with the stampede by U.S. multinational corporations to move production to offshore locations where labor and other operating costs were low, allowed the nation's manufacturing prowess to wither on the vine, undermining future growth prospects. All the while, the circle of dependency helped chip away at support for what has long been the world's major reserve currency.

Gaining Advantage

To be sure, those who have been feeding the beast have suffered some indigestion themselves, as dollar-denominated holdings have fallen in value. Nevertheless, their steady accumulation of cross-border surpluses and other economic resources has given them potent weapons, allowing them to secure geopolitical advantage. Nations like China and Russia, for example, have been aggressively wielding their financial firepower in Africa, Asia, Europe, and South America. In resource-rich regions, they've negotiated trade deals and built production and logistical facilities; they've provided grants and loans and underwritten infrastructure projects; they've supplied arms and high-tech defensive capabilities—increasingly, the currency of choice in a troubled world—all in exchange for what everybody else now wants.

Geopolitical up-and-comers have taken an increasingly aggressive tack in their dealings with established powers. In recent years, for example, China has revealed plans to diversify its $1.8 trillion of official reserves, showing just who is in charge of the United States' economic future. The Asian nation has also warned its ostensibly more powerful rival away from any moves that might undermine its export strategy, asserting that, if need be, China would resort to the so-called nuclear option—dumping its holdings of U.S. assets all at once, regardless of the damage it might cause to its own interests. Russia, meanwhile, has not been shy about increasing its stranglehold over energy supplies for Europe, or throwing its weight around in Asia, Africa, and the Middle East.

Such machinations have helped to augment an already growing antipathy toward free trade and increasing cross-border cooperation, in the West and elsewhere. Spurred on by the fallout from a global financial crisis and a quickening economic downturn, protectionist sentiments have gained strength. Increasingly, the harsh realities of dislocations and distortions have overshadowed the lofty theories of economic liberalization—neoliberalism. Fractures have developed in collective political arrangements. Monetary unions and currency pegs agreed to when times were good are being called into question as conditions worsen. Around the world, multilateralism is being subverted by regionalism, bilateralism, and unilateralism.

Meanwhile, the altered dynamic of key resource markets has set the stage for a debilitating and increasingly divisive struggle for advantage. *Financial Times* commentator Martin Wolf has made reference to a "zero-sum world," where a shortage of productivity-enhancing energy might turn back the clock to a time when gains could be achieved only at others' expense. The prospect of a further disorderly unwinding of numerous global imbalances—apart from the extraordinary eruptions already seen—also signals serious trouble ahead. So does a reversal of the productivity gains of recent years, brought on by heightened geopolitical unrest, rapidly diminishing economies of scale, and adverse demographic trends.

Further undermining the outlook, of course, is the United States' loss of standing—economically, politically, and militarily. Over the past several decades, booming global growth has had many forebears, though two, in particular, stand out. The first is the existence of the United States' protective umbrella, which has allowed vast resources to be channeled into productive peacetime activities. The second is a Western-fomented economic order, centered on the neoliberal-capitalist agenda. But with global stability in doubt, the rules and mechanisms of the established financial and trading system under assault, and the world's largest marketplace for goods and services becoming unhinged, advanced and developing countries alike will suffer the consequences.

It won't just be growth prospects that are affected. Economic shifts and shocks will destabilize other realms, too. Indeed, the schisms are already apparent. Growing wealth inequality and the scramble for key commodities have fostered tension and conflict between haves and have-nots. Long-distance, hydrocarbon-fueled global supply chains no longer offer the benefits they once did, lessening the attractiveness of increasing global connectedness. The fact that relatively few countries have managed to realize outsized gains under a trade regime ostensibly based on equality and fair dealings has raised suspicions about others' intentions. Instead of drawing people together, the successes of the past are driving them apart.

Around the world, economically inspired nationalism has stirred up feelings of arrogance and animosity toward outsiders. An emphasis on diversity has fostered an acceptance of divisiveness. Large populations of illegal immigrants, tolerated when booming growth created a seemingly insatiable demand for low-cost labor, are suddenly the targets of an angry backlash. In places like South Africa, Italy, and the United States, among many others, there have been grassroots movements to punish, prey on, and drive out foreign nationals. Popular anxiety has also spurred growing calls for a dramatic political response. In the United States, meanwhile, weariness and resentment over the long-drawn-out military actions in Iraq and Afghanistan have allowed isolationist sentiments to broaden their hold.

Responding to the End of the American Era

Taken together, these various developments constitute a clear and present danger to the economic well-being of every American, especially those who have been conditioned to believe that life can only get better in future. Dramatically changing times will require new ways of dealing with everyday routines. People will need to factor in the likelihood that livelihoods will be continually at risk. Many will be forced to expend a great deal of time and energy figuring out new ways of getting around and getting by. Living arrangements and lifestyle choices that once seemed second nature will have to be completely rethought when efforts to acquire the basics—fuel, food, water—are much more time-consuming and difficult than before.

Those in the United States and elsewhere will have to pay better attention to where and how they live, who they depend on, and what their options are when things go wrong. They will also need to think about the steps they need to take now in anticipation of the upheavals that will occur in future. Health- and security-related concerns, for example, will have to be a key focus of attention when deteriorating public finances, widespread business failures, and crumbling infrastructure boost crime, disrupt safety nets, and leave critical services, including medical care, that much harder to come by. No doubt the world will also be a more perilous place when competition for scarce resources is intensifying and powerful interests at home and abroad are vying to gain the upper hand—in any way they can.

Most, if not all, businesses will quickly discover that existing models either are irretrievably broken or will have to be dramatically reworked to accommodate the risks and challenges associated with a more uncertain and unstable operating environment. Unlike during the era of globalization, bigger won't necessarily be better. In fact, large size will likely be a serious disadvantage when flexibility and fast response times are imperative. Growth for growth's sake will be the road to ruin when the costs and risks of boosting payrolls, increasing plant and equipment, and taking on hefty financial obligations more than outweigh the potential benefits.

Mounting logistical disruptions, tighter borders, heightened geopolitical instability, rising costs of key inputs like water and energy, and an assortment of dislocations will shoot holes in many of the old theories about how to improve efficiency and boost growth. For most firms, approaches that might once have increased the odds of success, including just-in-time inventory management, the development of long and intricate supply chains, and outsourcing of functions to other locales, will lead to their undoing. What is more, instead of focusing on aggressively pruning back operations to reduce costs, owners and managers will be forced to strike a tenuous balance between what they might be able do without and what they must have on hand to remain in business when disaster strikes.

Needless to say, investors will have a much more difficult time preserving and expanding wealth under these sorts of conditions. Not only will economic and financial circumstances create a far more treacherous trading environment than has been seen before in modern times, but even ostensibly correct decisions could prove calamitous when other, previously less likely developments intervene. Betting against the dollar, for example, makes sense on many levels. However, the risks stemming from investing in or moving funds into other currencies, markets, and economies during a time of turbulence and growing geopolitical conflict may well offset all of the potential rewards—and then some. Paradoxically, having what others really want might not necessarily be such a good idea in the new scheme of things. At a time when everything is suddenly up for grabs, some things are best left out of reach.

In the end, the road ahead will be fraught with myriad dangers that will be impossible for anyone to ignore or avoid, regardless of current circumstances. Even worse, developments that have brought us to this point make it clear that a new, far more challenging environment is not just a passing storm, poised to quickly blow over. Instead of looking forward to a return to the way things once were, Americans—and investors in particular—will have to get used to a "new normal," where only those who are flexible, open-minded, resilient, and fully prepared for the worst will be able to survive, let alone come out on top. Those who refuse to take these threats seriously risk losing everything. Now more than ever, it is time to become attuned to an entirely unique roadmap.

Part I

FAULT LINES OF
A FADING EMPIRE

Chapter 1

Descent into Disorder

"General Secretary Gorbachev, if you seek peace, if you seek prosperity for the Soviet Union and Eastern Europe, if you seek liberalization, come here to this gate. Mr. Gorbachev, open this gate. Mr. Gorbachev, tear down this wall!"

—PRESIDENT RONALD REAGAN

There was electricity in the air when America's 40th president spoke those words during a June 1987 address at the base of the Brandenburg Gate, near the imposing concrete wall that divided the German city of Berlin into East and West. Many believe Reagan's now famous speech heralded the end of the Cold War and of the Soviet Union, which had been under the control of the Communist Party, then led by General Secretary Mikhail Gorbachev. Not long after, the United States stood alone, the one and only superpower.

But for much of the world, the commanding presence of the United States on the international stage and its metamorphosis into a seemingly unassailable modern day *empire* had been apparent for some time. Indeed, with the arrival of World War II, the United States revealed breathtaking military capabilities and unparalleled economic strength. Not only did the United States play a major role in the Allies' defeat of the Axis powers of Germany, Italy, and Japan, but the nation also helped rebuild the crippled postwar economies of friend and foe alike.

Whether willingly or through grudging acquiescence, countries across the globe welcomed what the United States had on offer in the decades after that devastating conflict, though the assistance frequently had strings attached. Along with financial and other aid came the promise of security and stability, bolstered in large measure by the formidable nuclear arsenal of the United States and its active and expanding military presence on almost every continent. In fact, American geopolitical dominance has, up until recently at least, benefited nations of all stripes and sizes, including those with political, social, and economic regimes that were and are at odds with the tenets of democracy, capitalism, and liberalism.

By providing what economists describe as "public goods," including maintaining political stability and acting as the world's policeman of last resort, the United States facilitated closer integration among nations—globalization—and underwrote an era of unprecedented prosperity. Many countries have also gained from their relatively open access to the American market, the largest by a wide margin until the establishment of the European Union. According to the *Washington Post*'s Robert J. Samuelson, citing historian Angus Maddison in "Farewell to Pax Americana," "the world economy expanded by a factor of six" from 1950 to 1998, while "global trade increased twentyfold."

Under the circumstances, it's not hard to see why most nations have historically been reluctant to challenge American hegemony—or what modern commentators describe as a "unipolar" world. Now, though, there is mounting evidence that our circumstances and others' attitudes are in flux and that American authority is being called into question on a number of fronts. The costly and drawn-out wars in Iraq and Afghanistan have revealed the limitations of our military capabilities. Our nation's significant external imbalances and a devastating financial crisis have undermined acceptance of our leadership on economic matters. Increasingly, countries have been willing to stand up to or exclude the United States from the table when they believe it is in their interests to do so.

Signs of Imperial Demise

These and other factors indicate that a geopolitical reckoning day is near. Additional evidence can be seen in the light of harbingers from the past. Historians such as Edward Gibbons, who wrote *The Decline and Fall of the Roman Empire*, and Paul Kennedy, author of *The Rise and Fall of the Great Powers*, are among those who have identified characteristics that have rung the bell for sprawling imperial predecessors who also believed—mistakenly—in their own eternal destiny.

One of the most commonly cited warning signs is "imperial overstretch," which scholar and author Fred Halliday has described as "a mismatch between political and strategic goals and economic and fiscal reality." Examples include Rome and Great Britain, both of which promulgated costly, far-flung empires that sowed the seeds of their eventual ruin. Does this describe the United States? Some would say no. Among other things, they would point to the fact that defense spending of $643.9 trillion for the fiscal year ending September 30, 2008, represented just 4.5 percent of gross domestic product (GDP)— the nation's output of goods and services—considerably below a multidecade median of nearly 6 percent, as well as a Vietnam War–era extreme of 9.4 percent, according to official government reports.

But experts like Chalmers Johnson, a historian and author of *Nemesis: The Last Days of the American Republic*, argue that Defense Department data doesn't take a great deal of other military-related spending into account. By his calculations, which include the costs of fighting the global war on terror, State Department–budgeted military assistance to foreign nations, Department of Veterans Affairs spending on injured soldiers, and various other programs, the actual figure is at least $1.1 trillion, or approximately 8 percent of GDP.

Yet even without the assumption that reported tallies are vastly understated, other evidence paints a clear picture of overstretch. According to the Stockholm International Peace Research Institute, U.S. military spending in 2006 was nearly equal to that of all other nations combined—46 percent of the global total. Statistics also reinforce the notion of an empire that is extraordinarily "far-flung" (Stålenheim et al.). Defense Department data reveals, for instance, that the United States has 737 bases in 130 countries around the world. According to Brown University professor and author Catherine Lutz, the "military owns (or rents) over 28 million acres of land and $600 billion worth of real estate." That is in addition to the 6,000 bases, as Chalmers Johnson has noted, that exist in the United States and its territories.

Moreover, the process of waging long-running campaigns in two Middle Eastern countries has laid bare the extent to which the United States has strained its available resources. A January 2006 *BBC News* report, "U.S. Military 'at Breaking Point,'" cited two studies, one by a former Clinton administration official and the other by the Pentagon itself, warning that the military had "become dangerously overstretched because of the scale of its operations in Iraq and Afghanistan." A 2008 survey of 3,400 active and retired officers at the highest levels of command by *Foreign Policy* and the Center for a New American Security, dubbed the "U.S. Military Index," found that 60 percent of those polled believed "the U.S. military is weaker today than it was five years ago. Asked why, more than half cite the wars in Iraq and Afghanistan, and the pace of troop deployments those conflicts require. . . . Nearly 90 percent say that they believe the demands of the war in Iraq have 'stretched the U.S. military dangerously thin.'"

Another sign of impending imperial demise stems from a seemingly intractable pattern of fiscal irresponsibility and increasing economic malaise, with national output regularly falling below the high-water mark of prior decades. To be sure, historians have noted a strong link between economic vitality and a nation's war-making prowess. Indeed, few would doubt that the global standing of the United States has been bolstered by military capabilities that owe much to its past fortunes. At the end of World War II, for example, the United States was producing around half of the world's goods, which allowed for a dramatic buildup of our military might. Since then, the country has lost ground economically, in part because of strong growth elsewhere, but also because of policies that have encouraged outsourcing of jobs and production to low-cost locales, an overemphasis on financial engineering, and a decaying work ethic.

But the nation's fiscal health hasn't only suffered from a loss of focus and a "hollowing out" of our industrial base, which many have traditionally regarded as a sign of strength in and of itself. The world's sole superpower has also been afflicted with the overspending and overborrowing disease that has long been a distinguishing feature of ailing third world nations—and dying empires. These include a 2007 current account deficit—the difference between what we produce and what we consume—of 5.5 percent of GDP, down from a record 6.6 percent a year earlier, but alarming, nonetheless.

Making matters worse is the fact that this persistent and growing financial imbalance with the rest of the world has required inflows of capital amounting to $2 billion or more per day, much of it borrowed from countries like China, Japan, and the oil producers of the Middle East. The precariousness of our nation's finances can also be seen in our net international investment position, which measures the gap between the value of the foreign assets we own and U.S. assets held by foreigners. At last count, this indicator was in deficit to the tune of around 20 percent of GDP, a hitherto unseen extreme and a far cry from the surpluses of the early 1980s.

Other data also paint a picture of a nation bereft of fiscal discipline. At the end of 2007, for example, total public and private debt reached an extraordinary 340 percent of GDP, based on data from the Federal Reserve and Commerce Department, far surpassing the multi-decade record of 265 percent seen at the height of the Great Depression. Stagnating inflation-adjusted wages, worsening household balance sheets, rising inequality between rich and poor, and the fallout from a devastating and far-reaching financial crisis only add to a sense of backsliding and decay. Under the circumstances, it shouldn't have been surprising to anyone when 40 percent of Americans surveyed in a February 2008 Gallup Poll (reported by Lydia Saad) believed that China was the "leading economic power in the world today." Only 33 percent, less than the clear majority seen eight years earlier, thought the United States deserved to be in the top spot.

Also marking the twilight days of past empires has been what might be described as an epidemic of cultural, moral, and social decline, though this aspect is not so easy to quantify. Sometimes, it is a case of "you know it when you see it." But the evidence is hard to miss.

Simply put, the United States has gone soft. People prefer watching or pretending, instead of doing. Education has been dumbed down. According to "PISA 2006," the 2006 Programme for International Student Assessment (PISA), a triennial survey of 15-year-olds around the world, the United States ranked 29th in science and 35th in mathematics out of 57 countries in terms of overall performance. A 2008 poll by Common Core found that a significant share of teenagers lived "in 'stunning ignorance' of history and literature," Sam Dillon of the *New York Times* reported in "Survey Finds Teenagers Ignorant on Basic History and Literature Questions."

Social standards have slipped. Manners and respect for the elderly have fallen by the wayside, replaced by coarse language, thuggery, widespread disrespect for authority, and YouTube exhibitionism. Sound arguments are overrun by sound bites, discourse is drowned out by diatribe, and facts and fundamentals are eclipsed by feelings and fantasy. There are faith-based government initiatives and moves to replace Darwin's science with the tenets of creationism. According to author Susan Jacoby, one-half of American adults believe in ghosts, one-third in astrology, and four-fifths in miracles. A National Science Foundation survey found that an astonishing one in five think the sun revolves around the earth.

Our health care system is an apt reflection of where we are as a nation. Though we've long prided ourselves on the idea that the United States is the best where it counts, an assortment of data—including the surveys noted earlier—suggest otherwise. U.S. infant mortality rates are among the highest for industrialized nations. Over the past three decades, the number of obese Americans has more than doubled. When average life expectancy is compared with per capita spending on health care, the United States ranking is off the charts relative to other countries—but not in a positive way.

Days of Diminishing Respect

Some parallels between the twenty-first-century United States and the last days of the Roman Empire seem particularly telling, though now, of course, developments are cast in the light of a supposedly more sophisticated age. Instead of bread and circuses, suggests historian Niall Ferguson (in his article "Empire Falls"), and others, we have NASCAR, video games, and reality TV. But the truth is, it isn't just about warning signs. Other evidence suggests that our power, our ability to dictate and dominate the global agenda, is also on the wane, a development that most Americans likely never envisaged in their lifetimes.

In general, there are two kinds of power, which go hand in hand. The first, soft power, stems from our reputation as a nation, the good will we've garnered over time, the allure of our values, and our ability to lead by example and have others naturally follow in our footsteps. Foreign policy expert and author Joseph Nye describes this concept as the "ability to get what you want through attraction rather than coercion"—that is, to influence by words rather than actions.

Now, though, the circumstances that have made the United States a beacon of light and the economic and cultural agenda setter over the course of many decades are changing. Many blame the disastrous military adventures in Iraq and Afghanistan, as well as the newfound acceptance of barbaric torture techniques and scandals like the mistreatment of prisoners at Iraq's Abu Ghraib prison. Others put it down to a general sense of arrogance, of unilateral decision making, and hubristic exceptionalism, especially during the two terms that President George W. Bush was in office. Or, perhaps, it reflects an accumulated dissatisfaction, the kind that spawns lurching shifts in democratic societies from the left to the right and then back again.

Whatever the reasons, more than a few developments seem to confirm our loss of status. A 2007 Pew Global Attitudes Survey, for example, found that distrust of the United States had grown around the world. The poll revealed that 26 out of 33 countries viewed the global image of the United States as "less favorable" than in 2002, with opinions influenced to a great extent by growing unease over the country's unsettling foreign policy and its willingness to act preemptively, aggressively—and alone. Another poll by Harris Research for the *Financial Times* (reported by Daniel Dombey and Stanley Pignal) revealed that Europeans regarded the United States as the "biggest threat to world stability."

Joseph Nye highlighted an even more dramatic shift in attitudes that he picked up on while attending the 2008 World Economic Forum in Davos, Switzerland. In a brief commentary for the *Huffington Post*, he noted a reference by Angela Merkel, Germany's first female chancellor, "to the importance of soft power in her keynote [speech]. But my strongest take-away of the day," Nye wrote, "was a seasoned Asian diplomat telling me that in all his travels, he has never seen American soft power at such a low ebb. In his words, only the Israelis, Indians, and Vietnamese have a positive view of the U.S."

Compounding the widespread sense of diminishing respect for the longtime superpower, rivals have become more and more outspoken in their anti-American rhetoric—and have found an increasingly receptive audience. For example, Venezuelan President Hugo Chávez "earned laughter and ovations from the world leaders on hand," Neil King Jr. of the *Wall Street Journal* reported in "Anti-Americanism Is a Big Hit at U.N.," when he called President George W. Bush "the devil" and "compared the U.S. to a 'sword hanging over our heads'" during a September 2006 speech at the United Nations.

Similarly, in a February 2007 address at the 43rd Munich Trans-Atlantic Conference on Security Policy, Russian President Vladimir Putin said that "one country, the United States, has overstepped its national boundaries in every way," noted Dilip Hiro, author of *Blood of the Earth: The Battle for the World's Vanishing Oil Resources*, in a *TomDispatch.com* column. "Condemning the notion of a 'unipolar world,' Putin added: 'However one might embellish this term, at the end of the day it describes a scenario in which there is one center of authority, one center of force, one center of decision-making. . . . It is a world in which there is one master, one sovereign. And this is pernicious.'" According to Hiro, Putin's "views fell on receptive ears in the capitals of most Asian, African, and Latin American countries."

A Corroding Currency

But it isn't just our influence and global standing that are being undermined. Our core strength—what geopolitical analysts describe as "hard power"—is also under assault. Hard power mainly refers to our military capabilities, though it also includes other key resources we have at our disposal, such as our ability to print what has been, up until recently at least, the world's reserve currency, a widely valued store of wealth, and a universal medium of exchange. History has shown that financial wherewithal and power projection go hand in hand. Without access to cheap funding, for instance, it is impossible for any nation to underwrite the costs of sustaining a global empire for long without eventually bankrupting the public purse.

By the same token, historians such as Niall Ferguson have highlighted a body of research that confirms the importance of sound finances for maintaining a superior military standing. Evidence suggests, however, that this lesson has gradually been lost on the leadership of the twentieth-century superpower. Over the course of two decades, rising budget and trade imbalances have transformed the United States from the world's largest creditor to its largest debtor, a turn of events that has proved detrimental to predecessors who embarked on a similarly profligate path. The United States is now literally dependent on the kindness of foreigners, especially China and other nations whose political, military, and social agendas aren't necessarily aligned with ours. That naturally limits policy making options and leaves the United States exposed to the possibility of economic blackmail.

But such dependency is not the only reason we are vulnerable. Up until recently, many of our vast funding needs have been met through foreign central bank purchases of U.S. government and government-sponsored agency securities, on terms that reflect a gold-plated past rather than what might be characterized as a lead-weighted future—in a currency that has shed a third of its value in less than a decade. Indeed, dollar weakness has forced our largest creditors to take substantial losses. Consequently, a growing number of countries have begun to rethink the composition of dollar-heavy foreign reserves, which have traditionally been used to pay import bills and counteract market disruptions. China, among others, has accumulated large greenback holdings in connection with aggressive export-oriented trade policies.

In October 2006, for example, *MarketWatch* reported that Russia's central bank, following on the heels of a comparable shift several months before at its state-controlled Oil Stabilization Fund, aimed to broaden its holdings of foreign currency by raising the proportion of Japanese yen in its portfolio from zero to several percent ("Russia Diversification Talk Hurts Dollar, Boosts Yen"). Earlier in the year,

China hinted at plans "to diversify its rapidly growing foreign exchange reserves away from the U.S. dollar and government bonds," according to the *Financial Times* in an article by Geoff Dyer and Andrew Balls entitled "China Signals Reserves Switch Away from Dollar."

Increasingly vociferous adversaries have pushed to marginalize the dollar's use in cross-border trade and as a benchmark for pricing key global commodities. At the November 2007 Organization of Petroleum Exporting Countries (OPEC) summit, Iranian President Mahmoud Ahmadinejad repeated earlier calls for a non-dollar-denominated OPEC Oil Exchange and OPEC Bank. Venezuela's Hugo Chávez and Ecuadorian President Rafael Correa voiced support for oil prices based on a basket of currencies. In addition, nations that have traditionally anchored their currencies to the greenback as a means of achieving economic stability have begun to weigh alternatives. That is because persistent dollar weakness has spawned unwanted inflationary pressures and rising social instability.

A December 2007 article by Ambrose Evans-Pritchard in London's *Daily Telegraph* noted that 26 leading Saudi Arabian clerics had called upon rulers of the decades-long U.S. ally to abandon its "dollar peg" in what the newspaper described as a "fatwa"—a religious decree—against the American currency. Qatar, which hosts the Middle East's largest U.S. military base, was also considering breaking its link to the greenback, Simeon Kerr of the *Financial Times* reported a month later. Data from official sources suggests such concerns have had a contagiously corrosive effect over time. According to the International Monetary Fund, the dollar's share of global currency reserves fell from 81.1 percent in the first quarter of 1999 to 63.8 percent in the third quarter of 2007.

Other factors have also stirred growing doubts about the currency's future. Up until the past few years, for example, no small number of foreigners seemed happy to own dollars and invest in the United States as long as they believed in the nation's structural underpinnings, including its financial system. That faith has been sorely tested by a devastating credit crisis and severe financial woes at iconic institutions whose fortunes have been seen as reflective of U.S. global dominance. The sight of so many large American banks going cap in hand to Asian investors in late 2007 didn't exactly convey a reassuring sense of stability and strength. The autumn 2008 bailouts of Fannie Mae and Freddie

Mac, the nation's largest mortgage lenders, and American International Group, formerly the world's largest insurer, only made matters worse. Indeed, an assessment of banking systems by the World Economic Forum ranked the U.S. in 40th place, according to an October 2008 *Reuters* report by Rob Taylor, "Canada Rated World's Soundest Bank System: Survey."

Commentators assert that the fallout extends beyond economic considerations, because a struggling greenback has helped to "undermine Washington's place on the international stage," according to a December 2007 *Financial Times* report by Daniel Dombey, "America Faces a Diplomatic Penalty as the Dollar Dwindles." " 'This is the neglected dimension of the dollar's decline,' says Flynt Leverett, a former senior National Security Council official under President George W. Bush. 'What has been said about the fall of the dollar is almost all couched in economic terms. But currency politics is very, very powerful and is part of what has made the U.S. a hegemon for so long, like Britain before it.' " Indeed, it is unrealistic to assume that a shaky currency would not, at some point, cause others to question our leadership role on many fronts.

Chinks in the Armor

It's not surprising, of course, that those who disagree with the premise that the United States' star is losing its luster are quick to steer the discussion back to the nation's war-making capabilities. Indeed, few people, in the United States or elsewhere, would challenge the notion that the world's longtime superpower has the deadliest and most technologically advanced military machine on the face of the planet. But is the United States truly as unrivaled as many seem to think? For one thing, the long-running military campaigns in Iraq and Afghanistan have revealed serious chinks in the nation's armor. In particular, the United States is less prepared for counterinsurgency operations than for an archetypal war against a traditional nation-state rival.

Brent Scowcroft, national security adviser to two presidents, has noted as much. "Part of the problem is that the nature of power has been changing. I've often said that our defense and intelligence communities are still finely honed for dealing with the military threats of the twentieth century," he wrote in a July 2007 commentary for the *National Interest*. "But, as we are finding in Iraq, we are being wrestled to a draw by opponents who are not even an organized state adversary. Our carrier battle groups, our heavy-tank divisions, our satellite imaging systems—all the pillars of our ability to project power to contain and beat back the challenges of a conventional superpower rival—aren't of much use." Indeed, U.S. Defense Secretary Robert Gates provided further confirmation in a September 2008 speech to rising military officers at the National Defense University, according to *Agence France-Presse*, in "Gates Warns of the Limits of US Military Power."

Aside from the question of whether U.S. military capabilities are well suited to new geopolitical realities, there is another concern: whether we have enough boots on the ground to accomplish all that is desired—or required. A June 2007 *Economist* report, "The Hobbled Hegemon," noted, for instance, that although the United States has 1.5 million men and women under arms around the globe, the number of troops was insufficient to meet outstanding obligations and "keep forces ready to deal with unexpected developments elsewhere." Clearly, the magazine added, "America needs a bigger army."

Needless to say, the financial pressures associated with escalating deficits, record amounts of borrowing, a vulnerable currency, and the costs of a deepening economic malaise will only make matters worse. In early 2008, reports already indicated that various fiscal challenges were threatening to "elbow defense priorities aside," according to the *Christian Science Monitor*, in a report by Gordon Lubold entitled "Record U.S. Defense Spending, but Future Budgets May Decline." " 'There are just too many competing demands for resources and an unwillingness to raise taxes for an overall increase,' says Vincent Reinart, a resident scholar at the American Enterprise Institute." In addition, the newspaper added, "the [2009 fiscal year] defense budget itself seems 'to hint that military spending may be at its peak,' says Steven Kosiak, a senior budget analyst at the Center for Strategic and Budgetary Assessments. . . . 'Under the [military spending] plan, between fiscal year 2010 and 2013, [the Defense Department's] base budget would be cut by 1.5 percent,' he says. 'Thus, the administration is proposing that the buildup, begun in earnest after the terrorist attacks of September 2001, should come to an end in fiscal 2010.'"

Meanwhile, amid the numerous headwinds the U.S. military has had to contend with, other nations have been boosting their own war-making capabilities, aided by years of burgeoning trade surpluses and the post-2000 boom in energy and other commodity prices. Research by the Stockholm International Peace Research Institute, for example, reveals that China's official military expenditures continued to accelerate in 2006, surpassing those of Japan for the first time and making China "the biggest military spender in Asia and the fourth biggest in the world" (Stålenheim et al.). According to author and foreign policy analyst Mark Helprin, "China is transforming its forces into a full-spectrum military capable of major operations and remote power projection." No doubt many defense-related efforts are hidden from view in a country that is not known for transparency when it comes to its strategic interests.

Instead of simply playing catch-up, rivals have zeroed in on U.S. vulnerabilities, minimizing the risks that might be associated with a head-on clash. The *Economist* noted in "The Hobbled Hegemon," cited earlier, that China was "emphasizing 'asymmetrical' means designed to blunt America's technological superiority: hoping to deny America the use of the seas with long-range anti-ship missiles and submarines, paralyze its highly computerized forces through cyber-warfare, and neutralize spy communications satellites." Reports suggest the strategy is paying off. In addition to the U.S. navy's unexpectedly close encounter with a Chinese submarine noted previously, the emerging power has also conducted a successful test using ground-based ballistic missiles to shoot down an aging weather satellite orbiting more than 500 miles above the earth.

Moreover, according to a *Financial Times* report by Demetri Sevastopulo, "Chinese Hacked into Pentagon," the emerging Asian superpower's "military hacked into a Pentagon computer network in June [2007] in the most successful cyber attack on the U.S. Defense Department. . . . 'The [People's Liberation Army (PLA)] has demonstrated the ability to conduct attacks that disable our system . . . and the ability in a conflict situation to re-enter and disrupt on a very large scale,' said a former official, who said the PLA had penetrated the networks of U.S. defense companies and think-tanks."

Other prospective rivals have taken a different, though equally unsettling tack, by focusing on developing firepower and logistical capabilities the United States doesn't have or is unlikely to have. In December 2007, for example, an Associated Press report, "Russia successfully Tests New ICBM," revealed that the U.S. Cold War rival "successfully test-fired a new intercontinental ballistic missile capable of carrying multiple nuclear warheads, a weapon intended to replace Soviet-era missiles." The missile was launched from a mobile platform, making it difficult for anyone, including the United States, to keep tabs on that nation's arms buildup. Nine months later, according to *Agence France-Presse*, in an article entitled "Russia Test-Fires New-Generation Strategic Missile," Russia announced "the latest launch [from a submarine] of a multiple warhead weapon designed to breach anti-missile shields."

In spite of these developments, many experts would still insist that the United States remains at the head of the pack militarily. Even with its tremendous nuclear arsenal, Russia is weaker than it appears because its conventional forces are in poor shape, notes the *Economist* (though, in fairness, some would argue that Russia's successful September 2008 military incursion into South Ossetia offers some evidence to the contrary). Meanwhile, social, economic, and political concerns at home may forestall attempts by the Chinese to engage the United States in a major conflict, especially over issues that aren't directly tied to regional interests. But these arguments don't take the bigger picture into account. Amid all the signs that have marked the waning days of past empires and evidence that U.S. power is, at the very least, less than it was, it's hard not to conclude that the end of American hegemony is near—if it hasn't already arrived.

Chaotic Unraveling

But what are the implications of such a shift? Some analysts maintain that a decline in the United States' relative standing won't necessarily lead to upheaval or conflict, as countries around the world have thrived under the existing system in spite of its origins. According to foreign policy expert G. John Ikenberry, writing in *Foreign Affairs*, "the postwar Western order is historically unique." In his view, any international order dominated by a powerful state is based on a mix of coercion and consent, but the U.S.-led order is distinctive in that it has been more liberal than imperial—and so unusually accessible, legitimate, and durable. . . . It is expansive, with a wide and widening array of participants and stakeholders. It is capable of generating tremendous economic growth and power while also signaling restraint—all of which make it hard to overturn and easy to join.

Even so, a number of developments suggest that past successes won't be enough to ensure the smooth functioning or even the survival of the current system as U.S. influence wanes. The 2006 collapse of the Doha round of global trade talks, for example, revealed numerous fault lines in the existing world order, especially between developed and emerging nations, and showed that there is growing disdain for U.S. and Western approaches to resolving differences. In the wake of the breakdown, there emerged a suddenly popular preference for bilateral and regional deals, giving more control to the countries involved—but also heightening anxiety for everyone else.

Geopolitical up-and-comers have also been pushing hard to overturn a regime they characterize as unfair and anachronistic. Russia's leader in June 2007 "called for a new world economic framework based on regional alliances rather than global institutions like the International Monetary Fund [IMF]," the *International Herald Tribune*'s Andrew E. Kramer reported in "Putin Wants New Economic 'Architecture.'" "The new system, he said, would reflect the rising power of emerging market economies like Russia, China, India, and Brazil, and the decline of old heavyweights of the United States, Japan, and many European countries." Six months later, Brazil, Venezuela, and six other Latin American nations sought to sever links to institutions associated with U.S. hegemony, including the IMF and the World Bank, by launching the Bank of the South. Venezuela also "conferred with Guatemala, Bolivia, and Cuba on the inception of a new development bank to provide development financing for its member nations," Fan Jianqing of the *People's Daily Online* reported.

Many countries, meanwhile, have already made it clear that they are committed to economic frameworks that are at odds with the established liberal order, which is ostensibly based on democratic-capitalist ideals and long-standing principles of free markets and unfettered cross-border commerce. Robert J. Samuelson has described the approach taken by China and other emerging powers as the "new mercantilism." In a December 2007 *Washington Post* commentary, "The End of Free Trade," he noted that countries around the world are "growing more nationalistic. They're adopting policies intended to advance their own economic and political interests at others' expense."

Other geopolitical jockeying suggests that nations are preparing for a more dramatic transformation. According to an August 2007 Associated Press report by Ivan Sekretarev, "Russia, China Hold Joint War Games," the two countries' "forces held their first joint maneuvers on Russian land . . . in a demonstration of their growing military ties and a shared desire to counter U.S. global clout. . . . The summit concluded with a communiqué that sounded like a thinly veiled warning to the United States to stay away from the strategically placed, resource-rich region." Months later, Russia and India "agreed to launch a joint unmanned mission to the moon, as well as to intensify deals on weapons and energy," Thomson Financial reported in *Forbes* ("Russia, India to Join in Moon Mission"). Leaders of both countries called for boosting links, "with a view to more than doubling trade by the end of the decade. . . . High-tech, and particularly military cooperation, are at the center of bilateral ties, Putin said."

A December 2007 United Press International report ("Saudis, Indonesia Buy Arms from Russia") highlighted what many observers viewed as an especially surprising development: "Saudi Arabia and Indonesia, both generations-long allies of the United States, independently conclude[d] giant $1 billion plus arms deals with the Kremlin within a few weeks of each other." Although spurred in part by Russia's offer of cheap financing terms amid the multiyear boom in that country's oil and gas revenues, the weapons accords likely also reflected a more pragmatic assessment of long-term partnership arrangements.

The winds of change haven't just been blowing in the East; they've also been wafting through the United States' backyard. A May 2006 article by Barbara Slavin in *USA Today*, "Beijing Builds Ties with Latin Countries," noted that "China [was] expanding military and economic ties throughout Latin America, taking advantage of a wave of

anti-American candidates who have come to power and a U.S. law barring military training and aid to a dozen Latin countries. . . . 'China's
profile in the region has been ratcheting up sharply,' said Thomas
Shannon, Assistant Secretary of State for Western Hemisphere Affairs."
The Associated Press's Steve Gutterman highlighted Russia's similarly
expansive ambitions in the region in a September 2008 report, "Putin
Says Ties with Latin America a Top Priority."

Hence, at a time when numerous portents are signaling an impending change in the international order, there's mounting evidence that
various interests are already taking steps to prepare for it. They are not
waiting for the moment of truth to arrive; they are maneuvering now
to capitalize on what is likely to be a yawning chasm in future. While
some might quibble about the timing, the real question, then, is how
things will unfold as U.S. dominance wanes. Is another country poised
to assume the leadership mantle, like the United States was when it
stepped into the shoes of its culturally similar predecessor? Given language, political, economic, and other considerations, analysts are hard-
pressed to agree on any one candidate, at least in the short run.

An Unsettling Transition

Some observers have argued that the most likely outcome is a relatively orderly transition to benign multipolarity, facilitated, perhaps,
by the United States itself. In their view, the nation's formidable arsenal of nuclear and conventional weapons will continue to keep the
most unruly factions at bay, even as the United States loses its place at
the very top of the heap. And because so many countries have bought
into the existing international framework, few will have any real
incentive to change things or otherwise rock the boat. Paraphrasing
Newton's First Law of Motion, the optimists believe that the current
system of rules and institutions has a momentum of its own and will
likely carry on in its present form unless some other influence acts on it.

But our nation's precarious financial condition *is* the countervailing force. Countries that once viewed the United States as a vital
economic stepping-stone and reliable financial partner will be forced
to reassess their views and reevaluate their support in the face of a

wrenching, long-drawn-out, and virtually unstoppable process of economic unraveling and rebalancing. Those that long depended on U.S. aid—or even outright bribes to their corrupt leaders—will look elsewhere as the flow of dollars quickly dries up. Growing isolationist stirrings in Washington and around the nation will be seen by outsiders as a clear sign that the old rules and relationships no longer apply.

In the meantime, relentless pressure to cut back on out-of-control public spending—exacerbated still further by the extraordinarily costly bailouts of the financial sector during 2008—and also shift resources in favor of social programs amid rapidly deteriorating economic conditions will spur ongoing efforts to downsize and dismantle the nation's vast military presence at home and abroad. The threat of aggressive U.S. intervention will undoubtedly be taken much more lightly when the trappings of empire are no longer as visible as they were. In places like Japan and the Middle East, for example, longtime opponents of U.S. bases will step up calls for America's withdrawal, while agitators will repeatedly test the limits of the United States' wavering commitment to long-distance imperialism.

More broadly, the onset of a deep and prolonged contraction in the United States, along with corrections of breathtaking but ultimately unsustainable investment booms in places like China and the Middle East, will lay the groundwork for chronic worldwide malaise. That will naturally call into question all sorts of relationships, treaties, systems, and structures that were premised on a continuation of favorable economic conditions. Developed and mature nations alike will become increasingly focused on ensuring they don't lose out, forcing others to do the same. Instead of an established world order, it will be a global free-for-all. Along with the emerging leadership vacuum, these struggles will provoke a shake-up of political, economic, and military alliances around the world.

In many ways, the chaotic unraveling of the Soviet Union, spurred on by an array of economic woes and the suddenly widespread realization that the center lacked legitimacy, will be a model for the kind of upheaval we can expect. Echoing the abrupt rejection of Moscow's authority by constituent republics, U.S. allies and adversaries alike will become unbound. They will step up challenges to American supremacy on myriad fronts. Emerging global powers, including China and Russia, along with established regional rivals like Iran and Venezuela, will assert their influence, prodded still further by the rumblings of sizable populations looking for their share of the economic pie. Other nations will join in as long-simmering hostilities rise to the surface, stirring calls for payback.

Years of arrogant and self-serving meddling in others' affairs will come back to haunt the United States. In the Middle East, for example, the changing world order will undoubtedly spur individuals, groups, and countries to put U.S. commitments in the area to the test, in the hope of undermining long-established relationships and forcing a dramatic reversal of fortune in the region's power balance. Longtime American allies, including Israel and Saudi Arabia, will almost certainly be the focus of attention.

As the existing framework breaks down and the threat of U.S. intrusiveness recedes, nationalist sentiments and a mood of rebelliousness will spring up everywhere, seemingly out of thin air. The idea-spreading contagiousness of the Internet and the emergence in recent years of state-supported news services and other alternatives to Western media sources will compound revolutionary stirrings. Around the world, there will a rejection of one-size-fits-all institutions, standards, and cultural norms. Localities, nations, and regions will be rocked by calls for secession, realignment, and bloody revolt. Those who are uncertain and afraid will look for ways to defend their interests. Those who are sure and newly emboldened will seek to turn their ideas into action.

All the while, a host of other influences will be rearing their ugly heads.

Chapter 2

Tides, Torrents, and Tsunamis

The superior power of population cannot be checked, without producing misery or vice, the ample portion of these too bitter ingredients in the cup of human life, and the continuance of the physical causes that seem to have produced them bear too convincing a testimony.

—Thomas Malthus

In his "Essay on the Principle of Population," published two centuries ago, Thomas Malthus, the English demographer and political economist, theorized that human populations tended to expand at a much faster rate than available resources, eventually triggering an abrupt return to subsistence living conditions. Yet while the number of people in the world has grown exponentially since then, various factors have also spurred a similarly dramatic increase in the world's supply of food and other necessities, forestalling what many have described as a "Malthusian catastrophe."

Among the developments accounting for the boost in output are the long-running global economic boom, spectacular technological innovations and productivity enhancements, and a free-flowing pipeline of low-cost energy, especially during the postwar period. Thomas Homer-Dixon, author of *The Upside of Down: Catastrophe, Creativity, and the Renewal of Civilization*, asserted in a 2007 *AlterNet* interview by Terrence McNally that access to a seemingly inexhaustible supply of oil and other fossil fuels has "allowed us to increase the amount of energy in our food production systems by 80-fold" over the past 100 years, leading to a significant rise in agricultural yields—though, it should be noted, to a much lesser degree.

Now, however, there is evidence that the world's population of 6.6 billion people—which, according to the U.S. Census Bureau, is around four times what it was at the start of the twentieth century and more than twice the number that existed in 1960—is beginning to place a huge strain on available resources, from food and water to a range of other important commodities. Interestingly, despite the rapid expansion that has taken place during the past two centuries, population growth rates aren't necessarily the main concern nowadays. Many experts argue, in fact, that the pace of increases actually peaked in the 1960s.

What is having a more pronounced effect on the resource supply-demand equation is a structural shift in regional consumption patterns, as populations in fast-growing countries like China and India look to savor the fruits long enjoyed by the United States and other economically advanced nations. Jared Diamond, author of *Collapse: How Societies Choose to Fail or Succeed*, wrote in a 2008 *New York Times* Op-Ed, "What's Your Consumption Factor?" that "the estimated one billion people who live in developed countries have a relative per-capita consumption rate of 32. Most of the world's other 5.5 billion people constitute the developing world, with relative per-capita consumption rates below 32, mostly down toward one." But if, for example, China were to reach the same level as the United States, overall rates of consumption would be twice what they are now; if India did the same, the total would be three times as much. "And if the whole of the world were suddenly to catch up," Diamond warned, "world rates would increase elevenfold. It would be as if the world population ballooned to 72 billion people (retaining present consumption rates)."

Demographic Dynamics

Other demographic trends pose no less of a threat, though for different reasons. While many might view a slowdown in the overall rate of population growth as a welcome development, country-by-country patterns vary considerably. This disparity causes problems in its own right. In Russia, Japan, South Korea, and various Western European countries, for example, United Nations and U.S. Census Bureau data indicate that fertility rates—the average number of offspring that women of child-bearing age are having—have dropped well below the equilibrium level of 2.1, putting downward pressure on population sizes. Such declines create economic stresses, including mismatches between societal needs and productive resources and a dampening of future demand. Another concern stems from the so-called demographic tsunami in the United States and other nations, where the costs of rapidly aging populations are being shouldered by a shrinking number of workers. Such a shortfall lays the groundwork for future generational clashes. The long-standing pattern of rising life expectancies only worsens matters.

Meanwhile, populations in many poorer, often Muslim-dominated countries have continued to expand at a hefty pace, bolstered by fertility rates that are more than three times as high as the equilibrium rate. According to columnist and author Mark Steyn, writing in a *Wall Street Journal* Opinion Journal commentary, "It's the Demography, Stupid," Somalia produces 6.91 babies per woman, Niger 6.83, Afghanistan 6.78, and Yemen 6.75. Compare that with rates of 1.1 in Spain—which effectively allows the nation's population to fall by half within a generation, all else being equal—and 1.2 in Italy and Russia. These regional birth-rate disparities have spawned a number of destabilizing trends, including large migrations of illegal immigrants into Western Europe. The influx has strained public resources and heightened xenophobia in the destination countries, many of which are already lumbered with costly welfare programs. A rise in indigent and uneducated populations has also fostered unrest at home and abroad, enhancing recruitment efforts by terrorists and extremists.

Meanwhile, in two of the world's most populous countries, long-standing social preferences, ill-conceived government policies designed to curb population growth, and an assortment of economic constraints have spawned another unintended consequence: gender imbalances. China, where the Communist-led government adopted a mandatory one-child policy three decades ago, and India have both seen a demo-graphically atypical rise in the male-female ratio, which has report-edly been helped along by gender-selective abortions and infanticides. Many analysts believe that a surfeit of single males leads to social insta-bility and a proclivity toward conflict. Indeed, a 2007 study by Lena Edlund and others, "More Men, More Crime: Evidence from China's One-Child Policy," found that "increasing maleness of [China's] young adult population may account for as much as a third of the over-all rise in crime" from 1988 to 2004. But that is not all. According to *Bloomberg*'s William Pesek, the concern in that region "goes beyond young men with no prospects of finding mates in the decades ahead. Economists say the gap may undermine Asian growth and productivity, and lead to bigger budget deficits."

The End of Abundance

Taken together, these demographic torrents compound other, largely interconnected threats to well-being and stability at a time when the geopolitical, economic, and social order is already poised for dramatic change. After decades—or, perhaps, a millennium or more—of having relatively easy access to what seemed like virtually limitless supplies of resources such as energy and water—and, perhaps, fresh air and sun-light—mankind is being forced to come to terms with a new reality: the end of the age of abundance.

Throughout the postwar period—the "American century," as former *Time* publisher Henry Luce once described it—the global economy has boomed, helping to improve living standards worldwide. Although the United States has been at the head of the pack for dec-ades in terms of per-capita income, others have not stood still. More recently, economic growth rates in many developing nations have raced past those of the United States and other mature powers, enabling China, for example, to overtake Japan and Germany to become the world's second largest economy. Aside from improving economic fortunes around the globe, the multidecade-long economic upswing has helped boost demand for—and the prices of—myriad resources, including oil and other carbon-based fossil fuels, as well as food-related products, potable water, and various industrial commodities.

For a long time, this appetite was satisfied by equally fast-growing sources of supply, stimulated by technological advances and the efforts of wealthy multinational corporations scouring the globe. Over the past decade, however, there has been a visible buildup of stresses and bottlenecks, signaling a seemingly intractable disparity between supply and demand. Basic resources and industrial materials that were once readily available at relatively low cost are now more expensive and harder to find. Moreover, the biggest consumers and most aggressive buyers aren't only located in traditionally resource-hungry regions like the United States or Europe; they are cropping up everywhere, including Asia, the Middle East, Latin America, and Africa. At the same time, many traditional suppliers are making it clear that they no longer wish to play by the rules of what has been a Western-dominated game.

One reason for the shifting dynamic stems from the fact that, for an expanding array of resources, most notably energy, the easy pickings are all but gone. More time, money, and effort are being spent now than in the past on getting the most out of existing sources and uncovering new wellsprings of supply. In many cases, even though important discoveries have been made, reserves still appear to be diminishing fast, raising the prospect that future availability will dwindle past the point of no return. Such perspectives underscore increasingly widespread acceptance of the concept of "peak oil." Based on a theory developed by geophysicist M. King Hubbert, whose 1956 prediction that U.S. oil production would top out in 10 to 15 years proved remarkably prescient, the term has come to describe a point in time when global petroleum output has reached its zenith and has rolled over into terminal decline. The inevitable result: higher prices for and shortages of a commodity that has been a primary driver of growth and prosperity.

To be sure, energy industry officials and peak-oil skeptics, many of whom are well informed, challenge the notion that the world's supply of oil and other hydrocarbons will eventually dry up. Many believe that higher prices, among other things, invariably stimulate efforts that help augment global reserve totals and boost available output. In late 2007, for example, Brazil's state oil company announced that it had "discovered as much as eight billion barrels of light crude in an ultra-deep field off the coast of Rio de Janeiro, an amount that could help transform the country into a major world oil exporter," Alan Clendenning of the Associated Press reported in "Brazil Oil Field May Hold 8B Barrels."

Others predict that technology improvements and various efficiencies will allow a lot more oil to be teased from existing sources of supply. Nansen G. Saleri, the former head of reservoir management for state-owned Saudi Aramco, wrote in a March 2008 *Wall Street Journal* article that "modern extraction methods will undoubtedly stretch" the "tipping point" assumptions of Hubbert—which Saleri argued were based on "Sputnik-era technologies"—by as much as two decades or more.

Some have even questioned whether petroleum derives from biological origins at all, undercutting the widely held belief that supplies are finite. This view gained a modicum of credence when a team of scientists at Johns Hopkins University discovered that Saturn's moon Titan had "hundreds of times more liquid hydrocarbons than all the known oil and natural gas reserves on Earth," according to a February 2008 *WorldNetDaily* report by Jerome R. Corsi.

Still, research from the Association for the Study of Peak Oil and Gas (ASPO) and others documenting the fact that output at large oil fields around the world has tracked the bell-shaped production curve first outlined by Hubbert tends to reinforce a more pessimistic outlook. In January 2008, Alan Abelson of *Barron's* highlighted a report from energy expert Matt Simmons, author of *Twilight in the Desert: The Coming Saudi Oil Shock and the World Economy*, arguing that "global production peaked in 2005 at 74,298,000 barrels a day," while consumption was "rapidly approaching 88 million barrels." According to an article by Neil King Jr. in the *Wall Street Journal*, "White House Sets Long View on Oil," the excess capacity available for emergencies was around two million barrels per day in early 2008, down from 3.1 million barrels eight years previously.

Michael T. Klare, author of *Blood and Oil: The Dangers and Consequences of America's Growing Dependence on Imported Petroleum*, wrote in a 2006 *Foreign Policy in Focus* commentary, "Ever since the 1960s, the most fruitful decade in the worldwide discovery of new oilfields, there has been a steady decline in the identification of new deposits, according to . . . the U.S. Army Corps of Engineers. Even more worrisome, the rate of oilfield discovery fell below the rate of global petroleum consumption in the 1980s, and since then has fallen to approximately half the rate of consumption. This means we are increasingly relying on deposits found in previous decades to slake our insatiable thirst for petroleum."

Even those who challenge the notion that oil, gas, and other fossil fuels are set to run out acknowledge that there are other, no less critical constraints to bringing fresh supplies to market. A November 2007 *Wall Street Journal* report by Russell Gold and Ann Davis, "Oil Officials See Limit Looming on Production," revealed, for example, that "a growing number of oil-industry chieftains are endorsing an idea long deemed fringe: The world is approaching a practical limit to the number of barrels of crude oil that can be pumped every day." Among the reasons cited were "restricted access to oil fields, spiraling costs, and increasingly complex oil-field geology." By the same token, other analysts have noted that while supplies of lower-quality grades of oil are more abundant than the benchmark light sweet variety, refineries and systems are largely configured to process the latter product, presenting a costly and time-consuming logistical challenge.

When Supply Doesn't Meet Demand

Arguably, then, the real concern is not whether peak-oil proponents are literally correct. Regardless of whether one is referring to full-scale exhaustion of global hydrocarbon reserves or the fact that existing output can't keep pace with demand, it's clear that a destabilizing gap has opened up between production and consumption. In fact, many experts would argue that demand-side developments, spurred in large part by the developments cited earlier, represent the most problematic aspect of the global energy equation. During the past four decades or so, global oil consumption has climbed sharply. Based on data from the *BP Statistical Review of World Energy 2007*, demand rose from 31.2 million barrels a day in 1965 to 83.7 million in 2006, an increase of around 170 percent. Over that span, India's and mainland China's combined share of the total grew eightfold, from 1.5 percent to nearly 12 percent, while the U.S. share fell from 37 percent to just under a quarter of world consumption.

In a November 2007 *Financial Times* column, "Welcome to a World of Runaway Energy Demand," Martin Wolf cited statistics from the International Energy Agency (IEA)'s *World Energy Outlook* highlighting the dramatic impact that rising standards of living were having on overall consumption. According to the IEA, "the increase in China's energy demand between 2002 and 2005 was equivalent to Japan's current annual energy usage." What's more, Wolf added, "if governments stick with current policies . . . the world's energy needs will be more than 50 percent higher in 2030 than today, with developing countries accounting for 74 percent, and China and India alone for 45 percent, of the growth in demand." He also noted the agency's forecast that fossil fuels will "account for 84 percent of the increase in global energy consumption between 2005 and 2030."

Explosive economic growth in populous nations like China and, to a lesser extent, India has fostered and accompanied their transformation from agrarian-based economic lightweights to modern industrial and commercial powerhouses, further bolstering their seemingly insatiable demand for energy. According to a *Wall Street Journal* article by Leila Abboud and John Biers, "Business Goes on an Energy Diet," businesses are "some of the world's biggest energy consumers. They need huge amounts of electricity to keep their factories humming and their stores air-conditioned, as well as countless gallons of gasoline for their delivery trucks. . . . The manufacturing sector alone accounts for nearly one-third of the world's global energy use."

Adding to concerns is the fact that a sizable share of oil-producing nations have seen a dramatic transformation in their own consumption habits in recent years, fueled by public subsidies for energy usage as well as increasing industrialization. A 2007 *New York Times* report by Clifford

Krauss, "Oil-Rich Nations Use More Energy, Cutting Exports," found that "the economies of many big oil-exporting countries are growing so fast that their need for energy within their borders is crimping how much they can sell abroad, adding new strains to the global oil market. Experts say the sharp growth, if it continues, means several of the world's most important suppliers may need to start importing oil within a decade to power all the new cars, houses, and businesses they are buying and creating with their oil wealth." In the same vein, a May 2008 *Times* (London) article by Carl Mortished suggested that some countries in the Middle East might "soon need coal imports to keep the lights on."

To be sure, certain developments cast doubt on the notion that the thirst for energy can continue to grow at the dizzying pace of recent years. For one thing, the combination of far-reaching economic slow-down in the United States and elsewhere, America's loss of standing on the world stage, a messy unraveling of global financial imbalances, and rising protectionism will undermine globalization-inspired prosperity. In addition, the pattern of price increases in recent years suggests the structural price band for oil has likely shifted upward, ruling out a return to the days of $10-a-barrel crude. Still, while both aspects will temper demand at one level, the impact will be partially or maybe even fully offset by marginal consumption increases in populous and economically emergent nations that have sought to catch up with the developed world.

Shifting consumption patterns will also exacerbate an existing source of tension, which has been highlighted by historian and author Niall Ferguson and others: the uneven geographical distribution of available supplies and a growing divide between haves and have-nots, in regard to energy as well as other vital commodities. For example, according to "Country Energy Profiles" data from the U.S. Energy Information Administration (EIA), the top five net oil exporting countries in 2006 were Saudi Arabia, Russia, the United Arab Emirates, Norway, and Iran, while the leading importers were the United States, Japan, China, Germany, and South Korea, with each group accounting for roughly half of the respective totals. Needless to say, the mismatch has already provoked plenty of standoffs and skirmishes.

However, when various interests are aggressively competing for geopolitical advantage, the troubles will be even more pronounced.

As far as the oil market is concerned, the prospect that output will be concentrated among a shrinking group of producers can only mean a much more contentious future for all involved. In its *World Energy Outlook 2007*, the *Financial Times*' Wolf reported, the International Energy Agency (IEA) forecast that the "share of world supply coming from members of the Organization of Petroleum Exporting Countries will rise from 42 percent to 52 percent [by 2030]. Moreover, 'a supply-side crunch in the period to 2015 involving an abrupt escalation in oil prices cannot be ruled out.'"

Interestingly, energy consumers aren't the only ones feeling vulnerable. Various news reports have detailed something of a scramble in recent years by Russia, the world's leading producer of natural gas and a supplier of 25 percent of Europe's gas needs, to diversify its customer base and reduce its reliance on marketing domestically generated output. The longtime U.S. rival has signed contracts with a wide array of producers in Central Asia, struck deals for additional gas distribution pipelines into Europe, and sought out new markets in Japan, China, and elsewhere. This has been done, in part, to lessen the threat of a collective push-back from its European customers, which together account for a substantial share of Russian hydrocarbon exports.

Collateral Damage

As it happens, supply-and-demand mismatches aren't the only concern. Years of energy-dependent growth and an overreliance on fossil fuels have also caused all sorts of collateral damage, especially in regard to the environment. Such will only worsen in future. The EIA, for instance, has forecast that the share of energy consumption accounted for by coal, which releases more carbon into the air—not to mention other hazardous by-products—per unit of energy than oil and other hydrocarbons, will rise from 26 percent to 28 percent of global consumption over the next three decades. The agency predicts that "China and India together [will] account for 72 percent of the projected increase in world coal consumption from 2004 to 2030. Strong economic growth . . . is projected for both countries, and much of the increase in their demand for energy, particularly in the industrial and electricity sectors, is expected to be met by coal." Of course, the EIA's assumptions may well prove overly optimistic, especially in light of recent economic woes, but other constraints could still leave those nations with few alternatives as far as their fuel choices are concerned.

Indeed, while one side effect of peak oil is higher prices for the commodity, which many view as a welcome means of curbing demand for petroleum-based energy products, the structural boost in developing countries' consumption patterns hints at other, less desirable consequences. According to Daniel Gros, director of the Centre for European Policy Studies, "coal's supply elasticity is much higher than that of oil, so rising demand encourages substitution to dirty coal from cleaner oil—and switching is easy ex ante but hard ex post. In the next 10 years," he argued in a column for *Vox*, "China will install more power-generation capacity than Europe's current stock. If it is all coal-burning, emissions will be difficult to reduce for decades."

Toxic discharges have already spawned serious problems in developing nations—as well as many other countries around the world. In a 2006 article, "Pollution from Chinese Coal Casts a Global Shadow," Keith Bradsher and David Barboza of the *New York Times* noted that "the sulfur dioxide produced in coal combustion poses an immediate threat to the health of China's citizens, contributing to about 400,000 premature deaths a year. It also causes acid rain that poisons lakes, rivers, forests, and crops." According to an article by Jacques Leslie in the *Christian Science Monitor*, "China's Pollution Nightmare Is Now Everyone's Pollution Nightmare," the fallout "severely damages forests and watersheds in Korea and Japan and impairs air quality in the U.S." A 2007 *Wall Street Journal* report by Robert Lee Hotz, "Huge Dust Plumes from China Cause Changes in Climate," described "an outpouring of dust layered with man-made sulfates, smog, industrial fumes, carbon grit, and nitrates" that had crossed the Pacific Ocean "on prevailing winds from booming Asian economies in plumes so vast they alter the climate."

For many experts, though, polluting emissions from the burning of dirty coal and other fossil fuels, as well as the environmental degradation caused by the unchecked industrialization that has taken place in China and other developing nations, may be no match for the damage being done to the earth's climate. Among the developments worth considering, notes the *Financial Times'* Wolf, citing a United Nations Development Programme report, are the following:

> Atmospheric concentrations of carbon dioxide continue to rise at a rate of 1.9 parts per million a year; over the past 10 years the annual growth rate of emissions has been 30 percent faster than the average for the past 40 years; if the rate of emissions were to rise in line with current trends, stocks of CO2 in the atmosphere might be double pre-industrial levels by 2035; and that, argues the [Intergovernmental] Panel on Climate Change [IPCC], would give a likely temperature increase of 3 degrees C, though rises of over 4.5 degrees C cannot be excluded.

Such concerns have caused many environmental groups and traditionally left-leaning politicians and political parties to raise the alarm and press for immediate and concerted action. That has fostered international agreements aimed at countering unwelcome climate changes, though the results have thus far been less than promising. One well-known example is the Kyoto Protocol, a treaty negotiated in 1997 and later ratified by more than 175 countries whereby signatories committed to reducing their emissions of carbon dioxide and other greenhouse gases. Many fault the fact that developing nations such as China, the world's largest emitter of CO2, according to 2007 data from the Netherlands Environmental Assessment Agency, have only been required to monitor and report emissions.

In fairness, some researchers have questioned whether human activities cause global warming. Yet despite their arguments that the evidence remains unclear, data is incomplete, models are unreliable, and factors like solar variations can affect the earth's climate, a landmark 2007 report from the IPCC asserted that there is "unequivocal" evidence that human activities do affect the climate, according to Richard Black of *BBC News*. Citing scientists who agreed with the assessment of the intergovernmental body set up by the World Meteorological Organization and the United Nations Environment Programme, the British news service noted that there has been "a warming trend of about 0.8 degrees C since 1900, more than half of which [had] occurred since 1979."

A March 2008 European Union study, prepared by two of the region's senior foreign policy officials, went even further, arguing that the "the risks of climate change have turned from a threat to reality impacting the conflict in Darfur, migration from flood-prone Bangladesh, and hopes for stability in the Middle East," *Agence France-Presse* reported in an article entitled "Climate Change a New Factor in Global Tensions: EU." "From Africa to Asia, and from pole to pole, climate change has become a 'threat multiplier which exacerbates existing trends, tensions, and instability.' " Those threats include a "reduction of arable land, widespread shortages of water, diminishing food and fish stocks, increased flooding, and prolonged droughts."

Wrong No More?

Indeed, while energy-related concerns have garnered almost constant attention since the oil-price shocks of the 1970s, the kinds of resource constraints that Thomas Malthus would have readily identified with have also come to the fore during the past few years. In a March 2008 article, "Already We Have Riots, Hoarding, Panic: The Sign of Things to Come?" Carl Mortished of the *Times* (London) reported that the "specter of food shortages is casting a shadow across the globe, causing riots in Africa, consumer protests in Europe and panic in food-importing countries," with concerns centering on the availability of basic staples. "Half of the planet depends on rice," he noted, while "stocks are at their lowest since the mid-1970s when Bangladesh suffered a terrible famine. Rice production will fall this year below the global consumption level of 430 million tons."

Many factors account for the relatively recent supply-demand gaps, including population increases and droughts in key growing regions. However, rising standards of living have also spawned a surge in demand for a variety of foodstuffs, including proteins like fish and meat. Terrence McNally, in an interview with Thomas Homer-Dixon, notes, "Since 1950, industrialized fishing has reduced the total mass of large fish in the world's oceans by 90 percent." In a December 2007 article, "The End of Cheap Food," the *Economist* reported that rising food prices were "underpinned by long-running changes in diet that accompany the growing wealth of emerging economies—the Chinese consumer who ate 20 kg (44lb) of meat in 1985 will scoff over 50 kg of the stuff this year. That in turn pushes up demand for grain: it takes 8 kg of grain to produce one of beef."

Making matters worse, modern food production has, as noted earlier, become very energy-intensive. "From farm to plate," wrote Danielle Murray of the Earth Policy Institute in a 2005 commentary, "the modern food system relies heavily on cheap oil. Threats to our oil supply are also threats to our food supply. As food undergoes more processing and travels farther, the food system consumes ever more energy each year." According to Murray, "The U.S. food system uses over 10 quadrillion Btu . . . of energy each year, as much as France's total annual energy consumption. Growing food accounts for only one-fifth of this. The other four-fifths is used to move, process, package, sell, and store food after it leaves the farm."

The *Economist* also highlighted another factor, closely related to energy concerns, that helped boost its food-price index to the highest level since it was created in 1845: "America's reckless ethanol subsidies." Biofuels took a third of the United States' record maize (corn) harvest during 2007, and "the 30 million tons of extra maize going to ethanol [that year amounted] to half the fall in the world's overall grain stocks," the magazine reported. In July 2008, Aditya Chakrabortty of the *Guardian* detailed a confidential World Bank report that found biofuels had "forced global food prices up by 75 percent." According to a *CNN* report, "Riots, Instability Spread as Food Prices Skyrocket," Jean Ziegler, United Nations special rapporteur on the right to food, "has called using food crops to create ethanol 'a crime against humanity.'" Surging demand for arable land—as well as the lumber needed for construction and for manufactured wood products—has spurred clearcutting and burning of carbon-absorbing forests and rainforests in South America, Southeast Asia, and elsewhere, adding to climate woes.

Along similar lines, the chairman and chief executive of Swiss consumer giant Nestlé has "warned the food industry would need to fight the biofuels industry for access to arable land as the world runs short of water," Jenny Wiggins of the *Financial Times* reported in "Nestlé Chief Warns of Land Resources Clash." In fact, evidence suggests that an even more precarious gap has opened up between the demand for potable—clean—water and available supplies. Helter-skelter economic growth, unconstrained industrialization, ill-conceived modernization programs, inadequate treatment facilities, lax environmental standards, and misguided government subsidies—along with the wasteful corruption that is often a way of life in many developing countries—have led to increasing shortages of what has been called "the elixir of life" in cities, countries, and regions around the world.

Data from the World Health Organization (WHO) and UNICEF reveal that 20 percent of the world's population lacks access to what is undoubtedly an essential resource. According to Jared Diamond, "something like 70 percent of the fresh water in the world is already utilized." In "Olympics Water Diversion Threatens Millions," Jamil Anderlini of the *Financial Times* quoted one local official who "warned of an impending social and environmental disaster [in China] because of overuse of scarce water resources." A March 2008 Reuters report by Gerard Wynn detailed research by Zurich-based Sustainable Asset Management arguing that "water shortage is already a serious problem in many regions of the world, . . . [including] southern Spain, the Maghreb, the Middle East, Central Asia, Pakistan, southern India, and northern China. In the Americas, the U.S. mid-west, Mexico, and the Andes are the worst-hit areas. Eastern Australia is also badly affected."

But that is only a part of the story. Experts also point to a related but potentially greater concern. According to WHO/UNICEF, about 2.6 billion people lack access to basic sanitation facilities, including simple latrines. Consequently, more than two million children die of diarrhea each year, while half of those who live in developing nations suffer from the same ailment or other diseases like cholera, typhoid, trachoma, and parasitic worms. In a column arguing that the issue of water, not oil, is the biggest threat to Asia's long-term prosperity, *Bloomberg*'s Andy Mukherjee noted that "it isn't so much the likelihood of Asian cities running out of fresh water that should bother the region's policy makers as the bigger danger of being overwhelmed by waste water."

The list of resource-related concerns doesn't end there, however. Markets for other important commodities have also been turned upside down by adverse shifts in supply-and-demand dynamics, especially during recent years. In a December 2006 *Wall Street Journal* commentary, Niall

Ferguson described how the boom in Asia had impacted demand for various industrial metals. "Between 2002 and 2005, according to the IMF, China accounted for literally all the global growth of zinc and lead consumption, and more than 80 percent of the increase in tin and nickel consumption." Rising standards of living in many developing nations have also spurred growing interest in precious metals—as jewelry, a hedge against inflation, and a store of wealth.

Meanwhile, supplies have been constrained by an assortment of obstacles, including, as Ferguson noted, a "lack of investment and increased political risk." In a February 2008 article, "Global Shortage of Metals Looming," Peter Hodson of Canada's *Financial Post* reported that cost overruns, financing difficulties, heightened environmental concerns, and even Mother Nature were hindering expansion plans and delaying the launch of new mining projects that would help ensure the future availability of commodities like copper, zinc, and gold.

Searching for Greener Alternatives

To be sure, there have been various efforts, some more successful than others, to counter growing resource constraints and related concerns. No doubt higher prices and the collateral costs associated with harmful emissions and untreated waste by-products, for example, have been a powerful motivating factor. Still, approaches have varied. In many cases, particularly in economically advanced nations, much of the emphasis has been on reducing consumption through education and jawboning, efficiency drives, and incentives, government-sponsored or otherwise. Businesses have also become more interested in reducing outlays for fuel and other inputs to maintain profit margins. An IEA study revealed, for instance, that "energy use in heavy industry could be reduced by 18 percent to 26 percent just by applying best practices and available technologies," according to the *Wall Street Journal* article by Leila Abboud and John Biers on businesses' energy use cited earlier.

Countries with a strong and growing appetite for oil and other vital commodities, especially in those instances where there is extensive state involvement in the private sector, have moved to develop, improve, and expand access to potential sources of supply—wherever they might be found. China and India, for example, have struck accords and established trading relationships with an expanding universe of energy and commodity producers, many of whom have long been hostile to U.S. and other Western interests. Large consuming nations are also sourcing supplies in extremely inhospitable regions of the world and are covering the cost of building pipelines and establishing logistical capabilities that allow materials to be readily shipped back to home markets.

Along with efforts aimed at reducing the demand for and increasing the supply of oil and other hydrocarbons, in particular, there has also been an intense scramble to come up with substitutes and alternatives. As noted earlier, one side effect of the relatively recent pattern of rising oil prices has been an increase in the use of coal in places like China—where domestic stocks of the mineral are plentiful—despite its damaging side effects. But even then, there has been belated recognition of the economic and social costs involved. In a December 2007 article, "China Eco-Watchdog Gets Teeth," Andrew Batson of the *Wall Street Journal* reported that "China's environmental controls, long criticized as ineffective, are starting to have real economic bite."

Such concerns have spurred a search for technology and processes that allow waste to be recycled or converted into useful by-products. A January 2008 *BusinessWeek* article by Chi-Chu Tschang noted plans by China "to take advantage of methane, a gas that is a by-product of coal mining, by using it to power steel mills, heat homes, and fuel public buses and taxis." The nation's air quality also stood to benefit from a reduction in emissions of methane, which "contains 21 times more carbon than the carbon dioxide," according to the magazine.

And while there have clearly been unintended consequences associated with attempts to achieve energy independence and reduce emissions through expanded use of biofuels, some countries have nonetheless garnered a measure of success in that regard. A February 2006 *Wall Street Journal* report by David Luhnow, "How Brazil Broke Its Oil Habit," detailed how the rising Latin American power had managed to end its "'addiction' to imported oil in part by using alternative fuels," including sugar cane–derived ethanol. The newspaper did note, however, that in order for the United States and other countries to achieve similar results, very difficult political choices would be required.

Still, odds are that biofuels won't be the key focus of attention. At the very least, the upheavals in global food markets that began in earnest during the latter part of 2007 will call many such efforts into question, spurring a major reappraisal by policy makers. Instead, there will likely be a much greater emphasis on other, greener alternatives, including wind power, solar power, and hydropower. According to the Renewable Energy Policy Network for the 21st Century, the latter already accounts for nearly a fifth of global electricity production. The U.S. Department of Energy, meanwhile, expects that "20 percent of the nation's power could be produced by wind by 2030," according to Lauren Berry of the *Charlotte Observer*, up from 3 percent in 2006.

The Irony of Going Nuclear

In what some might view as an ironic turn of events, a growing number of countries are also embracing nuclear fission as a clean alternative to burning fossil fuels. Until recent years, worries about safety stemming from the disastrous 1986 accident at Russia's Chernobyl nuclear power plant, together with problems associated with radioactive waste disposal, have impeded the industry's expansion. However, those fears have gradually eased amid improvements in technology and the increasingly widespread belief that conventional energy sources will prove inadequate in future. Even the green movement has come around to the idea that atomic energy makes more sense than biofuels, for example.

Various reports have chronicled the nascent change in attitudes. One example includes a January 2008 *BusinessWeek* article by Mark Scott, "In Europe, New Life for Nuclear," which reported that Britain was leading the EU's "bid to reconsider an energy source that can reduce oil dependence and emissions." The magazine added, "London isn't the only capital rethinking nuclear power. With its low carbon dioxide output and resistance to rising oil and gas prices, nuclear power generation meets many requirements of European countries looking to meet stringent European Union targets for greenhouse gas reductions and to reduce energy dependence on oil and gas imports from Russia and the Middle East."

To be sure, support for the nuclear energy renaissance hasn't been unequivocal, despite its newfound popularity. "Some countries hopping on the nuclear bandwagon have abysmal safety records and corrupt ways that give many pause for thought," George Jahn of the Associated Press reported in "Developing World's Role in Nuclear Renaissance Raises Safety Concerns." "Of the more than 100 nuclear reactors now being built, planned, or on order, about half are in China, India, and other developing nations. Argentina, Brazil, and South Africa plan to expand existing programs; and Vietnam, Thailand, Egypt, and Turkey are among countries considering building their first reactors."

The biggest concern, however, stems from fears that the spread of the technology sets the stage for an accelerating global arms race. According to a February 2007 *Christian Science Monitor* article by Howard LaFranchi, "Iran's Pursuit of Nuclear Power Raises Alarms," if a "sense of entitlement to nuclear power and the fuel that makes it possible is allowed to take root, [nuclear nonproliferation experts] say, the world soon could find itself with dozens of nuclear countries with the means to switch from peaceful energy production to building a nuclear arsenal virtually overnight. . . . Many of those countries would be in such hot spots as the Middle East and Southeast Asia, where a mounting temptation to keep up with worrisome neighbors could be too much to resist."

In reality, it is already too late. Along with the United States and Russia, at least seven other countries have admitted to having atomic weapons or are believed to be in the nuclear club. That alone has stimulated efforts by others to catch up. Despite the existence of the Nuclear Non-Proliferation Treaty and efforts to safeguard know-how and materials, breaches have occurred. In January 2008, for example, in an article entitled "For Sale: West's Deadly Nuclear Secrets," the *Sunday Times* (London) reported a "series of extraordinary claims" made by Sibel Edmonds, a 37-year-old former Turkish language translator for the FBI, "about how corrupt government officials allowed Pakistan and other states to steal nuclear weapons secrets." Six months later, Jay Solomon of the *Wall Street Journal* detailed the discovery by Swiss authorities of advanced nuclear-weapons designs in computer files seized from a Pakistani smuggling network.

To try to avoid the economic and social challenges posed by growing resource constraints, countries around the world have raced to find alternatives. Among the options they have chosen is one that will almost certainly have unwelcome and unintended consequences. Without meaning to, they have heightened the risks in a world already destined to become more dangerous and violent.

Chapter 3

A Future of Violence

"Yeah? Why don't you ask 'Tom' about his older brother Ritchie? Ask 'Tom' how he tried to rip my eye out with barbed wire, and ask him, Edie, how come he's so good at killing people."
—"Carl Fogarty" (as played by actor Ed Harris) in
A History of Violence

The tagline of the 2005 film *A History of Violence* is: "Everyone has something to hide." Directed by David Cronenberg and starring Viggo Mortensen as "Tom Stall" and Maria Bello as his wife "Edie," the story centers on a seemingly mild-mannered small-town bar owner whose life is turned upside down after he kills two would-be robbers to protect his waitress. His heroic deed sets off an unexpected and violent chain reaction that ensnares his family and eventually reveals Tom's hidden past as a brutal hit man. In broader terms, the film explores the question of whether humans are, at their core, prone toward violence, especially in the face of a Darwinian struggle for survival.

Many would say that aggressiveness is in our genes. Indeed, a January 2008 *LiveScience* article by Jeanna Bryner, "Humans Crave Violence Just Like Sex," noted research by a team of scientists from Vanderbilt University, published in the journal *Psychopharmacology*, that revealed mice brains process aggressive behavior in the same way as other rewards. "Mice sought violence, in fact, picking fights for no apparent reason other than the rewarding feeling." According to Bryner, "the mouse brain is thought to be analogous to the human brain in this study, which could shed light on our fascination with brutal sports as well as our own penchant for the classic bar brawl. . . . In fact, the researchers say, humans seem to crave violence just like they do sex, food, or drugs."

To be sure, it would be hard to argue that violence, in all its forms, is as pervasive as it once was. In many parts of the world, the long-running economic boom and seemingly widespread acknowledgement of the benefits of living in civilized society have tempered the brutal and sadistic urges that regularly revealed themselves during more barbaric times. And while armed conflicts have continued to flare up and fester around the globe as they did during times past, mankind has seen nothing like the sickeningly destructive chaos that took place more than six decades ago, when tens of millions of soldiers and innocent civilians died during World War II.

There's little doubt, of course, that the United States' military dominance and its formidable nuclear arsenal—as well as other nations' long-standing acceptance of our role as global policeman of last resort—have helped to foster a degree of peace in the postwar period that is unprecedented. Now, though, with the United States poised to lose its place at the head of the geopolitical table and the prospect of an intense scramble for key resources, several developments suggest the world is on the cusp of a destabilizing shift in favor of rising violence and more frequent outbreaks of hostilities between individuals, groups, and nations.

Arguably, such a transformation may already be under way. In its 2006 annual report, "States in Armed Conflict," the Uppsala Conflict Data Program (UCDP) at Uppsala University's Department of Peace and Conflict Research wrote that "the number of conflicts in the world is no longer declining. . . . The trend toward fewer conflicts . . .

since the early 1990s now seems to have been broken." According to the Swedish-based UCDP, the turnabout followed nearly a decade and a half of continuous declines. Moreover, researchers expressed concerns that current conflicts were "extremely protracted," because the development indicates "that the successful negotiation efforts of the 1990s are no longer being carried out with the same force or effectiveness."

Data on U.S. crime rates, while not necessarily applicable to other countries, also hint at a transition of sorts. According to the Federal Bureau of Investigation (FBI), violent crime in the United States rose 1.9 percent in 2006, the second straight annual increase. Prior to that, it had fallen for 13 consecutive years, though the pace of decline has actually decelerated since 1998. In fairness, FBI data for 2007 revealed that the rate of violent crime, which includes murder and nonnegligent manslaughter, forcible rape, robbery, and aggravated assault, slipped lower again, by 1.4 percent. Nevertheless, downward momentum has clearly waned.

Many would argue, of course, that apparent stabilization is not the same as a reversal of trend. Yet there are other signs that point to a souring social mood around the globe. Hostile rhetoric and facile assertions that armed conflict may be the best way to resolve differences have become increasingly commonplace. In March 2008, for example, Venezuela's Hugo Chávez warned that Colombia's attack on a rebel encampment across the border in Ecuador "could spark a war," according to Ian James of the Associated Press. A month earlier, London's *Daily Mail* had reported that "fear of a new Balkan war gripped Western capitals . . . after the powder-keg state of Kosovo declared independence from its powerful neighbor Serbia" ("War Fears Put British Troops on Standby as Kosovo Declares 'Freedom' "). Though both proved to be false alarms, they reflect a mood shift that seems increasingly inflammatory, rather than conciliatory, when conflicts arise.

A January 2008 Associated Press report by George Jahn, meanwhile, carried warnings from Russia's military chief of staff that "Moscow could use nuclear weapons in preventative strikes." That same month, according to Ian Traynor of the United Kingdom's *Guardian*, former armed forces chiefs from the United States, Britain, Germany, France, and the Netherlands put forth a "radical" plan for reorganizing NATO that argued "the West must be ready to resort to a pre-emptive nuclear attack to try and halt the 'imminent' spread of nuclear and other weapons of mass destruction." All of a sudden, the frightening and formerly taboo subject of a nuclear first strike is just another strategic option.

The Strains of Awareness

Increasingly widespread awareness of an evolving world order, where nations such as China and Russia, among others, are continuing to gain ground at the expense of the United States, is also helping to boost the geopolitical temperature. As foreign policy expert G. John Ikenberry has noted, "power transitions are a recurring problem in international relations" that are "fraught with danger. . . . When a state occupies a commanding position in the international system, neither it nor weaker states have an incentive to change the existing order. But when the power of a challenger state grows and the power of the leading state weakens, a strategic rivalry ensues, and conflict—perhaps leading to war—becomes likely."

The strains have manifested themselves in various ways. Longtime U.S. rivals such as Venezuela and Iran, along with Russia, have stepped up their anti-American rhetoric, seeking to spur a groundswell of resentment against U.S. and other Western interests. For example, in a July 2007 article, "Iran, Venezuela in 'Axis of Unity' Against U.S.," Reuters highlighted remarks by Venezuela's Chávez concerning the two countries' plans to "defeat the imperialism of North America." In February 2008, Russia's foreign minister "called U.S. plans to build a global missile defense shield an example of 'imperial thinking,' and suggested . . . that Washington was using the system to try to encircle Russia," the Associated Press' Ryan Lucas reported in "Russia Criticizes U.S. 'Imperial Thinking.' " Five months later, Russia said it would be forced to "react with military means" if the United States moved forward after agreeing on a related deal with the Czech Republic, according to BBC News ("Russia Warns over U.S.-Czech Shield").

In a growing number of cases, harsh words have been matched by provocative actions. For example, a March 2008 report by the *Daily Telegraph's* Richard Spencer, "North Korea Provokes U.S. with Missile

Test," revealed that the rogue nation "let off a salvo of test missiles, issuing a defiant response to American demands for action over nuclear decommissioning and to a new conservative government in the South." A November 2007 article by Nick Coleman of *Agence France-Presse*, "Russia Abandons Key Cold War Arms Treaty," highlighted a number of aggressive steps taken by Moscow over the course of the year, including its decision to "renew strategic bomber patrols [and] withdraw from . . . bedrock disarmament treaties." In May 2008, the French-based news-wire also reported that "nuclear missiles and tanks paraded . . . across Red Square for the first time since the Soviet era," as new President Dmitry Medvedev "warned other nations against 'irresponsible ambitions' that he said could start wars" ("Nuclear Missiles Parade across Red Square").

To a number of observers, however, Russian president-turned-prime-minister Vladimir Putin's August 2008 decision to send troops into the breakaway Georgian territory of South Ossetia following an assault on the capital city of Tskhinvali by Georgian forces revealed a bold new assertiveness. With a swift and direct challenge to a key U.S. ally in the region, Putin scored a victory "not just over Georgia but also over the West, which has been trying to prise away countries on Russia's western borders and turn them democratic, market-oriented and friendly," according to a August 2008 *Economist* report, "Russia Resurgent." "Now that Russia has shown what can happen to those that distance themselves from it, doing so will be harder in future."

Not surprisingly, the nation many see as the United States' most serious rival has also become increasingly assertive in both words and deeds. In a May 2007 article, "China Warns U.S. May Set Off Arms Race," *China Daily* reported that the emerging Asian power had joined Russia "in criticizing a U.S. plan to build a missile defense system in Europe, saying the system could set off an arms race." According to a Chinese Foreign Ministry spokeswoman, speaking in measured diplomatic language that did little to allay the seriousness of the response, "the impact of a missile defense system on strategic defense and stability is not conducive to mutual trust of major nations and regional security. . . . It may also give rise to a proliferation problem."

A December 2007 report by Rowan Callick in the *Australian*, "China Warns U.S. to Keep Out of Taiwan," detailed a "series of incidents" between the two countries, including China's refusal to allow two storm-swept American minesweepers to seek shelter in Hong Kong's deep harbor, its abrupt denial of permission for a long-planned Thanksgiving holiday visit to Hong Kong by the U.S. aircraft carrier *Kitty Hawk* and its eight-ship escort (which was then followed by an abrupt and unexplained change of heart after all the ships had left the area), and China's decision to halt a routine quarterly visit by a cargo plane carrying supplies for the United States' consulate on the island.

China also roiled the United States, as well as many other nations, when it shot down an aging weather satellite in January 2007—with apparently little advance warning—using a ground-based medium-range ballistic missile. According to a *New York Times* report by Joseph Kahn detailing the incident, "China Shows Assertiveness in Weapons Test," the move "was perceived by East Asia experts as China's most provocative military action since it testfired missiles off the coast of Taiwan more than a decade ago. Unlike in the Taiwan exercise," the newspaper said, "the message this time was directed mainly at the United States, the sole superpower in space."

To some, these challenges are but a taste of what's to come. A July 2006 *Barron's* article by Jonathan R. Laing, "What Could Go Wrong with China?" highlighted an assertion by John Mearsheimer, a political scientist at the University of Chicago, "that an 'intense confrontation' between the United States and China is 'inevitable' in 20 years if China continues to grow at its current pace." The paper added that "similar predictions about Japan and the U.S. were made in the decades before the two nations went to war." Other analysts have noted various catalysts that could trigger a dangerous clash between the two countries. In January 2008, for instance, Robert Kagan, the founder of the Project for the New American Century, a neoconservative think tank that had pressed for the invasion of Iraq, told German weekly *Die Zeit*, "The Taiwan problem can explode at any moment" ("PNAC Founder Predicts U.S.-China War"). Jin Riguang, a Chinese government oil and natural gas adviser and a member of the Standing Committee of the Chinese People's Political Consultative Conference, said he expected to "see China and the U.S. coming into conflict over energy in the years ahead," according to an October 2006 *International Herald Tribune* report by William Mellor and Le-Min Lim.

Heat from the Hot Spots

But these sorts of eruptions are not the end of it. Along with the prospect of potentially devastating large-scale military encounters, evidence suggests that global terrorism is becoming a more pervasive threat than in past decades. Many observers believe this development has been fostered to a great extent by the military debacles in Iraq and Afghanistan and related forms of what author Chalmers Johnson describes as "blowback"—hostile responses to U.S. interventions, covert or otherwise, in the Middle East and in various hot spots around the globe. In its annual *2006 Country Reports on Terrorism*, the State Department reported that "new terrorist tactics and a spike in Iraqi violence led to a 25 percent increase in terrorist incidents worldwide," according to a report by David McKeeby.

To be sure, the energy-rich Middle East has long been a cauldron of geopolitical instability. In recent years, however, anxiety has been heightened by mounting anger and resentment toward Israel and the United States over the plight of the stateless Palestinians, as well as continuing conflicts between Israel and terrorist groups like Hamas and Hezbollah, many of which are believed to be supported by Syria, Iran, and other hostile interests in the region. Tensions also stem from the expanding influence of radical Islamism, with the demographic crosscurrents noted earlier helping to exacerbate a tendency toward instability and violence in areas where economic and social pressures naturally inflame anti-Western sympathies.

Iran's strategic intentions in the region, especially insofar as they relate to the country's nuclear ambitions, have stirred fears of a far-reaching and deadly conflict. Even though a December 2007 U.S. intelligence estimate concluded that the world's fourth largest oil producer had ended its nuclear weapons program four years earlier, many observers continue to believe that Iran's persistent interest in bolstering its atomic power-generating capabilities is part of a broader plan aimed at developing an aggressive nuclear presence. Such fears have prompted increasing speculation that Israel or the United States might launch a preemptive attack against the Middle Eastern nation. Iran, for its part, has threatened to "hit Tel Aviv, U.S. shipping in the Gulf, and American interests around the world if it is attacked over its disputed nuclear activities," according to a July 2008 Reuters report by Parisa Hafezi, "Iran to 'Hit Tel Aviv, U.S. Ships' If Attacked."

Pressure to keep up with this nettlesome neighbor, together with the search for fossil-fuel alternatives, has spurred others nearby to seek out nuclear technology—again, for ostensibly peaceful purposes. In January 2008, for example, the United Arab Emirates revealed plans for an atomic energy program, "becoming the first Arab state to go ahead with announced ambitions to develop nuclear power," Rhoula Khalaf of the *Financial Times* said. Arab states in and outside the Persian Gulf region have expressed a similar interest, he added. The urge to go nuclear has spread quickly, hinting at an accelerating scramble as countries press forward in fear of being left behind. Among the would-be nuclear-energy acquirers, according to reports, are Albania, Nigeria, Ghana, Venezuela, Georgia, Indonesia, and Vietnam. Yet as the numbers grow, the likelihood increases that there will be others like Iran—or worse. According to one expert cited by the *Christian Science Monitor* in "Iran's Pursuit of Nuclear Power Raises Alarms," by Howard LaFranchi, it is not "too difficult to foresee a world of dozens of virtual nuclear-weapons states, capable of building a bomb because of the nuclear material and technology they have, and Iran represents the danger of this future scenario."

Indeed, after North Korea announced that it had tested a nuclear bomb in October 2006, the head of the United Nations watchdog International Atomic Energy Agency (IAEA) warned that "as many as 30 countries might develop the capacity to produce nuclear weapons swiftly unless more is done to tackle the spread of the technology," according to Reuters. "Five countries—the U.S., Russia, China, France, and the U.K.—have formerly declared their nuclear weapons and signed the Nuclear Non-Proliferation Treaty," the newswire said, in an article by Karin Strohecker entitled "More Countries Could Develop Nuclear Bombs," while "the four other states . . . known to have an atomic bomb are India, Pakistan, Israel, and now North Korea."

More alarming still, reports suggest that terrorists and other rogue elements have stepped up efforts to get their hands on nuclear weapons. In March 2008, for example, Colombia's vice president "accused Communist guerillas in his country of trying to obtain radioactive material that would give the group the potential to develop a so-called dirty bomb," according to a *Wall Street Journal* article by John Lyons entitled "Colombia Says FARC Sought to Make 'Dirty Bomb.' " A January *WorldNetDaily* report, "Hunt Launched for 'Dirty Bomb' Ingredients," revealed that "British intelligence agents at stations across Europe are spearheading a hunt for enriched uranium that may be missing from Russia's poorly guarded stockpiles."

For many observers, there's no question about the implications of an increasingly widespread drive to acquire nuclear technology and know-how—whether characterized as peaceful or not. A senior Israeli cabinet minister, quoted in a November 2007 *Agence France-Presse* report (" 'Apocalyptic Scenario' If Egypt, Saudi Go Nuclear"), asserted that "Egyptian and Saudi nuclear ambitions, on top of Iran's atomic drive, will lead to an 'apocalyptic scenario.' " Just 10 months earlier, a transatlantic group of prominent scientists warned that "the world has nudged closer to a nuclear apocalypse and environmental disaster," largely because of atomic standoffs with Iran and North Korea, and moved the big hand of its symbolic Doomsday Clock by two minutes, to five minutes before midnight, according to Alex Morales of *Bloomberg*.

Buildups in Conventional Firepower

The prospect that even a small group of unstable or unfriendly regimes will have access to nuclear weapons undoubtedly represents the worst kind of threat to humanity. But in reality, the concerns don't end there. A growing number of countries and groups have also sought to build up large and potentially devastating stockpiles of conventional firepower. They have been aided by the aggressive deal-making efforts of global arms makers, including the United States and Russia. In the latter case, windfall gains from the sale of oil, gas, and other commodities have allowed Moscow to offer attractive terms on surface-to-air missiles, fighter jets, and other high-tech weaponry in its bid to project power around the world.

Deteriorating geopolitical conditions in the Middle East have motivated the financially stretched United States to remain an active supplier of weaponry, both there and elsewhere. In July 2007, for instance, the United States "announced new military pacts worth $US20 billion for Saudi Arabia, $US13 billion for Egypt, and $US30 billion for Israel in a bid to counter Iran," *Agence France-Presse* reported ("U.S. Arms Pacts to Counter Iran, Syria"). According to Secretary of State Condoleezza Rice, the goal of the accords was " 'to support our continued diplomatic engagement in the region.' " Was it merely a coincidence that only three months earlier, David Brunnstrom of Reuters reported that the United States had "expressed concern . . . about Russia's arms sales to Iran, Syria, and Venezuela and accused Moscow of bullying its neighbors"?

But while the oil-rich Middle East has been a key focus of attention, developments suggest that future instability could emanate from any number of locales, including what has traditionally been called "America's backyard." As with Iran, an increasingly assertive and well-armed Venezuela has spurred considerable unease, especially among nations that are within shooting distance of the South American troublemaker. According to a February 2008 *El Universal* report ("U.S.: Venezuela Purchases Four Times More Weapons Than It Needs"), two senior U.S. intelligence chiefs claimed Venezuela had "purchased up to four times the number of weapons it needs for domestic defense, with a goal to destabilize countries in the region that are close to the United States."

Not surprisingly, those efforts have inspired others in the vicinity, worried about the risks posed by their belligerent neighbor, to do the same. According to a January 2008 article by Andrew Downie, "Is Latin America Heading for an Arms Race?" in the *Christian Science Monitor,* "increased defense spending by Venezuela, Brazil, and Ecuador, coupled with significant arms purchases by Chile and Colombia, may mark the start of an arms race in South America—a region that hasn't seen a major war between nations in decades. . . . 'There is a real risk of it escalating and it could become very dangerous,' says Michael Shifter, the vice president of policy at the Inter-American Dialogue in Washington."

Other parts of the world have also witnessed a seemingly headlong rush toward increasing militarization. "Since the dawn of the twenty-first century," notes John Feffer, co-director of Foreign Policy in Focus at the Institute for Policy Studies in Washington, in a March

2008 article for *Japan Focus*, "five of the six countries involved in the Six Party Talks [aimed at addressing the North Korean nuclear threat] have increased their military spending by 50 percent or more. The sixth, Japan, a regional military power, has maintained steady growth in its military budget while placing heavy bets on the U.S. military umbrella. Every country in the region is now investing staggering sums in new weapons systems and new offensive capabilities."

By the same token, a range of global suppliers is aggressively looking to match that demand with sophisticated technology and devastating weaponry. In a March 2008 article, "US, Russia, China in Fierce Battle to Sell Fighter Jets in Asia," *Agence France-Presse* reported that "the United States is bracing for tough competition from Russia and China as cash-flush Asian economies look up to the trio for a new breed of fighter jets to beef up their air forces, experts say. With Asia powering ahead with military modernization and capability growth," the newswire added, "the United States wants to maintain leadership in defense sales in the region attracted by low-cost offerings from Russia and China."

Tensions on the Rise

Strategic advantage isn't the only consideration, of course. Geopolitical frictions have also been stirred by social and grassroots pressures. These include demographic schisms; religious, ethnic, and other ideological differences; economic concerns such as wealth inequality and stagnating wages; and resource-related conflicts. In a March 2008 article, "High Rice Cost Creating Fears of Asia Unrest," Keith Bradsher of the *New York Times* reported that "shortages and high prices for all kinds of food have caused tensions and even violence around the world in recent months." Along with troop deployments in Pakistan, protests in Indonesia, and price controls in China, "food riots have erupted . . . in Guinea, Mauritania, Mexico, Morocco, Senegal, Uzbekistan, and Yemen," the newspaper said. Similarly, Ben Russell of the British *Independent* wrote an article carrying the headline: "Water Will Be Source of War Unless World Acts Now, Warns Minister."

There seems little doubt, in fact, that growing gaps between the supply of and demand for essential resources, as well as uneven distribution of supplies, will be a powerful driving force provoking confrontation and armed conflict in countries and regions around the world. Most observers believe, for example, that the United States' long-standing and—up until recently, at least—escalating involvement in the Middle East, including two ill-fated wars in Iraq and Afghanistan, has everything to do with securing supplies of energy for what has long been the world's largest per-capita energy consumer. Similarly, the seemingly insatiable thirst for oil, natural gas, and other commodities in China and other economically emergent nations has spawned increased aggressiveness on every continent.

In a January 2008 article, "Gazprom Plans Africa Gas Grab," Matthew Green and Catherine Belton of the *Financial Times* reported that Russia's state-owned energy group was "talking tough" and "seeking to win access to vast reserves in Nigeria, [heightening] concerns among western governments over its increasingly powerful grip on gas supplies to Europe." Separately, a June 2007 report ("Putin's Arctic Invasion") detailed "an astonishing bid" by Russia—described as "muscle-flexing" by Putin—"to grab a vast chunk of the Arctic [to] tap its vast potential oil, gas, and mineral wealth." According to the *Daily Mail*, the "dramatic move provoked an international outcry." While the United States and other nations rejected Russia's claim on the basis of established international law, today's realities indicate things won't end there. Indeed, an August 2008 *Canwest News Service* article by Randy Boswell highlighted remarks by the United States' top Coast Guard official that revealed "a planned shift in American foreign policy from scientific research to 'sovereignty' and 'security presence' in Alaskan waters bordering Canadian and Russian territory."

Other, equally remote frontiers have also stirred up a broad interest—as well as the threat of violent clashes and all-out war. A December 2007 report by Leo Lewis in Britain's *Times* revealed, "The Japanese Government is secretly hatching plans for a huge underwater treasure hunt in the depths of the East China Sea in an urgent effort to secure supplies of the 'vitamins of industry' . . . 'huge, black submarine boulders' for possible deposits of rare metals extruded from the Earth's core." While "Japan may realize an old dream of resource independence from its sometimes troublesome neighbor China," the newspaper added, "the prospecting itself could become a trigger for acrimonious disputes between Tokyo and Beijing."

Odds are, in fact, that waning U.S. influence, declining cross-border trade, and the strains of ongoing economic deterioration will provoke increasingly aggressive claim-staking that is oblivious to established international rules and obligations to other nations. Up until recently, most countries have stood by treaties and trade agreements. Yet these deals have been "based on the logic of economic prosperity," author and geopolitical analyst Jeffrey R. Nyquist wrote in a December 2007 commentary. When "win-win" becomes "zero-sum," many will fall by the wayside. *Washington Post* columnist Robert J. Samuelson has also noted that the world economic order "depends on a shared sense that most nations benefit." However, "the more some countries pursue narrow advantage, the more others will follow suit."

To that end, it appears, China and Russia are already on the prowl, creating stiff competition to the United States, Europe, Japan, and other nations in the rush to secure first-mover access to key markets and vital resources. A January 2007 *Time* article by Michael Elliott, "China Takes on the World," detailed the expansive approach the Asian power has already been pursuing. According to the newsweekly, China's appetite for raw materials has "transformed economies from Angola to Australia." Around the world, the report noted, the nation was actively seeking to turn "commercial might into real political muscle." Eleven months later, a headline by Andrew Grice in Britain's *Independent* proclaimed: "China the Victor as Europe Fails to Secure Trade Deal with Africa."

Asia's third largest energy consumer has also entered the fray. In a March 2008 report, "Iran, India to Sign Oil Deals," the *Persian Journal* revealed that India's Oil and Natural Gas Corporation was preparing to sign deals with Iran to develop huge oil and gas fields in that nation. Moreover, under the headline "Energy Race between India and China," *AsiaNews* revealed that after being "beaten by China over oil fields in Kazakhstan and Myanmar," India was "launching its own worldwide strategy": negotiating exploration deals with Russia, fine-tuning oil agreements with Venezuela, and competing against China and others for access to Angolan oil. Indeed, Angola, Nigeria, Libya, and other countries in the region are increasingly being seen as prime hunting grounds. Once the "world's most neglected continent," Christopher Thompson of the *New Statesman* wrote in June 2007, Africa is "suddenly assuming an increasing global importance."

Jockeying for Spheres of Influence

Some observers have likened developments in Africa to a modern-day gold rush; others argue that the United States, China, India, and Russia are reenacting the nineteenth-century "scramble for Africa," when European nations laid claim to territories in the region during a four-decade-long span prior to World War I. The jostle for advantage has spawned a bustling arms trade, along with a stepped-up foreign military presence. According to the Stockholm International Peace Research Institute, Russia supplied Sudan, the civil-war-torn oil producer, with most of the weapons it received between 2003 and 2007. The rest came from China, which has also been looking to enhance its military ties with the Khartoum government. Overall, the Chinese accounted for 10 percent of all weapons sales to Africa from 1996 to 2003, according to the Congressional Research Service.

Suddenly cognizant of the region's growing strategic importance, the United States has begun to pick up the pace of its diplomatic efforts and arms sales to African nations over the past few years, though from relatively low levels. More recently, the United States has moved to reorganize disparate military operations on the continent into a unified structure known as the United States Africa Command (AFRICOM). According to Christopher Thompson of the *New Statesman*, "This significant shift in U.S. relations with Africa comes in the face of myriad threats: fierce economic competition from Asia; increasing resource nationalism in Russia and South America; and instability in the Middle East that threatens to spill over into Africa."

Another resource-rich region just north of Africa, and adjacent to Iran, Afghanistan, and Pakistan, has also become a target of consuming nations' attentions—as well as their angst. According to an August 2007 Associated Press report by Ivan Sekretarev, "Russia, China Hold Joint War Games," the "United States, Russia, and China are locked in an increasingly tense rivalry for control over Central Asia's vast hydrocarbon riches. Washington supports plans for pipelines that would carry the region's oil and gas to the West and bypass Russia, while Moscow has pushed strongly to control export flows. China has also shown a growing appetite for energy to power its booming economy." In a December 2007 article, "Russia, Kazakhstan and Turkmenistan Sign Caspian Gas Pipeline Deal," the Associated Press detailed the three nations' plans "to build a natural gas pipeline along the Caspian Sea coast that would strengthen Moscow's monopoly on energy exports from the resource-rich region.... But the plan also [delivered] a strong blow to Western hopes of securing alternate energy export routes." Another article from the same newswire, "New 'Great Game' for Central Asia Riches," by Douglas Birch and Mansur Mirovalev, highlighted the vast quantities of Chinese-made goods flooding markets "along the old Silk Road in former Soviet Central Asia," saying they were "the most visible sign of Beijing's growing power in the region." In the struggle for financial and strategic advantage, the reporters noted, China seemed to be "gaining the upper hand."

Not all of the geopolitical jockeying is taking place on terra firma. Outer space has also become a key battleground for geopolitical leaders and challengers alike. In a November 2007 *Asia Times* commentary, Nicola Casarini, the Jean Monnet Fellow in the Robert Schuman Center for Advanced Studies at Florence's European University Institute, asserts that "Asia's main powers are warming up for a big space race . . . largely driven by what scholars call 'techno-nationalism.' Successful space missions generate pride domestically and demonstrate prowess internationally." Along similar lines, other analysts have noted that "deals and advantages" tend to "flow toward leaders," especially those who are seen as smart and aggressive up-and-comers.

But there's more to it than the warm glow of achievement and recognition by other nations. Casarini contends that "China's space missions aim to foster both the economic and military sectors." He points out that policy makers have "emphasized the link between the space and information fields as well as the need for China to modernize its space forces to counter the technologically advanced U.S. military." Casarini also notes remarks by India's air chief of staff, who "declared that the 'Indian air force is in the process of establishing an aerospace command to exploit outer space.'" Such efforts have sparked considerable anxiety. In February 2008, for instance, Iran conducted its first successful space-rocket launch, according to the Islamic Republic News Agency. *WorldNetDaily*'s Jerome R. Corsi, who highlighted the development, wrote that "western observers continue to express concern that the space program could be a cover for Iran's attempt to develop a military ballistics missile program capable of delivering an atomic warhead."

Only months before, Reuters revealed that "Russia's military space commander vowed to retaliate with an arms race if any country started putting weapons systems into orbit" ("Russia Warns of Arms Race in Space"). The news service added that "tensions between Russia and Washington have deepened over U.S. plans to rekindle the stalled 'Star Wars' program from the 1980s with a new generation of missile shields." The strategy involves placing parts of a proposed missile defense system in some former Soviet bloc countries, including Poland and the Czech Republic. This development has, not surprisingly, heightened Russian concerns about Western intentions in the region. Indeed, an August 2008 Associated Press report by Jim Heintz, "Russia: Poland Risks Attack Because of U.S. Missiles," detailed remarks by a top Russian general who said that "Poland's agreement to accept a U.S. missile interceptor base exposes the ex-communist nation to attack, possibly by nuclear weapons."

Russia isn't the only emerging power that is sensitive to "interference" and other unwelcome intrusions in its sphere of influence. As noted earlier, China's unsettled relationship with Taiwan, which the mainland government has long treated as a wayward province, has often been viewed as a potential catalyst for conflict in that part of the world. Even though the Kuomintang, or KMT, has independently ruled the island since Chinese Nationalists fled there in 1949 following civil war with the Communists, the mainland government has repeatedly warned that any move by Taiwan or other nations to assert formal independence for the island would have serious consequences.

Whether or not the Taiwan question can be resolved peacefully— which appeared, to some at least, a bit more likely following the island's March 2008 election of a pro-China presidential candidate— remains to be seen. But that isn't China's only stress point. Prior to the 2008 Olympics, for example, trouble flared up in Tibet and the Muslim-dominated province of Xinjiang amid growing resistance to Chinese rule. Still, it's worth bearing in mind that such problems are not necessarily limited to certain countries or regions. Arguably, the conflicts that triggered the unrest in China constitute part of a broader undercurrent that may well be energized by an unfolding global power vacuum, among other things. By one account, secessionist and separatist pressures are smoldering in more than 100 countries worldwide.

Potential catalysts for upheaval run the gamut from economic disparities to strategic concerns. A December 2007 *CNN* report by Helena DeMoura revealed, for example, that "members of [Bolivia's] four highest natural gas–producing regions declared autonomy from the central government," presided over by its controversial socialist president, Evo Morales. Four months later, Christian Lowe of Reuters reported a senior Russian official's assertion that "Georgia's Moscow-backed rebel regions will secede if NATO moves to make Georgia a member." In light of Moscow's aggressive intervention in South Ossetia the following August, such warnings cannot be taken lightly.

Planting the Seeds for Economically Debilitating Violence

The sorts of tensions that can quickly escalate into violence and armed conflict often stem from long-standing blood feuds and intractable ethnic and cultural differences. In some cases, ill will has already been stirred by political boundaries laid down during earlier times, when lifestyles and living conditions were much different than they are today. Moreover, what some might describe as tribal bonds can easily undermine social cohesiveness and a commitment to liberal ideals. As Robert J. Samuelson put it in a December 2006 *Washington Post* commentary, "Farewell to Pax Americana," "Iraq has reminded us that religious and ethnic loyalties dim the appeal of democracy, freedom, and materialism."

Such divisiveness can transcend nation-state borders and geographical dividing lines. In a September 2006 report ("Kissinger Warns of Possible 'War of Civilizations'"), *Agence France-Presse* highlighted a *Washington Post* commentary by former U.S. Secretary of State Henry Kissinger in which he warned of a "global catastrophe" and a possible "'war of civilizations' arising from a nuclear-armed Middle East." Following the 9/11 attacks in New York City, Americans and U.S. allies were quick to acknowledge President Bush's call for a "global war on terrorism." In his *Wall Street Journal* Opinion Journal commentary noted earlier, Mark Steyn argued that "whatever its merits for the believers, [the Muslim faith] is a problematic business for the rest of us. . . . There are many trouble spots around the world," he added, "but as a general rule, it's easy to make an educated guess at one of the participants: Muslims vs. Jews in 'Palestine,' Muslims vs. Hindus in Kashmir, Muslims vs. Christians in Africa, Muslims vs. Buddhists in Thailand, Muslims vs. Russians in the Caucasus, Muslims vs. backpacking tourists in Bali. Like the environmentalists, these guys think globally but act locally."

Deteriorating economic circumstances and a growing backlash against the disastrous campaigns in Iraq and Afghanistan raise the prospect of an abrupt and destabilizing U.S. retreat from the Middle East. Yet regardless of how that plays out, the combination of religious tensions, resource conflicts, and social inequities suggest the region is destined to become an even more fertile breeding ground for insurgency and violence than in the past. Some countries are already preparing for the worst. A September 2006 *Wall Street Journal* report by Yochi J. Dreazen and Philip Shishkin, for example, entitled "Growing Concern: Terrorist Havens in 'Failed States,'" detailed plans by Saudi Arabia "for an unusual and hugely expensive project: a multibillion-dollar electrified fence along its 560-mile border with Iraq" amid fears about militant incursions by residents of its troubled neighbor.

Similar concerns will come to the fore in other hot spots, including nearby Pakistan, "a country routinely marked by turbulence and turmoil since it first became independent in 1947," notes Bill Schiller of the *Toronto Star*. Following the assassination of pro-Western opposition leader Benazir Bhutto in December 2007, many commentators have downgraded their outlook for the culturally divided, economically impoverished, strife-torn, and nuclear-armed nation, which shares an increasingly lawless border with Afghanistan. In a January 2008 *Independent* report by Saeed Shah, Bhutto's widowed husband, Asif Ali Zardari, warned that "Pakistan was hurtling towards disintegration, a failed state"—as he described it, "another Somalia."

Upheaval in these and other regions will breed lawlessness and invite dangerous alliances with criminal elements. *Foreign Policy* detailed one such example in its "Failed States Index 2007":

Fighting by a resurgent Taliban in Afghanistan and in the lawless Northwest Frontier Province of Pakistan has the potential to spread instability across Central Asia. Pakistan and Uzbekistan have shown only marginal gains in their index scores during the past year and are at risk not only from spillover but from growing internal dissent. But it is Afghanistan's record poppy yield that has neighboring states most concerned. Drug trafficking routes, fueled by underground heroin factories, cut swaths through the former Soviet republics to the north, bringing crime, addiction, and HIV/AIDS in their wake.

The U.S. National Intelligence Council (NIC) has warned of similar developments further east. In its 2020 Project report, "Mapping the Global Future," the government-sponsored think tank maintains that "if China's economy takes a downward turn, regional security would weaken, resulting in heightened prospects for political instability, crime, narcotics trafficking, and illegal immigration." Meanwhile, Yossef Bodansky, author of *Chechen Jihad: Al Qaeda's Training Ground and the Next Wave of Terror*, has suggested that the terrorist group that Washington has identified as a key threat to American security has smuggled nuclear weapons into the United States from Russia, aided by organized criminal gangs in the embattled Chechen Republic.

The intersection of crime, politics, and economics is just one of the many factors that will undermine stability and spawn an upsurge of economically debilitating violence in the years ahead. Worries and resentments over falling wages, surging unemployment, and the widening gap between rich and poor will also rouse nationalistic, protectionist, and xenophobic hostility. Throughout the world, there will be push for tighter borders and controls on the flow of people, goods, and capital. Immigrants and foreigners will become scapegoats for domestic ills. Meanwhile, a variety of home-grown woes will stir up social unrest, triggering obstructive and antagonistic responses. In many cases, governments will implement ill-conceived policies, including hyperinflationary expansions of the money supply, which will engender further instability. Enfeebled nations will see the reins of power commandeered by populists or tyrants. Some will tap the destructive energy of old rivalries or demonize wealthier rivals, including the

United States, or actively seek out conflicts that divert attention from domestic woes.

Odds are, too, that nations controlling vital resources and stock-piles of foreign reserves will look to put those advantages to tactical use. Already, some have begun to test the capabilities of their economic firepower. As in the political and social realms, the financial world is set to become a dangerous frontier.

Chapter 4

Money Talks

We are thus in the position of having to borrow from Europe to defend Europe, of having to borrow from China and Japan to defend Chinese and Japanese access to Gulf oil, and of having to borrow from Arab emirs, sultans, and monarchs to make Iraq safe for democracy. . . . We borrow from the nations we defend so that we may continue to defend them. . . . To question this is an unpardonable heresy called "isolationism."

—Patrick J. Buchanan, Author and commentator

According to the Concord Coalition's "Debt Facts," foreigners owned a record $2.354 trillion—or nearly half—of all publicly held U.S. government debt at the end of 2007. Overall, foreign ownership of Treasuries has grown by more than $1 trillion since 2000. To some observers, the fact that the United States owes so much money to the rest of the world is not necessarily a cause for alarm. On the contrary, they view it as positive, because it reflects others' faith in the nation's future. Besides, it is creditors who ultimately bear the risk of loss, just as banks do when they make loans that eventually turn sour.

There's much more to it, however. Nearly 70 percent of foreign holdings are in the hands of official institutions, mainly central banks. By definition, that indicates factors other than traditional investment criteria have been involved in the decision-making process. Moreover, Japan and China account for the largest share, according to Treasury Department data, with $581.2 billion and $477.6 billion, respectively, while oil exporters—Venezuela, Iran, Saudi Arabia, and others—ranked fourth after the United Kingdom. Together, those four country-categories comprised 58 percent of the foreign-held total—a level of concentration that naturally raises questions.

In the case of China, substantial holdings of U.S. securities are an offshoot of mercantilistic trade policies that were designed and put into place to keep production engines humming at home, in the hope of powering continuing strong economic growth, rapid industrialization and modernization, and plenty of jobs for its sizable population—which, if unemployed and hungry, would constitute a serious threat to social stability. As part of its strategy, the emerging Asian superpower has for many years maintained the value of its currency, the yuan—which is also known as the renminbi—at depressed levels relative to the U.S. dollar. Such a strategy gives Chinese manufacturers a pricing advantage over rival exporters in world markets.

One by-product of China's approach has been the Asian nation's accumulation of substantial foreign currency reserves, most of which have been kept in dollars. Instead of allowing domestic firms to convert export earnings into yuan by way of global foreign exchange markets, which would almost certainly trigger a rise in the relative value of the local currency and thus undermine overall export competitiveness, China has put strict controls in place that ensure most cross-border surpluses flow straight through to government coffers. Although China itself has been mum on the details, analysts reckon its portfolio of foreign currency assets is the largest in the world, having swelled from an estimated $100 million in 1996 to more than $1.8 trillion in 2008, according to *Agence France-Presse* ("China's Forex Reserves Hit 1.8 Trillion Dollars: Report").

China isn't the only country whose economic star has burned brightly. Other emerging nations have also experienced eye-catching booms. In a January 2008 *Financial Times* column, "Challenges for the

World's Divided Economy," Martin Wolf wrote that it "is astonishing how widespread rapid growth has now become in the developing world. In 2007, for example, growth is estimated by the World Bank to have run at 10 per cent in east Asia, 8.4 per cent in south Asia, 6.7 per cent in eastern Europe and central Asia, 6.1 per cent in sub-Saharan Africa, 5.1 per cent in Latin America, and 4.9 per cent in the Middle East and north Africa." In some countries, the driving force behind rapid expansion and a string of cross-border surpluses has not been manufacturing prowess. Rather, the gains have largely stemmed from tight markets in oil and other commodities during most of the past decade. Key beneficiaries include Russia, Brazil, and the hydrocarbon-rich members of the Organization of Petroleum Exporting Countries (OPEC), many of which are based in the Middle East. They, too, have accumulated large portfolios of dollars, along with smaller holdings of other currencies and assets like gold. As of 2006, International Monetary Fund (IMF) data indicated that nearly 70 percent of global reserves were in the hands of developing countries.

Up until recently, various factors reinforced the popular decision to keep the lion's share of official foreign currency assets in dollars. Chief among them has been a near-universal acceptance of the greenback as an international reserve currency. Exceptional liquidity, the benchmark pricing of oil and other commodities in dollars, and a global system of finance and trade anchored to the U.S. unit of account have also played a role. In addition, many countries have viewed allegiance to the United States—and by extension, its national currency—as the quid pro quo for its protective umbrella and other public goods the long-time superpower has provided. One consequence of this long-running appetite for greenbacks, however, has been an extraordinary buildup of global financial imbalances.

Where the Exposure Lies

Is the lopsided accumulation of dollars by other countries—which, arguably, they hold mostly out of choice—necessarily a cause for concern? How about the concentrated ownership of U.S. government securities by geopolitical challengers, as well as those who have made little secret of their animosity toward the United States and its interests? Some analysts would say no. They would argue that such worries are misguided or overblown, if only because the balance of financial power is often transformed when significant sums of money—especially the borrowed kind—are involved.

Indeed, no matter how or why the United States reached this point, there is an argument that says the sizable dollar claims of a relatively small number of countries actually represent a problem for them, not the United States. Simply put, the imbalance has altered the traditional creditor-debtor dynamic. As James Surowiecki wrote in an April 2005 *New Yorker* column, "In Yuan We Trust": "To paraphrase John Paul Getty: If you owe the bank a hundred dollars, you've got a problem. If you owe the bank three trillion dollars, the bank's got a problem." For countries with an outsized vulnerability to swings in the value of the U.S. currency and dollar-denominated assets, any moves they make to reallocate or restructure holdings, to rework economic strategies and political agendas, or to otherwise reorient themselves to an evolving global order could have self-defeating consequences.

Over the past few years, for instance, even rumors that China was weighing plans to rebalance its foreign currency assets have triggered abrupt and dramatic market reactions—the kind that that can cause substantial damage to portfolios that are chock-a-block with greenbacks. One such example was detailed in a November 2007 *Bloomberg* report by Agnes Lovasz and Stanley White, "Dollar Slumps to Record on China's Plans to Diversify Reserves," which attributed a sudden burst of forex market volatility to remarks by Chinese officials that were not especially well received by traders and investors. " 'We will favor stronger currencies over weaker ones, and will readjust accordingly,' Cheng Siwei, vice chairman of China's National People's Congress, told a conference in Beijing. The dollar is 'losing its status as the world currency,' Xu Jian, a central bank vice director, said at the same meeting."

By the same token, there's little doubt that other countries' willingness to finance the United States' propensity to spend more than it earns has benefited the nation in certain ways. University of Virginia scholar Frank Warnock has published research, for example, showing that "foreign buying of U.S. Treasuries has kept long-term U.S.

interest rates about one to one-and-a-half percentage points lower than otherwise," according to George Hoguet, a senior portfolio manager and chief global strategist at State Street Global Advisors, writing in a December 2007 *Financial Times* commentary. Through their accumulation of large dollar hoards, foreigners, especially those overseeing state-controlled funds, have also helped to underwrite a relatively long span of economic stability in the United States. In addition, their support has dampened inflationary pressures that might have run rampant in a nation with a current account deficit greater than 5 percent of gross domestic product (GDP). On the flip side, the bursting of the global credit bubble has revealed that such generosity was not without consequences, if only because it had allowed untenable imbalances to grow and fester, undermining the United States' longer-term economic well-being.

The Dollar's Growing Loss of Favor

In recent years, attitudes toward the greenback have changed. Private investors, in particular, have become increasingly reluctant to acquire or hold dollar assets. In a March 2008 *RGE Monitor* blog post, economist Brad Setser highlighted data revealing that inflows of private capital into the United States had slowed to a trickle, with foreign governments picking up the slack. The fact that the nation "depends so heavily on central bank financing," he wrote, "makes the U.S. all the more sensitive to any change in the dollar's status." Indeed, Setser concluded, the United States

> relies on exorbitant privilege not so much to live well as to sustain the otherwise unsustainable. . . . Without a lifeline from the world's central banks, the U.S. wouldn't be able to finance its external deficit by selling under-performing financial assets. And if the U.S. ever had to finance its deficit by selling financial assets that outperformed comparable assets, watch out. The U.S.' external position would deteriorate rapidly. . . . That leaves the United States in a position of intrinsic vulnerability.

That is not necessarily the greatest concern, however. The United States is also exposed to a more ominous threat. In a May 2006 *Wall*

Street Journal commentary, "Thinking Global: Why Economists Worry about Who Holds Foreign Currency Reserves," Frederick Kempe highlighted extant fears that "China or some other American rival could someday use its vast holdings of U.S. debt as a geopolitical weapon, despite the great harm that would also cause to the attacker's own economy." According to Kempe, a journalist and chief executive officer of the Atlantic Council of the United States, "those gaming the odds typically speak of the danger that a rising China, in defending its vital interests—Taiwan's status or threats to a key ally—might risk such a move despite the economic backlash."

Given China's emergence as a potentially formidable rival in the quest for global dominance, concerns about what the nation—or others like it—might do in future are not surprising. Yet even established allies seem to be growing more antagonistic amid the fallout from the United States' deteriorating fortunes. In a December 2007 report by Liam Halligan, Britain's *Telegraph* asserted that "Europe has finally had enough of America's 'benign neglect' dollar policy. . . . Over the past seven years, the single currency [euro] has risen by a shocking 82 per cent against the greenback. That's hammered eurozone exports—provoking serious trade disputes between the EU and US, the world's two biggest trading blocks. No wonder French President Nicolas Sarkozy describes America's drooping dollar as 'a precursor to economic war.' "

Another *Telegraph* article published four months later, "Foreign Investors Veto Fed Rescue," by Ambrose Evans-Pritchard, described a similarly unnerving development in a capital market that has long been viewed as a gilt-edged financial oasis. "As feared, foreign bond holders have begun to exercise a collective vote of no confidence in the devaluation policies of the U.S. government. The Federal Reserve faces a potential veto of its rescue measures [in response to growing credit market turbulence]. . . . Asian, Mid East, and European investors stood aside at last week's auction of 10-year U.S. Treasury notes. 'It was a disaster,' said Ray Attrill from 4castweb. 'We may be close to the point where the uglier consequences of benign neglect towards the currency are revealed.' "

The fact that the United States no longer rules the global roost as it once did has jeopardized its economic and financial well-being in other ways, too. For one thing, events of recent years have demonstrated that oil- and gas-producing companies, international commodity traders, and emerging-nation governments—not, as many might expect, the world's "sole superpower" and a leading oil importer—dictate the rules of the game in global energy markets. Venezuela, for instance, has been redirecting oil exports away from the United States toward China and other U.S. rivals. Russia is considering pricing hydrocarbon exports in rubles. Iran has proposed a regional oil exchange that competes with Western bourses.

Meanwhile, in a global trading arena where the United States was once the principal pacesetter, what takes place on a day-to-day basis is increasingly in others' hands. According to Frederick Kempe, the proliferation of substantial, state-controlled pools of capital represents a "radical shift [that] increases the volatility in—and decreases U.S. influence over—the world's largest market, the $2 trillion in foreign exchange that changes hands daily. Nowadays, the forex market "can increasingly be shifted by decisions that foreign governments make about selling dollar assets. What's also at stake," he adds, "is leverage on matters as diverse as U.S. home-mortgage rates and America's global political clout."

The ways in which sizable holdings of foreign currency assets might be used or invested have spawned other worries. Traditionally, these resources have been somewhat akin to a financial safety net. But as Eliot Kalter, a fellow at Tufts University's Fletcher School of Law and Diplomacy and a former International Monetary Fund official, noted in a March 2008 Associated Press report, "Dollar Losing Clout around the World," " 'the accumulation of reserves has become so large in most emerging market countries that the balance is way beyond what's needed for precautionary reasons.'"

Then there is the issue of where and in what form the funds are held. Historically, official reserves have been invested in conservative, low-yielding assets like government bonds. To a considerable extent, that strategy reflects a bureaucratic aversion to risk. Typically, the reserve pools have been overseen by public officials on fixed salaries with little incentive to maximize returns. A desire to maintain ready access to resources that might suddenly be needed to offset sudden bouts of financial turbulence has also favored investments in safe and liquid markets.

But as surpluses from manufacturing and commodity exports have multiplied, developing nations have sought to enhance the value of what many—especially oil and gas producers—perceive as one-off windfalls. Approaches have varied: Some countries have chosen to aggressively manage portions of their holdings, hoping to match private-sector returns and foster an overall increase in national wealth. Others have focused on improving future economic prospects through increased spending on infrastructure—roads, seaports, and airports—and similar large-scale needs. In resource-rich countries, the emphasis has also been on developing and improving production, storage, and logistics capabilities.

One strategy that has become especially popular in recent years centers on shifting a notable percentage of government-controlled assets into sovereign wealth funds (SWFs), which generally have a broader investing mandate than state treasuries or central banks. Rather than accumulating government bills and bonds, for example, SWFs may have discretion to buy (or even bet against) stocks, corporate bonds, and commodities. Longer time horizons also give some sovereign funds leeway to acquire illiquid or risky assets, including stakes in hedge funds and private companies.

As of 2007, the International Monetary Fund estimated that SWFs controlled as much as $3 trillion in assets—up from $500 million in 1990—and that overall totals could reach $10 trillion by 2012. Many SWFs are based in the Middle East, including the world's first, the Kuwait Investment Office, established in 1953, and its largest, the United Arab Emirates' Abu Dhabi Investment Authority, with assets of $250 billion and $875 billion, respectively, according to a January 2008 *Economist* report ("The Invasion of the Sovereign-Wealth Funds"). In addition, Henny Sender, David Wighton, and Sundeep Tucker of the *Financial Times* revealed in late 2007 plans by Saudi Arabia to establish a fund that was "expected to dwarf Abu Dhabi's . . . and become the largest in the world," though later reports suggested more modest goals. Overall, *BusinessWeek* notes in a report by Emily Thornton and Stanley Reed, Gulf-based funds "earned about $180 billion from their sovereign wealth fund investments in 2007—more than half of the $315 billion they collected in oil and gas revenues."

Effects of a New Economic Framework

The amounts involved make these state-run pools, whether referring to traditional foreign currency reserve funds or SWFs, a force to be reckoned with. Overall, their size and geographical concentration, along with the potentially dramatic impact that portfolio strategy shifts can have on market psychology and investor behavior, have spurred growing unease. As Brad Setser noted in a January 2008 commentary at *RGE Monitor*, "State-Led Globalization," a set of developments and policies "has concentrated the world's financial firepower in the hands of states in emerging economies. . . . State flows, after all, now dominate global capital flows."

The suggestion by HSBC Group economist Stephen King—highlighted by Setser in the same column—that "the increasing financial power of emerging market states is likely to trigger a reassertion of the state in advanced economies" hints at an even more dramatic turn of events. In fact, with myriad imbalances already starting to unwind and economic conditions likely to be further undermined by geopolitical uncertainty, resource constraints, and the specter of growing divisiveness, the groundwork seems laid for a broad move away from American-style free-market capitalism. Some would even argue that unprecedented government support for the financial sector—in the United States and elsewhere—following the global credit meltdown that began in 2007 confirmed the shift.

Needless to say, the implications for individuals, businesses, and governments of such a radically altered framework are profound. But even without them, certain developments have already been reshaping the landscape. In a November 2007 *Financial Times* commentary, "Insight: The Pitfalls of Financial Globalization Grow Clearer," John Plender highlighted two, in particular. First, "China and other emerging market countries are unilaterally rolling back the high tide of liberalization. Thanks to their rise, more of the world economy operates under mercantilist pegged exchange rate regimes." Second, says Plender, "sovereign wealth funds are indirectly reversing the privatization trend that began in the 1980s through a re-expansion of state ownership, but on a cross-border basis. That in turn will spawn an illiberal political reaction that will inhibit global capital flows."

Analysts have noted the prospect that state control of large pools of capital invariably leads to a muddying of public and private interests. Government stakeholders, for example, may not have the same goals as traditional lenders and shareholders. They may see their mission as strategic rather than economic, or seek to throw their weight around to achieve any number of aims. That can heighten market uncertainty, spawn a misallocation of resources, and create all sorts of unintended consequences. There is also increased potential for corruption and political meddling, especially in locales where principles of transparency, accountability, and corporate governance are out of line with traditional Western standards.

Such deficiencies have already caused problems. Most monetary authorities around the world, including the People's Bank of China, don't publish data on the size or composition of reserve portfolios. Although analyst estimates help to bridge the gap, the lack of transparency can boost anxiety and stir speculation about goals and policies. Rumors also serve to heighten volatility. In addition, sovereign funds, which are actively involved in markets that have traditionally been under the purview of private-sector investors, offer little insight on strategies or holdings.

Economist and former U.S. Treasury Secretary Lawrence Summers described a number of related concerns in a January 2008 *International Herald Tribune* commentary, "Different Money, Different Rules": "The first revolves around the issue of 'multiple motives.' What is the primus of capitalism? It is that people invest and own companies in order to maximize their value. If you think about national ownership of a stake in a business or a whole company, or even a direct investment made by a public pension fund in the United States, the same issue arises: There can be motives other than highest rate of return." Summers then detailed several instances where public and private interests might diverge:

> Perhaps a state-owned fund wants an airline to fly to its country. Perhaps it wants a bank to do extensive business in its country. Perhaps it wants suppliers from its country to be sourced. Perhaps it wants to disable an industry that competes with its nation's national champion. These other motives distort

the whole notion of capitalism that value maximization is the chief objective.

There is also the issue of "general politicization," as Summers describes it, where an aggressive trading strategy or failed investment might lead to conflicts of one kind or another.

Such consequences may not be entirely unintended. On the contrary, growing state involvement in economic matters in various parts of the world, along with mercantilist and other aggressive strategies that have ultimately served to boost the resources under government control, may be seen as part of a natural progression—that is, to a post-American era, where a variety of interests will be looking to gain the upper hand and asserting their influence militarily, politically, and economically. Under the circumstances, it's no surprise that Niall Ferguson and others described moves by Chinese, Middle Eastern, and other state-controlled funds to acquire stakes in beleaguered U.S. banks in late 2007 as a shift in the global financial power balance.

No Longer for Sale?

Initially, the flood of foreign money into a key U.S. industry did not provoke much of an outcry, either in Washington or in the hinterlands. Worries over the health of the financial system overshadowed other concerns. Yet even though complaints were muted, the mood seemed more fatalistic than supportive. In a December 2007 article, for instance, "China Controlling More of U.S. Economy," the Associated Press reported that "'both Chinese private and government interests are controlling more and more of the U.S. economy, and this is a result of the big trade and budget deficits we have,' said Alan Donziger, professor of economics at Villanova School of Business. 'These investments will make the U.S. somewhat less independent, but this is inevitable when we live in a global economy.'"

In future, however, the public and political response to such efforts will be much less welcoming. Reactions will likely mirror the vociferous opposition that sprang up in the wake of an attempt by state-controlled China National Offshore Oil Corporation to take over California-based Unocal in 2005, or the uproar over Dubai-owned DP

World's 2006 plan to acquire a business that managed sensitive port facilities in New York and New Jersey. In both cases, moves by foreign-government-dominated firms to acquire a U.S. foothold in strategically important sectors like oil and shipping were viewed as a threat to national security. More recent reports indicate, in fact, that Americans are growing wary of economic incursions by foreigners and the financial firepower they have at their disposal for a wealth of reasons, regardless of the benefits they—and their money—might offer.

A January 2008 *New York Times* article by Peter S. Goodman and Louise Story, "Overseas Investors Buy Aggressively in U.S.," highlighted the conflicting crosscurrents. "For much of the world, the United States is now on sale at discount prices. With credit tight, unemployment growing, and worries mounting about a potential recession, American business and government leaders are courting foreign money to keep the economy growing. Foreign investors are buying aggressively, taking advantage of American duress and a weak dollar to snap up what many see as bargains, while making inroads to the world's largest market." In the meantime, the newspaper added,

> the surge of foreign money has injected fresh tension into a running debate about America's place in the global economy ... [and] has reinvigorated sometimes jingoistic worries about foreigners securing control of America's fortunes, a narrative last heard in the 1980s as Americans bought up Hondas and Rockefeller Center landed in Japanese hands.... With a growing share of investment coming from so-called sovereign wealth funds ... lawmakers and regulators are calling for greater scrutiny to ensure that foreign countries do not gain influence over the financial system or military-related technology.

Increasingly, Americans have come to believe that years of out-sized growth in China, India, and other developing nations, along with parallel accumulations of large surpluses, stems from unfair trade practices, offshoring of American jobs to low-wage regimes, and official policies that boost the profits of multinational corporations at the expense of U.S. workers. When asked in a December 2007 *NBC News/Wall Street Journal* survey detailed at Pollingreport.com if "the fact that the American economy has become increasingly global is good because it has opened up new markets for American products and resulted in more jobs, or bad because it has subjected American companies and employees to unfair competition and cheap labor," only 28 percent of those polled responded in the affirmative, down from 42 percent about a decade earlier.

But it isn't just those living in the United States who are disturbed by such developments. In a July 2007 *Asia Times* commentary, economist Max Fraad Wolff noted that while "the anger and sense of ability to go it alone are pronounced in the U.S., Russia seems to believe that this is the best option in leading sectors. France has embraced a national-champion conception and Germany contemplates protection for domestic firms against foreign funds. Sovereign wealth funds are viewed with suspicion by many as foreign-government plots." That same month, in fact, the *Wall Street Journal*, in an article by Niels C. Sorrells and Andrew Peaple entitled "Germany Seeks EU Curbs on Some Foreign Takeovers," reported that

> German Chancellor Angela Merkel called for the European Union to consider a comprehensive plan for protecting companies from unwanted foreign takeovers, mirroring a legislative initiative under way in Germany. While there is no imminent threat to German industry, the move comes as senior members of Ms. Merkel's Christian Democratic Union Party have identified foreign state-run investment funds, particularly from such countries as China and Russia, as requiring close scrutiny when investing in strategic sectors.

Tensions over trade and what might be described as the machinations of foreigner interlopers have begun to spur calls in the United States, Western Europe, and elsewhere—and, ironically enough, even in China—for a counterattack, including higher tariffs, tighter borders, and stricter controls on capital flows and immigration. While economists might view the displacement of workers and the angst that goes along with it as a predictable side effect of greater overall efficiency, policy makers—and the public—aren't so accommodating. Increasingly, countries will look for all kinds of ways to beat back the globalization tide. Their prospective targets, meanwhile, will rely on the economic and financial weapons they have at their disposal to try to gain—or regain—the upper hand.

Financial Firepower

Few would argue with the notion that the Chinese government has used its control over the economy and concentrated state resources to give locally based manufacturers an edge in global markets. Yet other nations' less systematic interventions, ostensibly aimed at ensuring that market conditions remain stable and foreign exchange rates don't get too far out of line with the fundamentals, have often achieved the same result. Either way, it seems that developing nations, in particular, have come to the conclusion that certain aspects of economic management are best not left to free markets and the vagaries of unfettered capitalism. Indeed, signs point to an increasing willingness to manipulate rules, rates, and financial relationships to local advantage.

Emulating established powers like the United States and the heavyweights of Europe, up-and-comers are increasingly employing financial resources as diplomatic weapons—though, it seems, in more blunt fashion. In a June 2007 report, "The Chinese Aid System," Carol Lancaster, a visiting fellow at the Center for Global Development, notes that "China has become a major source of foreign aid in Asia, Latin America, and especially in Africa." Yet while the country has lent support "to these regions since the 1960s," she avers, the recent largesse "appears tied more to Beijing's interests in raw materials, such as oil, minerals, and timber, necessary to fuel its incredible growth machine. It, like nearly all aid-giving governments, also has political and strategic interests it pursues with its aid."

In fact, countries such as Russia, China, and India are putting their own unique stamp on things, relying on tactics that are at odds with the more measured and liberal-minded approaches favored by the West. Among other things, that means foreign aid often comes without the human rights conditions attached that established powers usually insist on. The upstarts are also more pragmatic in their approach, preferring to focus on broader strategic goals. As Joshua Kurlantzick notes in an August 2007 Foreign Policy Research Institute commentary,

China has become a country that embraces trade agreements, which would shock U.S. trade officials of 15–20 years ago. China is now negotiating between 15–20 free trade agreements

[FTAs] all over the world at the same time. If you talk to people in the U.S. who negotiate FTAs, they'd say that's impossible, it takes a year to negotiate just one FTA. What the Chinese government does is negotiate an FTA that has very little substance in it, sign it, then work out the substance later. [That] brings a lot of good will.

State-run firms are also being used to do the bidding for these rising global powers. A February 2008 *BBC News* report by Duncan Bartlett, "Russia's Energy Giant Flexes Its Muscles," highlights one such example. "Many countries in Eastern Europe depend on Russia for energy, and it supplies about a quarter of the gas used in the European Union. But the company which runs the gas business . . . is controversially close to the Russian state. Critics say it is little more than an economic and political tool of the Kremlin." Bartlett reports that journalist and author Edward Lucas "claims that Gazprom's marriage of economic and political power is particularly threatening. 'It used to be tanks and submarines and missiles that we were frightened of, now it should be banks and pipelines, and Russia has made tremendous strides in consolidating its monopoly of gas exports.' "

Moreover, in an effort to catch up with the West, funds and firms in places like China, Russia, and the Middle East have increasingly gone on the acquisition trail, snapping up foreign companies and looking to acquire critical intelligence and know-how from outside their borders, especially in the economically advanced nations of the West. Reports suggest the impetus often comes from the centers of power. A January 2008 *Financial Times* article by Catherine Belton noted, for example, a call by Dmitry Medvedev that urged business leaders to "copy China and go on a global buying spree of foreign companies to bolster the economy and cut dependence on technology from abroad." Russia's then president-in-waiting also "pledged Kremlin support for companies seeking assets abroad."

Economic Espionage and Warfare

Such moves have raised security concerns, along with worries over what might be characterized as "Trojan horse investing." In March

2008, for example, plans by Bain Capital Partners LLC and China's Huawei Technologies Co. to acquire U.S. firm 3Com Corporation fell apart after "U.S. lawmakers objected to the bid because it would have put 3Com's anti-hacking technology, used by the Pentagon, in Chinese hands" ("Bain Backs Out of 3Com Deal"). As it happens, such fears are not unfounded. In a July 2007 article by David J. Lynch, "Law Enforcement Struggles to Combat Chinese Spying," *USA Today* reported that "the world's fastest-growing economy operates a shadowy technology bazaar where individuals offering trade secrets find a ready buyer." According to the FBI, "about one-third of all economic espionage investigations are linked· to Chinese government agencies, research institutes, or businesses."

In fact, one overview of the "global economic espionage landscape" claims these kinds of activities are burgeoning. Christopher Burgess, a 30-year veteran of the CIA's clandestine service, wrote in an April 2008 article for *CSO* magazine that

> more than eight years since the climax of the Cold War, the threat of industrial and economic espionage has percolated once again to the forefront, and the tools of the intelligence collector are again being dusted off and put to use, as nations make use of what is referred to as the "second oldest profession." They are willing to make the political decision to support their indigenous corporations and companies with the provision of competitors' intellectual property the old-fashioned way—they will just take it.

Among those near the top of the list of aggressive intelligence acquirers is a longtime U.S. rival. Burgess noted that in October 2007,

> Russian President Putin introduced the new head of Russia's external intelligence service, Sluzhba Vneshny Razvedki (SVR), former Prime Minister Mikhail Fradkov. According to Russian press coverage of the event, in addition to introducing Fradkov, Putin projected in a clear and unambiguous manner his expectations of the SVR, including continuing to fight terrorism and building up its "economic espionage" capabilities. Putin is quoted as saying the SVR "must be able to swiftly

and adequately evaluate changes in the international economic situation, understand the consequences for the domestic economy and, of course, it's necessary to more actively protect the economic interest of our companies abroad."

While spying and other, less controversial methods will continue to be employed as a means of gaining advantage, the United States' waning influence, unraveling global imbalances, ongoing economic woes, and various resource-related concerns suggest that more aggressive tactics—short of all-out war—will also be used. In fact, an increased emphasis on asymmetric strategies, like those intended to counter the United States' advantages in conventional military firepower, suggests geopolitical up-and-comers won't be loath to tap their arsenals of economic weaponry. Aside from controls on trade, currency, and investment flows; taxes and regulations that place foreign-owned firms at a distinct disadvantage; and "beggar thy neighbor" currency devaluations, countries will threaten cutoffs in cross-border financing, shifts in asset allocations at state-run funds, and reductions in holdings of certain securities. Although budgets everywhere will be constrained by dismal economic conditions, current and prospective allies are nonetheless likely to garner preferential treatment through generous loans and grants, assistance on development projects, and subsidized arms sales.

The Nuclear Option

Then there is the so-called nuclear option—not literally, but in the sense of one nation attempting to destroy another by dumping its holdings of the latter's currency and financial assets (or encouraging others to do the same) or, perhaps, by stirring up other mayhem, including counterfeiting currency and disrupting financial systems through cyber attack. During a time of war, odds are that most countries will look to play this card. But circumstances might not even have to reach that point before the pin is pulled on a devastating financial grenade. In an August 2007 article, "China Threatens 'Nuclear Option' of Dollar Sales," Ambrose Evans-Pritchard of the *Telegraph* reported that "the Chinese government has begun a concerted campaign of economic threats against the United States, hinting that it may liquidate its vast holding of U.S. Treasuries if Washington imposes trade sanctions to force a yuan revaluation." According to the newspaper, "two officials at leading Communist Party bodies have given interviews in recent days warning—for the first time—that Beijing may use its . . . foreign reserves as a political weapon to counter pressure from the U.S. Congress."

Another article by journalist and author James Fallows in the January/February 2008 issue of the *Atlantic Monthly*, "The $1.4 Trillion Question," suggests the catalyst could be any number of developments.

> Let's take [the] fears about a rich, strong China to their logical extreme. The U.S. and Chinese governments are always disagreeing—about trade, foreign policy, the environment. Someday the disagreement could be severe. Taiwan, Tibet, North Korea, Iran—the possibilities are many, though Taiwan always heads the list. Perhaps a crackdown within China. Perhaps another accident, like the U.S. bombing of China's embassy in Belgrade nine years ago, which everyone in China still believes was intentional and which no prudent American ever mentions here.

> Whatever the provocation, China would consider its levers and weapons and find one stronger than all the rest—one no other country in the world can wield. Without China's billion dollars a day, the United States could not keep its economy stable or spare the dollar from collapse. Would the Chinese use that weapon? The reasonable answer is no, because they would wound themselves grievously, too. . . . But that "reassuring" answer is actually frightening. Lawrence Summers calls today's arrangement "the balance of financial terror," and says that it is flawed in the same way that the "mutually assured destruction" of the Cold War era was.

According to Fallows, it might not take much to upset the existing equilibrium. A mistake, a rumor, a miscalculation of some sort or even "pent-up political tensions" could trigger a move by China that sets a far-reaching financial meltdown in motion. Whatever the reason, there seems little doubt that not only China, but other rivals and antagonists, including Russia, Venezuela, and Iran, understand this dangerous dynamic.

In the end, the fact that geopolitical up-and-comers are championing aggressive approaches and their own ways of doing things should not be all that surprising. Remarks by the leader of one longtime U.S. rival, detailed in a June 2007 *Financial Times* report by Neil Buckley and Catherine Belton, "Putin Calls for New Financial World Order," sum up the perspective of the new kids on the geopolitical block. "Russian president Vladimir Putin called . . . for a radical overhaul of the world's financial and trade institutions to reflect the growing economic power of emerging market countries—including Russia. Mr. Putin said the world needed to create a new international financial architecture to replace an existing model that had become 'archaic, undemocratic, and unwieldy.'"

To the majority of Americans, however, their nation's exposure to such risks is not yet a pressing concern. In the near term, few will be focusing on the economic harm that other nations' aggressive tactics might cause them in future. Instead, the emphasis will be, as elsewhere, on trying to reverse a long-running development that many will come to blame for a litany of existing ills. Around the world, growing numbers will be seeking to undo the damage caused, they believe, by globalization and free trade.

Chapter 5

Local Is the New Global

Free trade has been the most expensive trade policy this nation has ever pursued. There is nothing free about ever-larger trade deficits, mounting trade debts, and the loss of millions of good-paying American jobs.
— LOU DOBBS, *CNN* ANCHOR AND AUTHOR

For years, Alan S. Blinder, a professor of economics at Princeton University and former Federal Reserve Board vice chairman, proclaimed himself a "free trader down to his toes . . . like 99 percent of economists since the days of Adam Smith." But in March 2007, he acknowledged that he was having second thoughts. According to a report by David Wessel and Bob Davis in the *Wall Street Journal*, Blinder was "helping lead a growing band of economists and policy makers, who say the downsides of trade in today's economy are deeper than they once realized." In doing so, he lent further credence to the views of earlier skeptics like Nobel laureate Paul Samuelson, who had argued that "rich-country workers aren't always winners from trade."

Yet even with this admission, academics and policy makers remained behind the curve. Reports indicated that many Americans had already figured out for themselves that despite all the talk about the benefits that would accrue from increased access to fast-growing economies, they had personally lost out. Indeed, for those who had or still worked in manufacturing and other industries where high-paying jobs were once the norm, the reality seemed completely at odds with the promises of free-trade advocates. Increasingly, American jobs were being lost to those living elsewhere, while foreign-made goods came flooding in.

Not surprisingly, popular support for increasing cross-border commerce has eroded. A spring 2008 survey by the Pew Research Center, for example, revealed that 48 percent of Americans thought that free trade agreements "are a bad thing" for the United States, the highest tally among similar polls conducted over the course of the past decade. The same proportion also believed that such accords had an adverse impact on their personal financial situations. According to the pollsters, there was "broad agreement that free trade negatively affects wages, jobs, and economic growth in America. By greater than six-to-one (61 percent to 9 percent), the public says free trade agreements result in job losses rather than in new jobs. A solid majority (56 percent) says that free trade makes wages lower in the United States, and half (50 percent) say it slows the economy."

Globalization, in the words of the International Monetary Fund (IMF), is the "increasing integration of economies around the world, particularly through trade and financial flows" ("Globalization: Threat or Opportunity?"). As the IMF and other pro-trade adherents have long argued, any dislocations associated with the free flow of goods and services tend to be more than offset by gains in overall well-being. According to the IMF, globalization has contributed to "unparalleled economic growth" during the twentieth century, "with global per capita GDP increasing almost five-fold." Moreover, "the strongest expansion came during the second half of the century, a period of rapid trade expansion accompanied by trade—and typically somewhat later, financial—liberalization."

Advocates of globalization's continued march also point to the fact that increasing cross-border commerce has been a boon to what were once some of the world's poorest countries. A 2008 report from the

U.S. State Department, detailed at *America.gov* in an article by Elizabeth Kelleher, "Trade Spurs Economic Growth among Poorest Countries," claimed that "developing nations participating in liberal trade have enjoyed an average annual economic growth rate of five percent during the most recent wave of globalization from the 1990s to the present." David Dollar, a World Bank Country Director for China and author of the report, maintained that as countries like China and Vietnam "became more open to trade, they created confidence and attracted foreign investment and technology."

Some have put forth an even loftier view. An October 2007 commentary in *Barron's*, "Trade Also Serves the Cause of Peace," by Bryan Taylor, chief economist for Global Financial Data, suggested that the Nobel Peace Prize for 2008 should be awarded to the World Trade Organization (WTO), "an organization that has probably done more to raise millions of people from poverty and promote international cooperation than any other organization during the past 60 years." The free trade–facilitating WTO, Taylor wrote, "is an organization that is central to how the world shares resources and whose success will promote the 'fraternity among nations' that Nobel wanted."

Still, for ordinary Americans, and indeed, for a growing number of individuals around the globe, the promise of better times through greater integration and the opening up of formerly closed economies has not rung true. Indeed, surveys, news articles, and anecdotal reports indicate that legions of workers, especially those living in the more economically advanced nations, have come to believe, rightly or wrongly, that globalization has actually reduced their standards of living. There is also a sense that desirable opportunities are harder to come by and that overall job quality has declined, especially as employers have eliminated or scaled back benefits like health care coverage and pensions.

No Longer Ignored

Thoughtful observers have also given these sentiments a voice. They argue, among other things, that the original tenets of "comparative advantage," as set forth by David Ricardo, don't apply in the way they once did. The eighteenth-century economist proposed that all nations benefit if they concentrate on producing what they are best at and trade freely with others. However, modern circumstances have revealed flaws in this theory. For a start, Ricardo assumed that markets are genuinely free, unhindered by distortions such as artificially manipulated currency rates, and that the rules of the game, like those that protect intellectual property rights, are broadly similar among nations.

Moreover, as journalist and author Martin Hutchinson has argued, Ricardo's theorem assumed a static world. "In reality, the world was not quite static even in 1817, and it has been growing progressively less static ever since." In Ricardo's time, Hutchinson said, "it might have taken a Third World manufacturer a couple of generations to acquire not only the manufacturing techniques but also the design, control, and marketing know-how of its Western counterpart." Nowadays, "with modern business education, widespread travel, and ubiquitous communications, that process can be accomplished in well under a decade. Hence the calculus of comparative advantage changes quickly once outsourcing and technology transfer are undertaken, generally substantially to the disadvantage of the wealthier country's workforce."

Some experts place the blame for workers' losses on increased offshoring of production from the United States—as well as from other developed countries, including those in Western Europe—to low-wage countries. According to columnist Paul Craig Roberts, this trend has been powered by the collapse of world socialism following the demise of the Soviet Union, which gave corporations "access to the large pools of excess labor in China and India," as well as by the rise of the high-speed Internet, which enabled businesses to hire professional services from anywhere in the world. "These two developments," he contends, "meant that highly productive and highly paid American labor could be substituted out of production functions and replaced with equally productive but much cheaper foreign labor."

Skewed incentives have spurred widespread adoption of the strategy, which Roberts, a former assistant secretary of the U.S. Treasury, dismisses as "labor arbitrage." The maneuver has boosted economic inequality, too.

Jobs offshoring is dismantling the ladders of upward mobility in the U.S., polarizing the population into rich and poor, and, thereby, worsening . . . income distribution. Because of the . . .

cap on tax-deductible executive pay, executive incomes depend
primarily on performance-related bonuses . . . for making or
exceeding profit expectations by such practices as offshoring jobs
and lowering production costs. We have created an incentive system in which a few corporate executives are amazingly well paid
for destroying jobs and career opportunities for Americans.

Indirectly at least, the facts seem to bear this out. A July 2006
Financial Times article by Edward Luce and Krishna Guha, "Summers
and Rubin to Highlight Lagging Wages," noted, for instance, that the
United States was in

> its fifth year of growth since the last recession. Yet median weekly
> earnings ([by] wage earners who are at the 50th percentile of
> income distribution, with half the workforce earning more and
> half less) have fallen by 3.2 per cent in real terms since the start
> of the recovery in October 2001. Similarly, average hourly earn-
> ings for non-managerial workers have fallen by 0.6 per cent since
> the last quarter of 2001, according to the U.S. Bureau of Labor
> Statistics. This contrasts with previous U.S. recoveries, in which
> wage growth started to overtake inflation at a much earlier stage
> in the cycle.

To those who question the mantra of unfettered cross-border commerce, the impact is clear. " 'What we are seeing is a major structural
shift in the way the U.S. economy works,' says Rob Shapiro, head of the
New Democrat Network's Globalization Initiative, a centrist advocacy
group. 'The ripple effects caused by the supply shock of the entry of
hundreds of millions of Chinese workers into the global economy have
changed the way American workers benefit from trade,' " Edward Luce
and Krishna Guha of the *Financial Times* reported. By most accounts,
the opening up of the formerly isolated economies of China and India,
as well as others, added more than two billion workers to the global
pool of available labor.

But it isn't only Americans who have suffered. Reports indicate
the impact has been far-reaching. A May 2008 *New York Times* article
by Carter Dougherty and Katrin Bennhold, for example, entitled "For
Europe's Middle-Class, Stagnant Wages Stunt Lifestyle," revealed that

large numbers of individuals living on the eastern side of the Atlantic
had also fallen behind in recent years. While some of the blame
stemmed from inflationary pressures that had boosted the prices of
food and other necessities, the fact that workers were having a tougher
time making ends meet could also be traced "to policy decisions and
economic developments over the last decade when globalization began
to reshape Europe and the world." The *Times* added that

> in Germany, Europe's largest economy, the decline in pur-
> chasing power began in 2000, when employers started wrest-
> ing wage concessions from unions, or simply shifting jobs to
> Eastern Europe and China. Inflation-adjusted incomes rose
> from one percent to two percent in the late 1990s, but more
> than one million Germans lost full-time jobs during and after
> a recession in 2000 and 2001. Subsequently, workweeks got
> longer without extra pay, and from 2004 through 2007, infla-
> tion outpaced income increases for the average family.

A number of observers also believe that free trade has augmented,
rather than alleviated, the kinds of disparities that can fuel social tensions. In an October 2007 article by Bob Davis, "IMF Fuels Critics
of Globalization," the *Wall Street Journal* highlighted research by the
International Monetary Fund (IMF) suggesting that while wealth, overall, had increased through globalization, "in the great majority of countries, the income of lower-income workers has risen . . . at a slower
pace than for higher-skilled workers. As a result, the gap between haves
and have-nots has widened." That has been the case, the IMF acknowledged, "since countries in Latin America, Asia, and Eastern Europe
began to liberalize their economies."

Stagnant wages, lost jobs, and growing inequality haven't been the
sole concerns. In the United States, critics of offshoring and a variety of
"unfair" trading arrangements have complained about the dismantling
of the nation's manufacturing base, arguing that it has undermined the
country's long-term growth prospects. A February 2006 study by Joel
Popkin and Kathryn Kobe, "U.S. Manufacturing Innovation at Risk,"
asserted that the

> U.S. share of global trade in manufactures has shrunk, falling
> from 13 percent in the 1990s to 10 percent in 2004. The

U.S. share of global trade in some of the highest value-added export industries such as machinery and equipment is falling. Furthermore, the United States now runs a trade deficit in Advanced Technology Products, goods produced in the industries expected to lead U.S. exports in the 21st century.

A Growing Backlash

These negative developments have sparked a growing backlash against globalization. Increasingly, Americans and others are questioning a system that claims to be fair yet allows nations like China, India, and Japan to gain the upper hand through policies that protect domestic jobs and industries and that lead to a seemingly never-ending accumulation of large trade surpluses. Aggrieved workers have also found fault with an economic framework where the emphasis seems to be on boosting profits and share prices at the expense of wages and benefits. Indeed, commentator Lou Dobbs, who has repeatedly challenged the notion that unrestricted free trade is some sort of economic panacea, has characterized policies favoring government, corporate, and special interests as a "war on the middle class."

Countries in Asia haven't been the only targets. Increasingly, citizens on both sides of Mexico's border have complained about the damage that has been caused by the North American Free Trade Agreement (NAFTA), a trinational pact that also includes Canada. Labor groups in the United States—and in its southern neighbor—argue that instead of creating new opportunities, NAFTA has spawned major job losses and a race to the bottom in terms of overall working conditions. Mexicans complain that instead of reducing prices as promised, liberalized trade has caused the price of tortillas, a dietary staple, to rise by 738 percent since the deal was struck in 1994, according to a December 2007 *Frontera NorteSur* report, "NAFTA at Fourteen."

In recent years, opponents of increasingly unfettered cross-border commerce have called for substantial changes in the terms of trade and the introduction of measures that they believe would level the playing field. Interestingly, the impetus hasn't come only from the working class and those on the left, who have traditionally viewed globalization with a great deal of suspicion. Resistance has also spread among white-collar workers and conservatives, many of whom have become more sympathetic to environmental concerns, as well as policies that have allowed, among other things, an influx of illegal immigrants to continue pouring into the United States unchecked.

Time has faded memories that once buttressed the pro-trade agenda. Many economists believe, for instance, that what transformed the economic downturn following the 1929 stock market crash from a severe recession into the Great Depression was the passage of the Smoot-Hawley Tariff Act. That measure, voted into law in June 1930, increased U.S. tariffs to record levels on tens of thousands of imported goods and sparked retaliatory moves by other nations that eventually led to a sharp contraction in global trade. Historians also contend that cross-border commerce was the economic glue that brought nations together once the Cold War between the United States and Russia came to an end.

Ironically, concerns about the downsides of increasing globalization have also stirred interest in the United States' less-than-liberal beginnings. In an *Asia Times* commentary, Henry C.K. Liu, chairman of a private investment group, notes that "protectionism was the economic system believed in and practiced by the framers of our constitution. Protective tariffs were the principal source of revenue for our federal government from its beginning in 1789 until the passage of the 16th Amendment, which created the federal income tax, in 1913. Were all those public officials during those hundred-plus years remiss in not adhering to a 'moral obligation' of free trade?" On the contrary, notes author and history professor Eric Rauchway, in a commentary for the *New Republic*.

> Cambridge economist Ha-Joon Chang says in *Bad Samaritans* that you can learn lessons about economic development from American history, but the benefits of free trade, free enterprise, democracy, and strong protection for private property are not among them. During the years when the United States developed industrial strength, Americans avoided free markets and, indeed, democracy. Yet nowadays the United States, along with the United Kingdom, the International Monetary Fund, and other major financial players, now prescribes free trade and a

general withdrawal of the state from the economy as the only
method of economic development, defying the actual history
of today's rich nations.

Still, it's hard to dismiss the assertion that nations around the world
have benefited from their participation in a neoliberal-inspired economic order, with its pro-trade rules and mechanisms for increasing
cooperation. Indeed, for all its rhetoric about not wanting to kowtow
to an overbearing West, Russia has seemingly remained intent on join-
ing the World Trade Organization, even as it downplayed those ambitions following its August 2008 South Ossetia incursion and amid
ongoing U.S. efforts to establish a European missile-defense shield in its
backyard. In a March 2008 Reuters report by Gleb Bryanski, "Russia's
Kudrin Says WTO Entry Talks Near End," the country's economic
policy tsar said that accession to the global trade body "would be the
next major milestone in Russia's economic development after the 2006
liberalization of capital movement."

Hostile Forces Gather Steam

The reality is, however, that international cooperation has largely
depended on and been intertwined with booming global growth, with
much of it powered by consumers in the world's largest economy. In the
wake of the unraveling of a historic credit bubble, a wrenching adjust-
ment of structural imbalances, the drag from growing resource constraints, and the debilitating impact of geopolitical turmoil, there will be
much less impetus for nations to work together. Not that there haven't
already been signs of trouble. Although intractable differences over agricultural policies were the ostensible reason why the Doha round of world
trade talks failed, the breakdown also served as an early warning sign of a
change in the geopolitical temperature. Countries no longer feel inclined
or even compelled to agree to multilateral accords for the good of all.
Instead, many have taken the opportunity to strike out on their own and
cut deals that can be more closely tailored to national interests.

An ill-considered move by the United States has also laid the
groundwork for future schisms over cross-border commerce. In a

December 2007 article by Lorraine Woellert, "WTO Online-Gambling Edict Prompts U.S. Resistance," *Bloomberg* reported that "U.S. refusal to comply with a World Trade Organization decision on online gambling is threatening to undermine the entire set of rules binding the international trade system. The WTO is to decide soon on a demand from the tropical nation of Antigua and Barbuda for $3.4 billion in annual compensation from the U.S., whose law banning Americans from wagering on Internet gaming sites was first ruled illegal by the WTO in 2004."

According to the newswire, "the implications of the case go far beyond Antigua, a nation of 69,000. That's because, instead of rewriting its gambling laws, the U.S. rewrote its trade rules to remove the issue from the WTO's jurisdiction. The prospect that other nations, including China, may take a similar tack if cases don't go their way has spooked the international trade community." Although arbitrators at the 152-nation body eventually awarded Antigua damages that were only a fraction of what it had been looking for, the United States' arrogant and clumsy handling of the matter has given a green light to others to play games with trade rules if they feel so inclined.

Regardless, data published in the spring of 2008 indicated that the expansive free-trade pendulum had already started to swing back in the opposite direction. A *Financial Times* report by Alan Beattie, "World Trade Decelerates Almost to Standstill, Says Study," revealed that global cross-border commerce "slowed almost to a standstill over the new year, threatening to shrink for the first time since the U.S. economy went into recession in 2001. An indicator produced by the Bureau for Economic Policy Analysis, a Dutch research institute, revealed that in the three months to January world trade in goods rose at annualized rate of 0.2 per cent over the previous three months. . . . 'This is a substantial deceleration,' the institute said. 'World trade volume growth is on a downward trend.'"

If past patterns repeat themselves—which seems a certainty given the many other negative forces that are at play—faltering growth will energize and expand already nascent opposition to free trade and the forces of globalization. A rising tide of protectionist sentiment will wash over advanced and developing nations alike. The seemingly paradoxical combination of global shortfalls in supplies of critical resources such as energy, water, and food, together with gluts of textiles, mobile telephones, automobiles, and other products that have been churned out in recent years by export powerhouses like China and Japan, will drive nations apart. Calls for action will turn into a bitter and hard-edged reality.

Tough Talk on Trade

Indeed, various reports indicate that antitrade sentiments have been hissing and stirring for quite a while, especially near the centers of power. In a December 2007 article by Greg Hitt, "China Focus May Stall Bush's Trade Plans," the *Wall Street Journal* noted that "at the dawn of an election year, trade skepticism is on the rise in the U.S., roiling the fights for control of the White House and Congress. . . . Much of the anxiety is focused on the competition posed by China, which is the U.S.'s second-largest trading partner, after Canada. Democrats in the House of Representatives already are girding for action on legislation to address concerns over Chinese counterfeiting, product safety, and currency policy, among other things."

According to the newspaper,

> critics contend China keeps its currency artificially low, creating imbalances that give Chinese exporters an unfair advantage in the global marketplace. Beijing has allowed its currency to strengthen at a faster pace in recent weeks, though there is little indication this has satisfied U.S. critics of its currency policy. Rep. Sander Levin (D., Mich.), an important voice on trade policy in the House, said the recent negotiations [with China] showed the administration is "more talk than action." Rep. Levin, chairman of the Ways and Means trade subcommittee, said the talks' middling outcome has "increased the notion on the Hill that we really need to take a serious look at legislation." Members of the Senate also are pushing to give the White House new tools to toughen policy toward China.

Such efforts have spurred a similarly strident response from the other side. In June 2007, for example, in an article entitled "China

Warns of Countermeasures. If U.S. Congress Passes Trade Bill," *Agence-France Presse* reported that China had

> warned of unspecified countermeasures if . . . Congress adopts a bill on Beijing's foreign exchange regime that could lead to higher U.S. tariffs on Chinese imports. "China has all along held that the development of Sino-U.S. bilateral trade is in the interest of both sides," foreign ministry spokesman Qin Gang told reporters. But "the US Congress could pass this legislation which will lead to the problem of higher tariffs on Chinese goods. . . . If this happens then the Chinese departments concerned will make a response."

As economic conditions in the United States and around the world continue to worsen, public anger and political anxiety will swell. Increasingly, expansive trade policies and export-oriented trading partners will attract the blame for a wide array of economic and social ills, including surging unemployment, declining wages, social instability, and widespread apprehensions about the future. There will be a noisy clamor for tough measures that protect domestic workers, reduce or eliminate unfair competition, and limit the types and quantities of goods and services that can be sourced from other countries.

Early on, mainstream economists and those who fault the Ricardian model but nonetheless believe in the benefits of increasing cross-border commerce will likely call for ad hoc bilateral arrangements that address claims of unfairness but which also seek to keep trading channels open. Among the possibilities: an approach described by Gabor Steingart in *Spiegel Online* "that would require the Chinese, the Indians, and the Mexicans to introduce reforms in their countries in return for access to American markets, reform that would include more stringent environment standards, the development of their own social welfare states, and the revaluation of their currencies."

More level-headed political leaders will also rely on jawboning and tough, behind-the-scenes negotiations to forestall the most damaging of outcomes. They will call upon other nations to correct trade imbalances voluntarily, in order to reduce the risk of being blindsided by quotas, tariffs, and other measures. Based on recent history, such efforts may even have some limited success, at least initially. A December 2007 *Bloomberg* report by Helen Yuan, for example, entitled "China to Introduce, Raise Steel, Iron Export Tariffs," detailed the nation's plans to "introduce export tariffs on some steel products . . . and boost rates on other items to rein in a record trade surplus and cut energy consumption and pollution." In reality, the move apparently came about in response to threats by European Union policy makers that they would take aggressive action over alleged dumping of Chinese steel products in the European market.

A Rising Tide of Isolationism, Protectionism, and Xenophobia

Waning U.S. influence, heightened social unrest, and an array of economic pressures will ultimately cast doubt on the authority of organizations like the WTO. In the near term, however, calls for relief under established frameworks will rise sharply. The WTO's Anti-Dumping Agreement, which offers redress in cases where firms are found to have caused harm by selling goods below prices they would fetch in home markets, will form the basis of many challenges. Exporters, meanwhile, will fight back with complaints about protectionism. Eventually, nations will reject established multilateral mechanisms and confront matters more directly. Many will focus on bilateral deals, while others will organize collective arrangements and set up trading corridors that make it difficult, if not impossible, for outsiders to compete.

Tariffs, quotas, mandated preferences, and rules favoring domestic interests will become increasingly prevalent around the world. While most will stem from legislation and government policy maneuvers, some barriers will likely spring up, seemingly spontaneously, from the grassroots level. Labor unions, populist and nationalist groups, and various media outlets will promote ad hoc and official boycotts against companies that don't favor home markets. Firms will face unrelenting pressure to hire more domestic workers and buy more products locally or else risk losing business to competitors. Community heat will be turned up against foreigners, immigrants, and outsiders.

Trade won't be the only target. Fears about economic "family jewels"—corporate assets, infrastructure and critical logistical facilities,

arable land, and sources of basic resources and industrial commodities—
being sold off too cheaply, a deteriorating economic outlook, and
heightened concerns over national security and threats to public order
will spur the introduction of restrictive investment policies and much
greater scrutiny of who is buying what. At the same time, individuals
and institutional money managers will likely face demands, as well as
financial incentives and penalties, to repatriate funds invested abroad.
After tripling to nearly 14.5 percent of world GDP over the course of
a decade—according to IMF data—cross-border fund flows will shift
rapidly into reverse.

Increasingly, faltering growth and turbulent market conditions will
lead some governments, especially in developing nations, to cover trade-
related shortfalls by divesting some or all of their foreign assets. Many
will look to keep growth alive through increased domestic spending. In
China, for instance, government fears of slowdown-induced instability,
along with the fallout from years of environmental damage, will likely
spur greater spending on infrastructure, housing, health care, cleanup
projects, and other social needs. At least a portion of those funds will
come from the nation's large pool of official reserves. These withdrawals will exacerbate an ongoing rise in the value of the yuan and
undermine an already wavering export-oriented growth strategy. The
repercussions will be felt far and wide.

Proliferating trade barriers and growing constraints on the free
movement of goods, services, capital, and people will engender a tit-
for-tat spiral that heightens political and social differences and reduces
cooperation worldwide. This, in turn, will further fuel resentment toward
outsiders. Up until recent years, globalization and booming growth have
kept such feelings at bay; widespread economic contractions and a dramatic change in the global order will cause these sentiments to resur-
face. Attacks on immigrants, illegal or otherwise, will steadily increase. In
countries where xenophobia is running rampant, there may even be calls
for abhorrent programs like "Operation Wetback." Organized in 1954 by
the U.S. Immigration and Naturalization Service (INS), under the direction of President Dwight D. Eisenhower's newly appointed INS com-
missioner, General Joseph Swing, and carried out alongside state and
local police agencies, this initiative was designed to turn back a tide of
illegal immigrants. The yearlong crackdown, mainly targeted at Mexican

nationals, eventually led to the deportation of at least 130,000 people, and hundreds of thousands of others left of their own volition.

Amid deteriorating social and economic conditions, immigrants may not even wait around for such a development; they will seek greener pastures elsewhere. In the United States, at least, that trend seems to have already started. A spring 2008 Inter-American Development Bank survey of Latino immigrants, detailed in a report by Julia Preston in the *International Herald Tribune*, found that three million of them had "stopped sending money to their families because life is becoming more difficult for them here." A large majority of those polled "said they experienced increasing hostility as a result of U.S. government and state efforts to curb illegal immigration and punish employers who hire unauthorized immigrant workers." Because of the difficulties, those "who said they were considering going back to live in their home countries increased notably."

Such a pattern seems to jibe with research indicating that historically, at least, immigrant flows appear to correlate fairly closely with economic conditions. In a column in *Vox*, University of Zurich history professor Drew Keeling asserted that "the economic risks of working abroad, particularly the risk of cyclical recessions, and the availability of family networks to help cope with those risks, were crucial factors determining who migrated and how they migrated." In his view, "risks and business cycles" may "turn out to be even more important in shaping migration levels than border controls."

Recent years' relative increases in emerging-nation labor costs will also force businesses that had rushed into those countries to bring work back home. Indeed, evidence suggests such a retrenchment is underway. In February 2008, for example, in an article headlined "South Korean Companies Pull Out of China without Paying Salaries or Debts," *AsiaNews* reported that

> hundreds of businesses are not reopening after closing for the new year, without paying their employees or settling their other debts. Seoul is intervening to avoid a diplomatic crisis. Thousands of factories owned by Taiwan and Hong Kong are also closing. . . . New taxes (from which foreign companies were exempted at first), greater pollution controls, the appreciation of

the yuan, and the rise in labor costs (the new law recognizes employees' rights to health insurance and severance pay) have made it less advantageous to maintain production in China.

Divisive Forces

Sputtering growth, high costs, the clamor for protectionism, and xeno-phobia will be major drivers, but they won't be the only factors spurring an inward turn in nations around the world. Other pressures will also spark isolationist calls, including the cost and availability of key resources. No doubt, the jump in food and energy prices that began in 2007 will buttress arguments for greater self-sufficiency. As *CNN Money* reported in the spring of 2008 (under the headline "Food Prices on the Rise Worldwide"), "riots from Haiti to Bangladesh to Egypt over the soar-ing costs of basic foods have brought the issue to a boiling point and catapulted it to the forefront of the world's attention. . . . 'This is the world's big story,' said Jeffrey Sachs, director of Columbia University's Earth Institute." A June 2008 *Bloomberg* report by Matthew Benjamin and Mark Drajem summed up the mood succinctly with a headline that read: "Free-Trade Era May Be Nearing End amid Food, Growth Concerns."

And while a dramatic worldwide slowdown will naturally undercut energy demand at one level, peak-oil constraints and the step-change boost in developing-nation per-capita consumption levels will continue to put a floor under fossil fuel prices. That alone will force a dramatic rethink about the benefits of being (and staying) connected to other countries—except to harvest their resource wealth. Challenging the views of Thomas Friedman, Thomas Homer-Dixon (in a February 2007 interview by Terrence McNally) contended that the frictionless global economy envisioned by the "flat Earth" apostle is feasible only if "we have abundant cheap energy. As energy becomes more expensive, people will start moving production closer to consumers. It won't make sense to have your production facilities in China if you're selling goods in the United States. You're going to want them at least on the Mexican border."

Around the world, the offshoring boom will turn to bust. Along with higher overseas wage costs, various other influences—including bully-pulpit jawboning, name-and-shame campaigns, and changing tax policies—will force businesses to withdraw from the international arena and channel more activities back home. Indeed, a November 2007 *Los Angeles Times* report by Peter Pae, "Small-Town America: The New Bangalore?" suggested some businesses might have already seen the writing on the wall. At one U.S. firm, for example, outsourcing computer work to domestic locations was suddenly making more sense than it did before. "It costs Northrop [Grumman Corporation] about 40 percent less to have the work done in [the Texas city of] Corsicana than in Los Angeles—savings similar to what would be achieved by sending jobs overseas. 'We're getting very high quality and a dedicated workforce,' said Thomas Shelman, president of Northrop's Information Technology Defense Group and creator of the company's onshoring program." In time, hostile economic, political, and social realities will force firms to rethink these and many other aspects of how they operate—just to survive.

Fear Further Fuels Deglobalization

Concerns over foreign health and safety standards will push countries even farther apart. Jurisdictional disparities will intensify as waning American influence and crippled economies in the United States, Europe, and elsewhere lead many countries to either ignore or abandon Western-dictated norms in favor of local or regional rules—or perhaps none at all. Consumer advocates in places like the United States, meanwhile, will raise all sorts of alarms about foreign products, citing incidents like the importation from China of tainted samples of the blood-thinning drug heparin, which reportedly killed more than 19 people during 2007 and 2008, and of animal feed containing a chemical made from coal that was linked to illnesses and deaths of hundreds of American pets during 2007.

Recurring outbreaks of bird flu—and other diseases that could evolve into devastating epidemics—in Asia and elsewhere will also bolster efforts to lock down borders and limit the free flow of goods and services—as well as people. In a story reported by Clair Leow detailing an autumn 2007 fatality from a strain of avian influenza, "Indonesia Confirms Death of Boy from Bird Flu, 88th Fatality," *Bloomberg* reported that "the H5N1 virus is known to have infected

330 people in a dozen countries since 2003, the World Health Organization said. . . . Three of every five cases have been fatal. Millions may die if H5N1 develops the characteristics of seasonal flu and begins spreading easily between people, touching off a global outbreak, according to the Geneva-based agency."

Rejecting the tenets of globalization in favor of protectionism and isolationism, governments and groups will seek to augment an already expanding array of economic, political, and other barriers to immigration and integration. Measures will include figurative and literal walls designed to keep foreigners out—and, just as likely, to keep residents in. In the fashion of totalitarian regimes, many countries, including the United States, may boost restrictions not only on foreign travel, but on free movements within the nation's borders. Visa, residency, and naturalization requirements will be tightened—if immigration is permitted at all. Increased use of no-fly lists, background checks, and burgeoning red-tape entry requirements will create an increasingly hostile environment that discourages tourism and other nonessential visits.

More than likely, there will be an upsurge in antagonistic incidents like the one described in a May 2008 *New York Times* report by Nina Bernstein, where a foreign visitor to the United States was denied admission, held in custody, and subjected to needlessly humiliating treatment over unfounded concerns about the number of his prior trips—to see his girlfriend. In the past, regular visitors might have been welcomed with open arms and thoroughly appreciated for their willingness to spend money and aid businesses in the destination country. In the new scheme of things, those who show too much interest in the attractions of other places risk being branded as dangerous threats to economic and national security.

Last but not least, old-fashioned barbed wire and newfangled electronic gadgetry will increasingly be used to make borders ever more secure and menacing. In fact, an April 2007 essay by Simon Robinson in *Time*, "Notes on a Divided World," reveals a trend that has begun to gain some serious traction.

All around the world, countries are busy throwing up walls. Iran is building a bulwark along its border with Pakistan to stop illegal crossings. Botswana erected a 480-km electric fence along its boundary with Zimbabwe. Saudi Arabia is spending hundreds of millions of dollars on massive ramparts to separate itself from Yemen to the south and from Iraq to the north. Thailand wants a concrete barrier along part of its border with Malaysia. The U.S. is erecting a controversial fence along its Mexico flank. Israel is building a separation barrier between itself and the West Bank.

As deglobalization takes hold and the existing geopolitical order continues to crumble, hearts and minds will close along with borders. Nationalistic stirrings will rise up and overwhelm the integrative spirit of the past several decades. Cracks and stresses will appear virtually everywhere, souring attitudes and stoking suspicions. Instead of being drawn together in a flatter, more connected world, people will discover that new economic, social, and political realities are slowly but surely driving them apart.

Chapter 6

Multiplying Divisions

The tools of conquest do not necessarily come with bombs and explosions and fallout. There are weapons that are simply thoughts, attitudes, prejudices—to be found in the minds of men. For the record, prejudices can kill and suspicion can destroy, and a thoughtless, frightened search for a scapegoat has a fallout all its own—for the children and the children yet unborn. And the pity of it is that these things cannot be confined to the Twilight Zone.

—ROD SERLING, ACTOR, PRODUCER, AND SCREENWRITER

Until the early 1960s, the "twilight zone" typically referred to the lowest depths of the sea that sunlight could reach. But after Rod Serling created *The Twilight Zone*, an acclaimed series that ran for five years on the CBS television network, another definition became popular—that is, "an ambiguous or unsettled state or condition, especially between two opposing conditions." Drawing on that tension with science-fiction plotlines featuring paranormal events, Serling often used the shows as vehicles for social commentary. In one episode, "The Monsters Are Due on Maple Street," a town is gradually engulfed by suspicion, hostility, and, eventually, violence, following a number of mysterious incidents. Though none of the residents were responsible for what originally transpired, they are nonetheless quick to point fingers in a cascade of blame and recriminations.

Most likely, the years ahead won't witness—as the episode's final plot twist reveals—the presence of mischief-making aliens with an acute understanding of human nature. Yet other, real-world developments will induce similar schisms. Troubles won't be confined to small towns, either. They will unfold more generally, as the forces of fragmentation and divisiveness trickle down through all levels of political and social organization. Among the factors causing strains will be the fallout from unraveling economies and heightened resource constraints, waning U.S. power and global competition for influence, old wounds and reawakened rivalries, and emerging societal pressures, many stemming from demographic and other broad-based social trends.

Diminishing American power will play a major role in undermining global stability and unleashing a raft of disruptive forces. Boundaries will shift and alliances will unravel, much like they did when the Communist Party was no longer able to exert its authority over the Union of Soviet Socialist Republics and the nations in its broader sphere of influence. Individuals, groups, and countries around the world that were amenable to—or, perhaps, constrained by—rules and systems that emanated from U.S. economic and military dominance will rethink existing arrangements and formulate new ones. Many will probe the limits of waning American imperial resolve.

In a 2008 *Foreign Affairs* commentary, "The Age of Nonpolarity," Richard N. Haass, president of the Council on Foreign Relations (CFR), acknowledged that the United States' loss of standing will be fractious and potentially destabilizing.

> The increasingly nonpolar world will have mostly negative consequences for the United States—and for much of the rest of the world as well. It will make it more difficult for Washington to lead on those occasions when it seeks to promote collective responses to regional and global challenges. One reason has to do with simple arithmetic. With so many more actors possessing meaningful power and trying to assert influence, it

will be more difficult to build collective responses and make institutions work.

Moreover, he said, "nonpolarity will also increase the number of threats and vulnerabilities facing a country such as the United States. These threats can take the form of rogue states, terrorist groups, energy producers that choose to reduce their output, or central banks whose action or inaction can create conditions that affect the role and strength of the U.S. dollar." Haass believes that the transition can and should be managed by the United States to avoid a "cauldron of instability." However, he also allows for a less desirable outcome. "Left to its own devices, a nonpolar world will become messier over time. Entropy dictates that systems consisting of a large number of actors tend toward greater randomness and disorder in the absence of external intervention."

To be sure, many of those who recognize that the times are, indeed, changing don't accept that the risks are skewed to the downside. In a May 2008 *Newsweek* excerpt from his book, *The Post-American World*, Fareed Zakaria, editor of the magazine's international edition, wrote that

> it's true China is booming, Russia is growing more assertive, terrorism is a threat. But if America is losing the ability to dictate to this new world, it has not lost the ability to lead. . . . The post-American world is naturally an unsettling prospect for Americans, but it should not be. This will not be a world defined by the decline of America but rather the rise of every-one else. It is the result of a series of positive trends that have been progressing over the last 20 years, trends that have created an international climate of unprecedented peace and prosperity.

Short Shrift to New Realities

But such perspectives give short shrift to the enmity and resentment that have built up toward the United States, especially over the course of the past decade. Clearly, the disastrous wars in Iraq and Afghanistan, the scandals at Abu Ghraib prison and the Guantanamo detention facilities, and the arrogance and exceptionalism that have permeated U.S. dealings with the rest of the world—especially while George W. Bush was president—have had a corrosive effect. In fact, anti-American sentiment seems to have become ingrained in some key regions. An April 2008 *BBC World Service* poll (reported by Kim Ghattas) found, for example, that "eight out of ten people in the Arab world have a negative view of the U.S." and, by extension, "governments supported by the U.S. are unpopular."

The optimists also gloss over other, equally unsettling realities. These include an unfolding global economic contraction, heightened antagonism toward free trade and the tenets of liberalism, and intense competition for key resources. Energy-related concerns could prove particularly divisive. According to the *Financial Times'* Martin Wolf, in a commentary entitled "The Dangers of Living in a Zero-Sum World Economy," cheap and abundant energy has played a major role over the past two centuries in creating a "positive-sum world economy," where everybody "can become better off." This, he believes, "is why democracy has become a political norm, empires have largely vanished, legal slavery and serfdom have disappeared, and measures of well-being have risen almost everywhere. . . . Consistent rises in real incomes per head have transformed our economic lives," Wolf added, but they have also "transformed politics."

By the same token, he writes, "a zero-sum economy leads, inevitably, to repression at home and plunder abroad. In traditional agrarian societies the surpluses extracted from the vast majority of peasants supported the relatively luxurious lifestyles of military, bureaucratic, and noble elites. The only way to increase the prosperity of an entire people was to steal from another one. . . . In a world of stagnant living standards the gains of one group came at the expense of equal, if not still bigger, losses for others. This, then, was a world of savage repression and brutal predation"—and of empire building and war.

For Wolf, "the biggest point about debates on climate change and energy supply is that they bring back the question of limits. . . . If there are limits to emissions, there may also be limits to growth. But if there are indeed limits to growth, the political underpinnings of our world fall apart. Intense distributional conflicts must then re-emerge— indeed, they are already emerging—within and among countries." In such an environment, it is only natural that the prospective and, to some great extent, hypothetical gains from greater integration with nations that are competing for a share of a shrinking pie are called into question. Rather, the natural tendency will be toward protectionism, isolationism, xenophobia, and conflict.

Ironically, decades of increasing globalization have laid the groundwork for future schisms. Even those who, like Fareed Zakaria, are sanguine about the future accept that a large-scale redistribution of wealth has potentially unsettling ramifications:

> As economic fortunes rise, so inevitably does nationalism. Imagine that your country has been poor and marginal for centuries. Finally, things turn around and it becomes a symbol of economic progress and success. You would be proud, and anxious that your people win recognition and respect throughout the world. In many countries such nationalism arises from a pent-up frustration over having to accept an entirely Western, or American, narrative of world history—one in which they are miscast or remain bit players.

Yet while such a development is seen as natural and inevitable, signs already point to outcomes that are less than benign. In an April 2008 front-page article by Bob Davis, "Rise of Nationalism Frays Global Ties," the *Wall Street Journal* said as much.

> During the long march toward globalization, international borders and trade barriers came down. Communism fell. Protectionist walls in Latin America and elsewhere were dismantled. Governments—long prone to meddling in trade—took a back seat to broader market forces. . . . No longer. The global economy appears to be entering an epoch in which governments are reasserting their role in the lives of individuals and businesses. Once again, barriers are rising. Call it the new nationalism.

In fact, despite their apparent support for a global system whose foundations rest on increasing cooperation and free trade, many newly emerging powers have nevertheless stuck with state-sanctioned frameworks that have allowed them to gain significant economic advantage over trading partners and rivals. The "Russo-Chinese model," as the *Financial Times* described it in a January 2008 lead-in to a reader Q&A, "Illiberal Capitalism," "is authoritarian and attempts to marry capitalism with a large state role in the economy. Moscow and Beijing," the newspaper noted, "increasingly stress a combination of economic growth and nationalism." During the good times, complaints have been muted. As conditions sour, a growing number of nations will abandon a system that seems less than fair.

A Souring Reputation

With the United States losing its place at the head of the geopolitical table, individuals, groups, and countries around the world will be quick to move in and fill the void, both as a defensive maneuver—to forestall being left in a lurch either economically or militarily—and as a means of ensuring they will play a significant role in shaping the new global framework. Competition for influence will take many forms and come from many quarters, though it will frequently cluster along geographical lines. In Asia, for example, China's economic and military strength all but guarantees that the nation will be a major power broker and center of economic gravity in that part of the world, though Russia, India, Japan, and others nearby—not to mention outsiders like the United States—will also be pressing for advantage.

As events unfold, allegiances and alliances will remain in flux, varying, often dramatically, as economic, social, and political conditions either stagnate or, more likely, deteriorate. Many links will evolve on an à la carte basis, depending on the strategic interests at stake and the agendas of those in power. Other tie-ups involving nations that might not have a long history of cooperation will come about in response to shared threats. Indeed, such has already been seen in the relationship between China and Russia. In a May 2008 article by Vladimir Isachenkov, for example, entitled "China, Russia Condemn U.S. Missile Defense Plans," the Associated Press reported that leaders of the two countries "sharply condemned U.S. missile defense plans, . . . taking a harder common line that reinforces an already strong strategic partnership during Dmitry Medvedev's first foreign trip as Russian president."

The newswire added,

Pushing forward their robust energy cooperation, Russia also
signed a $1 billion deal to build a uranium enrichment facility
in China and supply low-enriched uranium for use in China's
nuclear power industry over the next decade. Rivals throughout much of the Cold War, Moscow and Beijing have forged
close political and military ties since the Soviet collapse, seeking to counter the perceived U.S. global domination. They
have spoken against the U.S. missile defense plans in the past,
but [the] declaration by Medvedev and Chinese President Hu
Jintao sounded tougher than before.

Along with warnings about U.S. attempts to unsettle the world's
"strategic balance," as well as any plans the United States might have
for deploying weapons in space, the Associated Press concluded, the
nations' "joint position appears to raise the stakes for Washington,
which has been trying to persuade Beijing and Moscow not to see the
missile shields as threatening. At the same time, the cooperation on diplomatic issues masks deep Russian unease at China's growing power
and differences over military and energy sales."

Another region where competition and conflict will intensify is the
oil-rich Middle East. While the United States, China, and Russia have
laid down the gauntlet that they seek greater influence, America's continued loss of standing may spur a messier and deadlier free-for-all than
has already been seen. According to Richard Haass, other entities in the
Mideast, "including local states (Israel, Iran, Saudi Arabia, Egypt, Iraq,
Syria), militias, terrorist groups, political parties and movements, sovereign
wealth funds, etc., will all have influence of their own and reduce what it
is the United States or any outside power can accomplish" in that part of
the world. Although the foreign policy expert believes the United States
"will retain considerable influence in the region," that perspective seems
at odds with crumbling popular and political support for the longtime
superpower. Indeed, the *BBC* poll cited earlier in the chapter revealed
that "across the Arab world, Hezbollah's leader, Hassan Nasrallah, is . . .
the most popular leader, followed by Syrian President Bashar al-Assad
and Iran's President Mahmoud Ahmadinejad" because, it seems, they are

"the only ones standing up against U.S. influence." Moreover, the survey indicated that "while Sunni rulers in the region worry about Shia Iran's growing influence, ordinary Arabs don't seem to view Iran as a threat. Almost half . . . believe that if Tehran acquires nuclear weapons the outcome . . . would be more positive than negative."

Public opinion can change, of course, but other evidence suggests the U.S. position in this longstanding cauldron of instability has been irretrievably undermined, paving the way for discord and disorder. In a May 2008 commentary, "The New Cold War," *New York Times* columnist and author Thomas L. Friedman wrote that "the next American president will inherit many foreign policy challenges, but surely one of the biggest will be the Cold War. Yes, the next U.S. president is going to be a Cold War president—but this Cold War is with Iran." According to Friedman, this "is the real umbrella story in the Middle East today—the struggle for influence across the region, with America and its Sunni Arab allies (and Israel) versus Iran, Syria, and their non-state allies, Hamas and Hezbollah. As [a recent] editorial in the Iranian daily *Kayhan* put it, 'In the power struggle in the Middle East, there are only two sides: Iran and the U.S.'"

In Friedman's view, "Team America is losing on just about every front. How come? The short answer is that Iran is smart and ruthless, America is dumb and weak, and the Sunni Arab world is feckless and divided." Commenting on what he characterized as an "Iranian-Syrian-Hezbollah attempt to take over Lebanon," Friedman cited Middle East watcher Ehud Yaari (who labels the foray and related developments as an evolving "Pax Iranica"): "'Simply put,' noted Yaari, 'Tehran has created a situation in which anyone who wants to attack its atomic facilities will have to take into account that this will lead to bitter fighting' on the Lebanese, Palestinian, Iraqi, and Persian Gulf fronts. That is a sophisticated strategy of deterrence," Friedman wrote.

Winds of Change

Although the Middle East will be one of the most active hot zones, entropic winds will no doubt blow through other parts of the world, too. Certain regions are destined to be hard hit, including Africa, which has not been grounded by a stable economic or military history. Latin America will also be exposed. Spurred on by a militant Venezuela and its socialist allies on the one hand, and an economically invigorated Brazil on the other, the South American continent may well become a major battleground for competing local, regional, and international powers in an era of growing resource constraints. Its substantial oil reserves and mineral deposits and large tracts of arable land have already attracted a great deal of foreign interest. China, as noted earlier, has been building strong ties to the region, as have Iran, Russia, and traditional Spanish- and Portuguese-speaking allies in Europe.

This represents a sea change from when South America was seen by many as something of a backwater, occasionally forced to go along with the wishes of its superpower neighbor. In recent years, Latin America's newfound attractiveness and accompanying self-confidence have altered the dynamic. Needless to say, the transformation has raised hackles in the North, provoking a fresh focus on securing trade deals with and boosting arms sales to countries in the region. However, the shifting geopolitical winds mean that, unlike before, proximity to the United States could make for a more, rather than less, contentious future in America's backyard.

In a January 2008 *Le Monde Diplomatique* commentary, "Latin America Breaks Free of the U.S.," Janette Habel, a lecturer at the Institute of Latin American Studies in Paris, argued that "the U.S. has lost ground in Latin America over the past decade, since the project to develop the Free Trade Area of the Americas flopped and . . . leftwing governments took power and used it with imagination and vigor. The U.S. continues to try to block such emancipation by promoting more free trade agreements, and increasing military cooperation in the name of the war on terrorism and narcotics and the defense of market democracy." Nonetheless, Habel noted, those moves appeared to be for naught:

Latin America is a lost continent, according to the editor of *Foreign Policy*, Moises Naim. The president of the Inter-American Dialogue organization, Peter Hakim, voiced the same concern when he asked: "Is Washington losing Latin America?" Over the past decade the United States has suffered many setbacks in this part of the world. Voters, rejecting neo-liberal policies,

have elected radical or moderate leftwing coalitions, claiming
degrees of independence. In April 2002 the attempt to overthrow Venezuela's president Hugo Chávez failed. In 2005 the
native movement brought Evo Morales to power in Bolivia
despite U.S. State Department efforts. Though it exerted pressure, the U.S. was unable to prevent Daniel Ortega from being
elected in Nicaragua or Rafael Correa in Ecuador.

Undoubtedly, sovereign nations will be at the forefront of efforts
to shape the emerging global order. Yet developments in the Middle
East, Asia, and even directly south of the U.S. border make it clear they
won't be operating on their own. Terrorists, criminals, and other rogue
elements will also be looking to fill the gap that opens up as American
influence wanes. In Mexico, for example, an ongoing war between the
government and powerful gangs has left some wondering if that country "could turn into the kind of battleground that existed in Colombia
in the 1980s when drug cartels held sway over several cities and operated with impunity," according to a May 2008 report by Greg Flakus
of *VOA News*. To George Friedman, a political analyst at intelligence
firm Stratfor, Flakus writes, "the private armies of the Mexican drug
cartels resemble the militias that have undermined governments in
other parts of the world. 'What we are seeing in Mexico looks more
like Lebanon, which are militias that are stronger than the Lebanese
army,' [Friedman] said. 'This issue that we are facing here today is can
the Mexican state with all of its power outfight the militias of the cartels? Now, it is not clear that they cannot, but, at this moment, it is also
not clear that they can.'"

Other factors will simultaneously exacerbate and undermine
the quest for local, regional, and global dominance. The growing gulf
between the haves and, in some cases, increasingly desperate have-nots
will serve as a powerful catalyst for realignments and revolts, as well as
a worldwide expansion of cross-border conflicts. Some recent developments offer a taste of what's to come. In South America's poorest
country, for example, tenuous threads of domestic unity have become
increasingly frayed by ongoing disputes over regional economic disparities and uneven distribution of resource-related wealth. A May
2008 Reuters report by Pav Jordan, "Bolivia's Richest Region Votes

'Yes' on Autonomy," revealed that "Santa Cruz voted overwhelm-
ingly for autonomy . . . in a vote widely seen as a rejection of President
Evo Morales' leftist reforms, exit polls showed. . . . The ballot was the
first of four referendums on greater autonomy from central government being planned by Bolivia's eastern lowland provinces, deepening
a divide between Morales' supporters and the conservative opposition." According to the newswire, "The growing demands for regional
autonomy have exposed a bitter divide between Bolivia's wealthier
lowlands and the poor Andean highlands, where tens of thousands of
people marched to show support for Morales—Bolivia's first Indian
president—in several cities."

To be sure, Bolivia isn't the only country—nor is Latin America
the only region—where economic, social, and political inequities
have triggered—and will increasingly spawn—unrest and separatist calls.
Divisive undercurrents have long simmered in many parts of Africa, for
example, as well as in Asia and Eastern Europe. Some well-known global trouble spots, including Pakistan, Lebanon, and Afghanistan, have
been on the boil for the better part of the past several decades, with
violent clashes and periods of near anarchy only briefly interrupted by
calm and seeming unity.

Spreading Divisiveness

More recently, though, divisive pressures are being felt in traditionally less unstable locales. In Europe, for example, tensions between
Belgium's wealthy, Dutch-speaking northern region of Flanders and
the French-speaking southern region of Wallonia have sparked a continuing leadership crisis that shows little sign of abating. At the root
of failed attempts to form a new coalition government that spawned
demonstrations by thousands in December 2007, *Agence France-Presse*
reported ("Thousands Demonstrate as Belgian Political Crisis Hits
Pockets"), is Flemish parties' desire for "more autonomy for their
region, including in economic matters." Wallonians, meanwhile, have
feared losing subsidies that flow from the north.

Scotland has also faced pressures to extricate itself from a centuries-
old tie-up with England. These forces have intensified, especially during

the past few years, following Scotland's 1997 vote for "devolution," or limited home rule. The secessionist movement has been motivated, in part, by the locally popular perception that too much North Sea oil wealth has flowed southward toward London. Although the Scottish Nationalist Party and other proponents of severing ties to the United Kingdom have called for referendums to be held in the immediate years ahead, some argue that the future is more or less ordained. Indeed, a November 2007 headline of an article by Simon Heffer in the *Daily Telegraph* proclaimed, "The Union of England and Scotland Is Over."

Even in the United States—a century and a half after a long, bloody civil war nearly tore the country apart—separatist sentiments have been stirring, albeit on a very limited scale. An October 2007 Associated Press report by Bill Poovey, "Secessionists Meeting in Tennessee," detailed the lead-up to a two-day gathering in Chattanooga of individuals who were looking to bring about a dramatic change in the political landscape.

> In an unlikely marriage of desire to secede from the United States, two advocacy groups from opposite political traditions— New England and the South—are sitting down to talk. . . . Tired of foreign wars and what they consider right-wing courts, the Middlebury Institute wants liberal states like Vermont to be able to secede peacefully. That sounds just fine to the League of the South, a conservative group that refuses to give up on Southern independence. "We believe that an independent South, or Hawaii, Alaska, or Vermont would be better able to serve the interest of everybody, regardless of race or ethnicity," said Michael Hill of Killen, Ala., president of the League of the South.

According to the report, organizers expected to "attract supporters from California, Alaska, and Hawaii, inviting anyone who wants to dissolve the Union so states can save themselves from an overbearing federal government."

To be sure, many of these efforts will fizzle out or remain firmly on the fringe. But it seems clear that a souring social mood will boost the appeal of new political systems and redrawn boundaries that offer the promise of a dramatic change in the status quo. Not all of the strains will come from within, though. Changing economic realities and competition for key resources will stir up a divisiveness that extends beyond internal borders. Again, there have been hints of what a more contentious future will look like. In February 2008, for example, *BBC News* reported that Venezuela's state oil company was suspending sales of crude oil to Exxon Mobil in response to the firm's legal claims for "compensation following the nationalization of a project in Venezuela's largest oil reserve" ("Venezuela Breaks Ties with Exxon"). At the same time, President Chávez "threatened to cut off oil sales to the United States in an 'economic war,'" according to Sandra Sierra of the Associated Press. Months later, amid its dispute with the four resource-rich, autonomy-seeking provinces, Bolivia's president asserted unfettered authority over hydrocarbon assets. Spanish newswire EFE reported that he was "preparing a decree to nationalize oil and gas fields in case foreign companies fail to invest in them," according to Laura Price of *Bloomberg*.

What might be described as geopolitical spread betting will further heighten tensions, as an array of interests seek to ensure that they end up in the winners' circle. In a January 2008 *New York Times* article, "Waving Goodbye to Hegemony," Parag Khanna, author of *The Second World: Empires and Influence in the New Global Order*, details an approach that some are already taking. "No doubt the thaw with Libya, brokered by America and Britain after Muammar el-Qaddafi declared he would abandon his country's nuclear pursuits in 2003, was partly motivated by growing demand for energy from a close Mediterranean neighbor. But Qaddafi is not selling out. He and his advisers have astutely parceled out production-sharing agreements to a balanced assortment of American, European, Chinese, and other Asian oil giants."

That's not all, says the foreign policy scholar (who also believes that "three hemispheric pan-regions, longitudinal zones dominated by America, Europe, and China," will define twenty-first-century geopolitics). "Mindful of the history of Western oil companies' exploitation of Arabia," Libya's Qaddafi—"like Chávez in Venezuela and [President Nursultan] Nazarbayev in Kazakhstan—has . . . cleverly ratcheted up the pressure on foreigners to share more revenue with the regime by tweaking contracts, rounding numbers liberally and threatening expropriation." Regardless, Khanna's vision of the future, like that of other experts cited earlier, seems curiously benign.

Given the changes that are unfolding, most notably the United States' loss of standing, it is not surprising that some up-and-comers are more assertively pragmatic in their dealings with the United States and other established powers. In a May 2008 report highlighting the difficulties that India and the United States were having in trying to reach agreement on a benchmark civilian nuclear power deal, Jay Solomon and Peter Wonacott of the *Wall Street Journal* spelled it out clearly: "Some Indian security analysts have argued that India can get better energy deals elsewhere." In fact, the newspaper said, "there are signs the Indian government is hedging its bets among a diverse group of energy suppliers. Last month, India hosted President Mahmoud Ahmadinejad of Iran . . . to help spur a number of new energy projects." The report also noted that "leftist politicians have objected to an accord that locks India into a strategic and economic embrace with an unpopular superpower."

Energy needs won't be the only source of contention, of course. So will food security, along with struggles to secure other important commodities and resources. Such could be seen in a May 2008 *Financial Times* report by Jamil Anderlini, "China Eyes Overseas Land in Food Push," which revealed that Chinese companies

> will be encouraged to buy farmland abroad, particularly in Africa and South America, to help guarantee food security under a plan being considered by Beijing. . . . If approved, the plan could face intense opposition abroad given surging global food prices and deforestation fears. However, an official close to the deliberations said it was likely to be adopted. "There should be no problem for this policy to be approved. The problem might come from foreign governments who are unwilling to give up large areas of land," the official said.

According to the newspaper, "the move comes as oil-rich but food-poor countries in the Middle East and North Africa explore similar options."

Over time, in fact, the notion of global connectedness will lose its appeal. Instead, a growing number of schisms will emerge as countries press to ensure that their domestic needs and interests come first. Offering a taste of things to come, a June 2008 report by Shawn Hattingh, "Liberalizing Food Trade to Death," in the left-leaning *Monthly Review* revealed that several states in Latin America, including

> Venezuela, Bolivia, and Nicaragua, have tried to address the food crisis through breaking with the dictates of neo-liberalism. These countries along with Cuba have attempted to establish a viable regional alternative to free trade in the form of the Bolivarian Alternatives for the America's (ALBA). Through ALBA, these states have created five major agricultural projects that are producing soy beans, rice, poultry, and dairy products. The goal of these projects is to guarantee food security in the ALBA member states.

A Mixture of Crosscurrents

Economic and resource-related strains will come on tap of other stresses that undermine domestic and international cohesiveness. As U.S. influence wanes, the shifting power balance will stir up a mixture of highly charged cross currents, from fear and insecurity to pride and arrogance these newly awakened spirits will, in turn, spark frequent and powerful urges to see desires and ambitions translated into action. All the while, a spreading global malaise will spur resentments and help unearlth dark and painful memories that have been long suppressed. Rising nationalism will not only call the existing geopolitical order into question; it will focus attentions on ethnic, cultural, and social differences within and across borders.

With multilateralism losing its luster, argues J.R. Nyquist, in a December 2007 commentary, "The Advantage of a Nation State," nationalist sentiments are

> bound to overtake the feeble rationalism of globalist ideology. As it happens, men are not "global creatures." They speak a specific language, relate to a specific culture, and share specific historical experiences. Although it may sound enlightened to say that we "are all one," it is nonetheless untrue. We are not one.

We are individuals with individual traits and attachments. What attaches me to the globe is nothing compared to the reality of language, culture, family, and tribe. Every individual has a motherland and a mother tongue. There are national sentiments and national interests.

Thus, while some collective arrangements will likely arise in response to concerns over near-term economic circumstances and various strategic threats, many of those that came to the fore during the integrative hey-days of the past several decades will likely fall by the wayside. In Europe, for example, despite seemingly widespread enthusiasm for unification, the zenith of cooperative sentiment seems to have already passed. Not long after European Union leaders signed a December 2007 landmark treaty altering the way the EU operates—meant to bring the 27 member nations even closer together—there were signs of serious discord. A report by James Chapman in the *Daily Mail*, for example, entitled "David Cameron: I'll Tear Up the EU Treaty Even If It Has Been Signed," noted that the British Conservative Party leader had "given his clearest commitment yet to tearing up the revised EU Constitution if he wins power, even if it has been signed." Cameron said "he will 'not let matters rest' if [Prime Minister] Gordon Brown succeeds in forcing the controversial treaty through Parliament and into law." According to the report, "Conservative MPs and a band of Labour rebels are promising the biggest parliamentary showdown over Europe since the Maastricht Treaty plunged John Major's government into turmoil in the 1990s."

Six months later, however, those threats became moot following a widely anticipated national referendum on the treaty in one of the EU's member nations. "In a blow to the ambitions of the world's largest economic and political union, voters in Ireland derailed plans aimed at making the European Union a stronger global player," Marc Champion and Charles Forelle of the *Wall Street Journal* reported in "Europe in Turmoil after Irish Vote." The Irish "rejected the so-called Lisbon Treaty by 53 percent to 47 percent, in the only popular vote that will be held on the treaty by any EU nation. Because all 27 EU countries need to ratify the treaty, Ireland's 'no' vote risks killing it." Although the outcome was blamed on domestic concerns, other reports suggested that public opinion elsewhere in Europe had also soured as well.

Another ostensible unifying element has also become an increasing source of friction for the world's largest economic zone. In a May 2008 article by Ambrose Evans-Pritchard, "EMU Is More Unworkable Than Ever," the *Daily Telegraph* reported that

> far from converging, the Germanic bloc and Latin bloc have moved ever further apart. . . . Since 1995—when the currencies were finally fixed—Germany has gained 40 percent in unit labor costs against Italy, 30 percent against Spain, and 20 percent against France. This yawning gap between North and South confirms what Germany's eurosceptic professors have always argued: that the inflationary habits, wage bargaining structures, and productivity levels of the . . . countries in euroland . . . vary too much to sustain a currency union over a long period.

A month earlier, in fact, a commentary in *Forbes* by Avi Tiomkin, "The Demise of the Euro," argued that it was

> only a matter of time, probably less than three years, until the euro experiment meets its end. The financial crisis in the U.S. is hastening the process, as investors flee the dollar, pushing the euro to a price of $1.59. But it will not stay high for long. Countries like Spain and Italy will withdraw and return to their old currencies. Once that happens, get ready for the return of the deutsche mark and the French franc.

Growing Hatred and Discord

Further undermining cohesion in Europe—and elsewhere, for that matter—is an array of destabilizing demographic, social, and economic trends. As noted earlier, these include the expanding gulf between rich and poor, as well as those who are stuck in the middle. In a May 2008 article by John Thornhill, "Poll Shows Wide Dislike of Wealth Gap," the *Financial Times* reported that "public opinion across Europe, Asia, and the U.S. is strikingly consistent in considering that the gap between rich and poor is too wide and that the wealthy should pay

more taxes. . . . Income inequality has emerged as a highly contentious ✓
political issue in many countries as the latest wave of globalization has
created a 'superclass' of rich people."

In addition, generational strains associated with the costs of rapidly
aging populations, talk of "gender wars" stemming from male resentment
over relative gains in female per-capita income, and clashes over diver-
gent political and religious beliefs will prove to be formidable obstacles
to cooperation and cohesiveness in the years ahead. Slowing economic
growth will also shine a harsh light on the unwelcome presence of large
numbers of illegal and unassimilated immigrant populations, especially
those with high birth rates. Again, history suggests that foreigners and
other outsiders are lightning rods for frustration and anger during hard
times. More recent trends appear to bear this out. During early 2008,
for example, reports pinpointed xenophobic attacks on immigrants in
places like Italy and South Africa. A May 2008 *Financial Times* article by
Sarah Laitner, Ben Hall, and Jan Cienski detailed proposals put forth
by French President Nicolas Sarkozy, ahead of France's ascendancy to the
EU presidency, for a Europe-wide crackdown on illegal immigration.

In fact, as Max Fraad Wolff noted in a June 2007 *Asia Times Online*
commentary, while

> Americans are suspicious of and hostile toward traditional allies
> and rising regional powers . . . the U.S. is not alone. Chinese,
> Japanese, Korean, Russian, Indian, Pakistani, EU, Middle
> Eastern, and South American citizens view one another with
> significant suspicion. Foreign suspicions of the U.S. and of one
> another define the day. Anger in Latin America has been boil-
> ing over in natural-resource debates, elections, and street pro-
> tests. Russian anger and suspicion take the form of increased
> affection for strong central leadership. Japanese fear of a rising
> China pushes it even closer to the U.S. Various factions inside
> India and Pakistan fear one another, Westernization, and . . .
> other internal factions.

Sentiments like these invariably fan the flames of hatred and
violence. By some accounts, an antipathetic spiral is already under
way in the United States. According to the Southern Poverty Law

Center (SPLC) ("The Year in Hate," a report by David Holthouse and Mark Potok), 2007 was

> another year marked by staggering levels of racist hate in America. Even as several major hate groups struggled to survive, other new groups appeared, and the radical right as a whole appeared to grow. The latest annual count by the . . . SPLC found that the number of hate groups operating in America rose to 888 last year, up 5 percent from 844 groups in 2006. That capped an increase of 48 percent since 2000. . . . At the same time, FBI statistics suggested that there was a 35 percent rise in hate crimes against Latinos between 2003 and 2006. Experts believe that such crimes are typically carried out by people who think they are attacking immigrants.

As a new, more unsettled order emerges, animosity toward outsiders won't necessarily be discouraged. That's because governments, especially authoritarian or otherwise less-than-democratic regimes, are often happy to tap such fears for their own ends. As Philip Bowring wrote in an April 2008 *International Herald Tribune* commentary on China's pre-Olympics efforts to subdue a rebellious Tibet, "Beijing plays up the foreign threat—much like the U.S. government used the Al Qaeda threat as a justification for invading Iraq. . . . Equally important is the way official Chinese media has depicted the violence in Tibet as attacks on Han Chinese. This predictably arouses the hackles of the Han, who comprise 90 percent of China's population, and who tend to view Tibet as a backwater they improve by their modernizing drive."

Around the world, the shifting geopolitical winds will boost tensions and make for increasingly volatile politics. In some countries, worried despots and power-hungry dictators will crack down hard, as they seek to tighten their grip over a restless citizenry. In others, constant threats from rivals, upstarts, rogue elements, and foreign powers will undermine the political resolve of weak leaders and tear away at the social fabric, leading to confrontations, random violence, and dangerous conflicts. Reactionaries will press for new approaches, while conservatives will push back hard. Turbulence in different countries and regions will quickly become contagious. Over time, resurgent nationalism and rekindled ethnicity will spawn more and more movements favoring redrawn boundaries and new alliances.

Such developments are often the precursors to armed conflict. In *Where Nation-States Come From: Institutional Change in the Age of Nationalism*, author Philip G. Roeder notes that 82 percent of 188 suicide bomb attacks recorded by Robert Pape between 1980 and 2001

> were associated with . . . campaigns to achieve independence. . . . Similarly, nation-state crises have been the single most common cause of internal wars over the last half-century. Nils Petter Gleditsch recorded 184 wars within the jurisdictions of sovereign states between 1946 and 2001. . . . More than half of these wars, 51.6 percent, were associated with nation-state crises in which parties challenged the existing state and demanded either statehood for themselves or unification with another state.

In the end, the world will be a much different place than it was only a few years back. There will be many more challenges, intense uncertainty, and heightened danger when the United States is no longer the sole superpower, globalization has reversed course, and critical resources are in short supply. For businesses, investors, and individuals, it will be time for an utterly new economic roadmap.

Part II

OPPORTUNITIES AND THREATS

Chapter 7

Everybody's Business

Ever bigger machines, entailing ever bigger concentrations of economic power and exerting ever greater violence against the environment, do not represent progress: they are a denial of wisdom. Wisdom demands a new orientation of science and technology towards the organic, the gentle, the non-violent, the elegant and beautiful.
— E. F. SCHUMACHER, BRITISH ECONOMIST

To cynical observers, the 1973 publication of *Small Is Beautiful* marked the peak of hysteria about the limits to growth. In light of more recent developments, some might view things differently. While the book's author, E. F. Schumacher, was certainly guilty of bad timing in questioning whether "bigger is better" just as globalization was poised to take off, his concerns have not proved unfounded. In fact, troubles stemming from treating fossil fuels and other resources as expendable income rather than precious capital have returned with a vengeance. Perhaps it is ironic that despite decades of apparent evidence to the contrary, Schumacher's vision of the future has not disappeared from view. His book has remained in print, brimming with ideas whose time may finally have come.

No doubt owners, managers, and stakeholders will challenge the notion that they must embrace a less expansive future. Yet those who don't will almost certainly pay the price. For one thing, the commodity price rises of the past decade, aggressive geopolitical maneuvering to secure adequate future supplies, and social upheaval in response to shortages and higher costs for energy, food, water, and other essentials make it clear that the game has changed as far as natural resources are concerned. Not only will countries and populations around the globe face constant struggles and mounting conflict over factors that grease the wheels of commerce and civilized society, but most, if not all, businesses will be forced to remake themselves to an extraordinary degree.

In fact, firms that have thrived in a globalized world will discover that key parts of their business models are either broken or obsolete. The economics of making, marketing, and shipping goods, or providing services over vast distances, will be dramatically transformed when energy is no longer cheap or plentiful—or even available at all. Some have already begun to acknowledge the new reality. In June 2008, for example, a *Financial Times* article by Jonathan Birchall and Elizabeth Rigby, entitled "Oil Costs Force P&G to Rethink Its Supply Network," revealed that Procter & Gamble, the world's biggest consumer goods company, was considering "shifting manufacturing sites closer to consumers to cut its transport bill."

As noted previously, businesses, especially those in heavy industries like chemicals, iron and steel, cement, paper, and aluminum, consume extraordinary amounts of energy. Yet it's not just the notoriously power-hungry sectors or the largest firms that drive this demand. Small businesses, for example, account for half of all U.S. energy use, according to Keith Girard, a senior columnist for *AllBusiness.com*. Even so, the facts suggest that large firms, as a group, stand to suffer most in a resource-constrained world. Companies that have profited from ever-increasing economies of scale, far-flung operations structured to capitalize on global wage and production-cost differentials, and labyrinthine networks that bind so many disparate parts together will see those advantages fall by the wayside. In addition, broad-scale efficiencies stemming from the widespread use of computers, networking, and other technologies will be less than assured when access to a steady supply of electricity, replacement parts, and well-trained workers is easily interrupted.

Higher relative costs for and diminished availability of a variety of other resources will also undermine foundations based on growth for growth's sake. Take water, for example. A May 2008 *Forbes* report by William Pentland, "The Water-Industrial Complex," noted that U.S. businesses consume more of it "than agriculture thanks to its use in power generation. The industrial sector uses an estimated 45 percent, . . . agriculture accounts for 42 percent, and domestic uses, like drinking water and sanitation, account for a mere 13 percent. Worldwide, agriculture uses about 70 percent of all water." Although the world's population likely won't keep expanding at the same pace as before, the gains in global per-capita living standards that have already taken place ensure that competition for this precious commodity—as well as others—will only increase.

Not all of the pressure that businesses will face will emanate directly from the bottom line. Consumers, advocacy groups, and governments will turn up the heat—figuratively, at least—on large users of energy, water, and other commodities, along with those that fail to rein in environmentally destructive footprints. Such concerns won't be raised only in developed nations. Even in places like China, where worries over environmental degradation have long been relegated to the back burner, the fallout from years of helter-skelter industrialization will spur a green backlash. Indeed, by 2007 there were already signs things were headed in that direction. Chinese policy makers sought to limit expansion and require businesses to clean up after themselves, seemingly less concerned than in the past about the impact on growth.

If Life Hands You Lemons, Make Lemonade

The coming changes represent a serious threat and, in some cases, an opportunity. Businesses that refuse to adapt or that assume austere conditions will only be temporary could face substantial risks, including bankruptcy. Those that map out plans based on growing smarter instead of bigger, that center on boosting efficiency as well as revenues, and that make serious allowances for disruptions and uncertainty will have an edge as times change. Many resource-dependent strategies that once made sense, or where the benefits were simply taken for granted, will have to be reevaluated. Outsourcing production to other firms or countries, especially those based thousands of miles away, could prove especially penny-wise and pound-foolish when the full array of logistical, economic, and political costs is factored in.

To some extent, staying ahead will boil down to paying much closer attention to how things are done. It will also be a matter of trying to turn operational lemons into lemonade. When key inputs are no longer cheap or available, several approaches make sense. One strategy is to mandate broad-based reductions in spending on energy, water, and other resources that will be harder to come by, forcing staff to figure out for themselves how to make do with less. Of course, it's worth keeping in mind that a cold-turkey approach can lead to solutions that are not entirely consistent with other key goals. The effect can be like squeezing part of a balloon, only to see the trapped air bubble up elsewhere—or the whole thing explode.

Businesses can also seek out or invest in better equipment, improved processes, and innovative methods that offer more bang for the buck in terms of overall usage and efficiency. No doubt the up-front costs may prove especially hard swallow when the economy is reeling, financial resources are in short supply, and an unsettled outlook can make a return-on-investment winner suddenly seem doubtful, at best. Calculations depend, of course, on assumptions about the future. However, if all of the developments now brewing are taken into account, the economics of some marginal projects might still be compelling. Either way, those issues can be addressed only by taking the first step of exploring the full range of options.

Another approach is to search for ways to transform waste—which may now be difficult or costly to dispose of—into usable products or even valuable resources. That process can also generate environmental benefits. The avenues for boosting efficiency in this way are endless. Examples include reusing paper and shipping boxes; shredding office waste to create inexpensive packing material; converting used fats, motor oils, wood scraps, and similar by-products into cheap fuel for internal consumption or resale; warming facilities with heat thrown off by production lines and other operations; trimming electricity costs with more efficient lighting and timers that automatically switch power and machines on and off; harvesting rain and used tap water for outside irrigation; and insulating and repairing leaks in pipes and ducts carrying air, water, oil, and hot or cold air.

Businesses can also rethink packaging, shipping, and marketing options, with an eye toward reducing storage and transportation costs. Oftentimes, relatively minor changes can have a powerful multiplier effect. If products are placed in smaller boxes, for example, packaging materials won't be as expensive as they were previously; storage areas can be reduced (meaning less of an outlay for rent, utilities, security, etc.); and the costs of shipping fall proportionally. A June 2008 *New York Times* article by Stephanie Rosenbloom, "Solution, or Mess? A Milk Jug for a Green Earth," reported that a new milk-jug design introduced by the Sam's Club unit of Wal-Mart had generated big savings, in part because the jugs no longer needed to be transported in crates.

> The company estimates this kind of shipping has cut labor by half and water use by 60 to 70 percent. More gallons fit on a truck and in Sam's Club coolers, and no empty crates need to be picked up, reducing trips to each Sam's Club store to two a week, from five—a big fuel savings. Also, Sam's Club can now store 224 gallons of milk in its coolers in the same space that used to hold 80.

Other steps, including consolidating multiple purchases from the same vendor into a smaller number of deliveries or revamping shipping schedules to make the best of known traffic patterns may also yield positive results.

Of course, there are trade-offs associated with offering products, for instance, that have less of a physically and functionally appealing footprint. In the Sam's Club example just cited, some customers were uncomfortable with the flat-topped design of the jugs, which made pouring the milk that much harder. Breakage-related concerns and industry standards can't be ignored, either. Yet discussion and creative energy can often lead to solutions even in these circumstances. Otherwise, a more environmentally friendly approach will likely engender goodwill in the community and in the marketplace at a time when the issue of sustainability is gaining in importance. That could compensate for some or all of what has been given up.

Whatever the mix of strategies, businesses will need to take steps like those that are used to break an addiction—which, after all, defines the relationship that many firms have had with respect to energy and other critical inputs. One overriding goal must be to raise awareness, foster acceptance, and demonstrate a clear and convincing emphasis on increasing resource efficiency. Given human nature, that means such efforts must be seen as mission-critical, dictating budgets and bonuses. Training is important. So are benchmarking and monitoring. Studies show, for example, that a weighing scale is one of the best ways to ensure that a diet works, if only because it offers an unrelenting and unequivocal gauge of success. Although this type of approach is suitable in almost any context, firms will, of course, have to tailor solutions to the unique requirements of their industries, business models, operational limitations, and locations. Those that interact directly with retail customers, for example, may need to adopt approaches that are altogether different from approaches by businesses that market to producers, wholesalers, and distributors. In some cases, the answer will be to centralize control of processes like heating and cooling. In others, the best bet may be to make employees individually accountable for ensuring that targets are met. Either way, the incentive structure must be aligned with strategic goals.

And while "thinking outside the box" has become something of a cliché, it nevertheless remains an appropriate way of describing the kind of mind-set that will be required when options are limited—literally. Indeed, incredibly tough times will require creative input from many minds. Ideas should and must be encouraged to flow from all corners of the business, including—perhaps, especially—the lowest reaches. To be sure, many suggestions will be familiar: retune, upgrade, or replace. But a changing world order, deteriorating geopolitical conditions, and an economic environment that will remain unsettled and uncertain for far longer than in the past means ideas must be vetted and reworked from many angles before they pass muster.

Finding answers won't necessarily require that firms spend large sums of money or come up with cutting-edge breakthroughs, especially when economic and financial challenges, including maintaining sufficient liquidity, are an unsettling fact of life. Solutions may involve both basic changes in methods and clunky workarounds that might once have been seen as anachronistic in a digital age. All options, however odd they seem, must be on the table. According to Leila Abboud and John Biers of the *Wall Street Journal*, one semiconductor maker, STMicroelectronics, was able to realize significant savings on its energy bill by regularly forcing little rubber balls through the clogged tubes of expensive machines that chilled water for production lines. It was a fairly simple solution, yet it produced satisfying results.

More Than Just Resource Constraints

To be sure, resource constraints won't be the only concern—or even the most daunting challenge. Deteriorating economic circumstances, especially in the immediate years ahead, will make for an extremely difficult operating environment, with consequences that go far beyond soaring unemployment rates and surging bankruptcies. Firms that have depended on free-spending American consumers, for example, will find that the structural underpinnings of their business models have been obliterated as incomes drop, attitudes sour, purchasing habits change, and easy credit disappears. Even retail-oriented businesses that have benefited during the early stages of these nascent shifts, including online and warehouse-style vendors, will be at risk because of their Achilles' heel dependence on hydrocarbon-fueled transportation.

A quick read of longer-term savings and consumption trends suggests the spending habits of recent years have been the exception, rather than the rule. Until the late 1980s, for example, personal savings as a percentage of disposable income, based on data from the Bureau of Economic Analysis (BEA), hovered roughly between 8 and 10 percent, with spikes above those levels during World War II and the late 1970s. Over the past two decades, however, the savings rate has swooned, hitting an unsustainably low 0.4 percent in the first quarter of 2008. A similarly anomalous pattern has been seen in terms of consumer spending. Prior to 2000, BEA statistics reveal that personal consumption as a percentage of U.S. gross domestic product had ranged between 60 and 68 percent, with a seven-decade median of 65.9 percent. In more

recent times, consumers have accounted for nearly 72 percent of overall activity, an incremental increase equal to $1.3 trillion in a $14.2 trillion economy.

Other factors already noted will also cast a long and suffocating
pall over prospects for growth. These include shortages of and higher
costs for energy, water, and other drivers of economic activity; growing
restrictions on trade and cross-border investment; crumbling infrastructure; disruptions stemming from social and geopolitical instability and
an increase in cross-border conflicts; rising taxes; diminishing economies of scale; turbulent financial markets; and dislocations associated
with aging populations.

Once a measure of normality returns—whenever and whatever that
might be—firms can expect to see a pattern of business cycle volatility that more closely mirrors the stomach-churning undulations of days
gone by. According to Pam Woodall of the *Economist*, during the 90 years
prior to World War II, the United States was in recession 40 percent of
the time—quadruple the rate of the past two decades. In a world where
market turbulence is the order of the day, cross-border trade has shifted
into reverse, and the struggle for global dominance favors spending on
guns instead of butter, a less stable economic future is all but assured.
Breakdowns in economic, social, and political relationships fostered during the era of globalization will undermine the more recent trend of
increasing synchronization among nations.

Further muddying the waters, both economically and socially, are
demographic-related concerns. Small nest eggs and deteriorating safety
nets in countries with graying populations, including the United States,
will provoke growing generational clashes that play havoc with business-
related lawmaking, tax rates, and consumption patterns. Meanwhile,
ongoing cash raising by aging baby boomers can only add to confidence-
sapping turbulence in real estate, stock, bond, and other markets.

Desperate moves by populist, weak, or economically illiterate policy
makers, at home and abroad, to address fiscal woes and social tensions,
will lay the groundwork for spasms of deflation and hyperinflation.
Even in a divided world, the fallout will likely be globally contagious.
Increasingly, governments of beleaguered nations—whether developing or advanced—will be left with little choice but to become more
intimately involved in the private sector. Many of their efforts will be

aimed at protecting powerful interests, shoring up vital industries, and trying to create jobs for the restless and hungry masses. Meanwhile, spurred on by the global scramble for influence and resources, a growing list of countries—which will almost certainly include the United States—will seize the opportunity to reverse years of liberalization, privatization, and laissez-faire oversight and emulate the Russo-Chinese approach to economic management.

Along with more state-controlled competition, firms will have to grapple with the effects of a troubled and increasingly unworkable global trading system. Among the threats they will face are currency devaluations; tariffs and quotas; crackdowns on the flow of goods, capital, and people; piracy and espionage; and armed conflicts. Increasingly, countries will look to rewrite, break, or ignore treaties, or draw up superseding agreements with geopolitical up-and-comers. Many will lose faith in multilateral bodies such as the World Trade Organization (WTO); some will assert they are no longer bound by rules they had no role in creating. Needless to say, such developments will negate the advantages of global cost shifting and labor arbitrage, long-distance supply chains, and ever-increasing economies of scale.

Firms with significant exposure to foreign markets, either directly or indirectly, will also see doubt cast on supply, production, research, and marketing agreements. Paradoxically, energy and mining companies—along with others in seemingly well-positioned industries—could be exposed to dangerous crosscurrents. Emboldened by the allure of resource nationalism and the belief that diminishing U.S. power lessens the odds of serious reprisals, commodity-rich countries will prey on foreign-owned properties through windfall taxes, nationalizations, and, increasingly, expropriations. The *Wall Street Journal* noted, for example, in a report by Bob Davis cited earlier (in Chapter 6), "Rise of Nationalism Frays Global Ties," that Royal Dutch/Shell was "investing heavily in unconventional oil sources, many of which have little prospect of expropriation." In failed states, criminals may simply move in and take over. Depending on how successful the first-mover usurpers are, it likely won't be long before a dangerous tide becomes a devastating flood.

Not all of the problems will stem from bellicosity and deliberate actions, of course. Ongoing economic deterioration, collapsing cross-border trade, upheavals in credit and other financial markets, and rising social and political instability will trigger a surge in defaults and bankruptcies of companies and countries around the world. Cascading failures of vendors and lenders and the accompanying supply disruptions could transform an already unsettled operating environment into a desperate struggle for survival. Under the circumstances, businesses must make allowances for the fact that many things can and will go wrong, often simultaneously, and constantly address the question of whether they have sufficient cash and other resources on hand to weather the storm.

The dollar's loss of status as a global reserve currency and a universal medium of exchange will pose another threat to stability, in the United States and elsewhere. For owners, managers, and employees who are unaccustomed to an environment where transactions are mainly denominated in other nations' currencies, the logistics could be daunting, especially when the free flow of goods and capital is no longer assured. In addition, the continuing decline of the greenback will spur a structural shift higher in U.S. interest rates. Add that to the fallout from ongoing economic disorder and a banking system lumbered with the long-lingering pain of a massive credit-bubble bust, and the result is an operating climate that is, to say the least, precarious.

Other developments could further complicate planning and financial management. Among them is the prospect that currency unions, dollar pegs, and political accords that have been designed to ensure stability will be circumvented or will come apart at the seams. A disorderly unwinding of the European Monetary Union—and the accompanying demise of the euro—could be the most notable casualty. Strains over economic and cultural disparities, once held in check by global prosperity, will spill out into the open, spurred on by the lack of political will for increasing integration. Potentially more unsettling for U.S. firms, the North American Free Trade Agreement (NAFTA) will also be at risk of blowing apart, undermined by protectionism, xenophobia, and drug war–driven strife south of the U.S. border.

Amid the unfolding chaos, expanding state influence in economic and commercial affairs, together with more frequent bouts of government intervention and market manipulation, will lay the groundwork for all sorts of distortions, disruptions, and dislocations, many of which will be wholly unfamiliar to U.S. owners and managers. A growing number of politically connected and increasingly powerful firms that benefit from direct access to state coffers and rule making that favors local and regional interests could hold greater sway over the prices of key materials and access to important markets. Over time, corruption and cronyism will become an increasingly debilitating fact of life.

The quest for power and influence in Southeast Asia, Eastern Europe, the Middle East, and South America will engender a great deal of angst for businesses based outside those regions. Nations such as China, Russia, Iran, and Venezuela will likely orchestrate repeated attempts to close ranks against foreign interests through collective security and economic arrangements. Under these circumstances, U.S. firms, in particular, could be prime targets. Those that haven't already retreated from international markets will be blamed for worsening economic and social ills and for any role, however remote, they might have played in creating a system that will be seen as having failed the developing world.

Potentially more troubling realities include the fallout from geopolitical upheaval and domestic unrest. The witches' brew of waning U.S. influence, power struggles among heir apparents, disintegrating global growth, and heightened worries over food, energy, water, and other resources will be just the formula for a surge in protests, uprisings, revolutions, and wars, both at home and abroad. In many areas, concrete and high-tech walls will sprout like weeds to protect both longstanding and newly created borders and enclaves. At the same time, political and ethnic pressures, along with cross-border encroachments and incursions, will splinter cities and countries. Secessionist movements will gain strength virtually everywhere. Around the world, chaos will reign.

The kinds of concerns that were seen even before globalization took hold will also come into play. After years of ever-growing profits, easing regulations, and a yawning gap between the incomes of workers and those at the top, political and social pressures will force the pendulum back the other way. The result will be increasing taxes on businesses and their overseers, restrictive legislation and political interference, tougher rules on governance and executive compensation, and pressure for payoffs and handouts. Businesses may be offered incentives to expand domestic hiring; those that try to stick with their offshoring ways will almost certainly be penalized. Firms will also face intense grassroots pressure to boost local hiring and rescue communities from the yoke of hard times.

One Problem after Another

All of these developments will naturally spawn frustration, anger, and hostility. Tensions will also flare up over cultural, ethnic, religious, and generational differences. A range of social ills will cause people to lash out at others or band together in groups for protection. Many will also join forces with populists, agitators, and extremists promoting revolutionary causes and violent change. Unions will gain favor as workers try to take back what was lost during the era of globalism. Frustrations will boil over into strikes, marches, and random violence. In this kind of environment, owners, managers, and employees will quickly come to realize that security and safety concerns have assumed far greater importance than in the past.

But that's not all. Businesses will also have to contend with what might be described as second-order effects. In the United States, for example, ongoing dollar woes, worsening economic conditions, a disorderly unwinding of structural imbalances, and the financial strains associated with heightened security concerns will do serious damage to public-sector finances. That will, in turn, have a negative impact on critical elements of an advanced society. Roads, bridges and tunnels, water and sewage treatment plants, power-generation facilities, electrical transmission grids, and other infrastructure that has, in many cases, already been deemed deficient by experts like the American Society of Civil Engineers will malfunction or break down as capital spending falls and maintenance efforts slip. Souring municipal finances will also see police budgets slashed, courts overloaded, and crime rates shoot up. Businesses could find that their dependence on computers, telecommunications networks, the Internet, and other components of digital-age plumbing have serious drawbacks when electrical and other systems don't function as intended—or at all.

Under the circumstances, owners, managers, and employees will be faced with a constant, tenuous, and nerve-wracking balancing act. They will have to continuously evaluate the benefits of efforts aimed at cutting costs and improving efficiency against the risks of serious disruptions, heightened economic volatility, and dangerous geopolitical crosswinds. Among other things, these various developments will increase the need to maintain adequate liquidity and have backup financing in place. They will also spell the death knell of an approach that has proved popular in recent years. Instead of operating on a just-in-time basis, businesses will have to worry about getting enough of what they need—in enough time. Otherwise, it won't really matter how efficient they are.

In the end, a growing number of firms will be left with little choice but to relocate, scale down, or become more_locally focused_, in terms of both how and where they operate and who they market their goods and services to. Tighter labor markets and the increased costs of doing business in countries like China have already led some companies to _bring functions home_. While it is not clear whether the moves were driven solely by short-term considerations, they hint at a trend that will become increasingly commonplace.

Businesses will have to become much more flexible and accommo-dating, which, by definition, tends to work against sprawling, populous, or rigidly hierarchical organizations. Some companies have already been tweaking business models in that direction. They are adopting four-day workweeks because of fuel price increases and are allowing—even encouraging—employees to _work from home,_ thereby reducing the cost of providing office space and related amenities while also eliminating for the employee the time and expense involved in commuting. Even so, such efforts won't be anywhere near enough to compensate for the sorts of challenges that can be expected in the_ troubled times ahead._

Living by Other Nations' Rules

A new global order will force U.S. businesses, in particular, to adapt in a number of other ways. Most are accustomed to American-centric rules, standards, and modes of behavior. They have long operated under a Western-dominated legal and cultural framework, with an assertive-ness—and an arrogance, perhaps—that comes from being tethered to the most powerful nation on earth. While many firms have tailored production and marketing operations to suit local market conditions, broader perspectives haven't necessarily changed.

Once the rest of the world realizes, however, that it no longer needs to pay much heed to U.S. interests and desires, there will be major shifts in how things are done. Foreign governments, banks, and exchanges will hold increasing sway over key markets. Currencies like the yuan and the ruble will become benchmark units of account for energy and other commodities. Organizations that set regulatory, technological, commercial, and other standards with mainly local or regional interests in mind will see their influence grow, leaving outsiders—including American companies—at a distinct disadvantage. These changing circumstances will naturally create risks for businesses that try to maintain global aspirations. Yet even domestically oriented firms will be affected when it comes to the prices of and access to goods that must be sourced elsewhere.

Other developments will be just as hard to handle in a world that has largely been shaped by Anglo-American ideals. In April 2008, for example, *BBC News* reported that "Muslim scientists and clerics have called for the adoption of Mecca time to replace GMT [Greenwich Mean Time], arguing that the Saudi city is the true centre of the Earth." One geologist present at the conference where the proposal was made said that the "English had imposed GMT on the rest of the world by force when Britain was a big colonial power, and it was about time that changed." Meanwhile, with other countries increasingly brandishing their economic, political, and military swords, English could be supplanted as the universal language of business.

By the same token, developing and other nations around the world may no longer feel compelled to align commercial and regulatory frameworks with those of the West, especially as deteriorating economic circumstances diminish the allure of what has been the world's most vibrant marketplace for goods and services. Muslim Shariah law could overtake the Anglo-American system of justice in many jurisdictions, creating havoc for so-called infidels. Nationalists and others looking to roll back the tide of globalism may press for policies and rules that take only local interests into account. Americans—and U.S. businesses—will suddenly have to pay much more careful attention to what everyone else is doing and saying, whether they like it or not.

These changes will make life very difficult for owners, managers, and employees who have a twentieth-century mindset. From now on, they will have to contend with an operating environment that is far riskier, much more uncertain, and much less stable than what they've known before. For larger firms, the challenges will be that much greater. According to a February 2008 *BusinessWeek* report by Michael Mandel, "Multinationals: Are They Good for America?" businesses with more than 500 employees accounted for the lion's share of U.S. exports in 2006—a telling illustration of the advantages of size in a globalized era. But as the world is transformed, many will raise objections that echo the title of that article. Eventually, people will question whether the unfolding times are good for big size at all.

Thoughtful commentators like James Howard Kunstler, author of *The Long Emergency*, would answer with a resounding "no." He argues that the realities of a resource-constrained world will dramatically reshape the overall structure of society, especially in countries like the United States that are dependent on cheap energy. To survive, communities will be forced to become increasingly self-reliant, with a localized commercial framework that rests on "rich, fine-grained, multi-layered networks of people who make, distribute, and sell stuff (including the much maligned 'middlemen')." Heightened geopolitical strife, growing isolationist sentiments, and intense pressures to hire and purchase locally—coming from many different directions—will reinforce that pattern.

In the new scheme of things, decisions about product lines, staffing, facilities, logistics, finances, and virtually every other aspect of running a business will have to take much greater account of where customers, suppliers, and employees are located, the level and quality of infrastructure, security-related concerns, and the kinds of operational issues that seemed to matter much less in the age of abundance. Fluid conditions and increasing disruptions will force organizations to grant more decision-making leeway to those at the front lines. Yet at the same time, firms must be capable of responding as a cohesive whole to broader threats and opportunities. Many will find the seemingly paradoxical prospect of making their operations stronger, more secure, and more resilient, as well as more efficient, creative, and responsive, overwhelming. However, that is only the half of it. The challenge will be that much greater for those who don't have a clear sense of the broad range of uncertainties, shocks, and threats that lie ahead. It won't be a time for misplaced fantasies that the worst has passed or that difficulties will be fleeting. Instead, it will be time for realistic visions of a sobering future.

As is generally the case, owners and managers will find that the most promising strategies for surviving—and, perhaps, thriving—spring from a combination of eyes-wide-open analysis, creative and open-minded input from many sides, and hard-nosed planning. Data, trends, expectations, and assumptions will have to be checked and rechecked to ensure they are not simply legacies of the golden era of globalization. The prospect of sudden disruptions or dangerous upheavals will need to be factored into every equation, and various scenarios will have to be considered before there is even a hint of their actualization. Threats and vulnerabilities will need to be reviewed in the light of many different types of credit, operational, and political risks. Contingency, crisis, and disaster planning will assume a degree of importance that is substantially higher than before.

For the most part, existing operational infrastructure will have to be treated as a sunk cost. As a matter of survival, reforms must overcome hurdles like management pride, corporate tradition, and a potential loss of face. In a hostile, nerve-wracking, and rapidly changing environment, success will depend on quickly admitting mistakes, cutting losses, and playing to core competencies. There can be no room for procrastination or regrets when it comes to pruning weak or unproductive lines, functions, assets, employees, vendors, and distributors. Keeping active tabs on how customers, competitors, and suppliers react to changing economic, social, and political circumstances may offer valuable clues about the road ahead. Nonetheless, it is likely that most will be flying blind.

Less Than Straightforward

None of this will be straightforward, of course. The drive for greater efficiency, for instance, will require a continuous assessment of the supply-and-demand fundamentals of energy and a host of other turbulent markets. Models that depend on seemingly optimal strategies like hub-and-spoke systems will repeatedly be undermined by economic, logistic, and geopolitical challenges. Contrary to the preferences of recent decades, no small number of businesses will have to become more vertically integrated. Many will also need to shift some or all operations closer to customers and suppliers, or at the very least, rigorously scrutinize existing logistical arrangements. Firms may have little choice but to align with others that have complementary advantages, including direct access to key markets or raw materials. More broadly, owners and managers will have to completely rethink the businesses they are in.

For those operators who are intent on sticking around for a while, the watchword for the future will be a throwback to the past: "just-in-case" systems. Not only will businesses have to make sure they have adequate liquidity and inventories of raw materials, supplies, and finished products on hand, but they will also need to line up backup sources of financing and alternative vendors, distributors, and logistics capabilities, favoring, if at all possible, those based nearby or in readily accessible locales. Such resiliency comes at a price, of course, which could be quite steep in many circumstances. But without taking the necessary steps in advance of breakdowns and other problems to avoid being blindsided, firms could find that they are at risk of being put out of business—perhaps overnight.

Every spending and investment decision will need to be assessed in light of the broader structural changes that are taking place. The dollar's fading fortunes, ongoing economic deterioration, declining cross-border trade, turbulent financial markets, a hobbled banking system, and heightened geopolitical conflict all signal one thing: Money will be tight and increasingly difficult to come by. Managers and owners will have to work hard at boosting cash flow and freeing up funds from working capital while also keeping sufficient inventories on hand to weather inevitable disruptions. Amid widespread risk aversion, firms seeking financial assistance may have to make an impossibly foolproof case. What's more, while a realistic outlook will emphasize investment that is oriented toward efficiency and survival rather than growth, prospective stakeholders might not be so convinced. For the most part, a dependence on capital, like a dependence on energy, will have to be completely rethought or totally undone.

One way forward may be for businesses to adopt a variant of E. F. Schumacher's "appropriate technology" strategy. This approach emphasizes finding solutions that are ideally suited to economic and environmental realities, where "the aim ought to be to obtain the maximum amount of well-being with the minimum amount of consumption." The British economist argued, for example, that in labor-rich and capital-poor countries like those found in the developing world, progress could best be achieved by introducing sustainable, low-technology methods that make the most of comparative advantages—such as pool of prospective workers seeking to improve their lives.

As noted previously, demographic trends indicate that no small number of nations, including the United States, will see working-age populations diminish over time. In the short run, however, a plethora of economic woes, inadequate savings and shrinking safety nets, and the fallout from unraveling global imbalances will lead to a significant rise in the numbers of those seeking employment. Many areas will see more elderly entering or remaining in the labor force, more former stay-at-home spouses and young family members looking for jobs, and more of those who once depended on charity or state assistance seeking ways to survive. It is possible these developments could more than offset resource-related and protectionist constraints, for a while at least.

Of course, a more labor-intensive orientation won't be without pitfalls. For one thing, rising unemployment and efforts to counter a loss of individual power will spur some to seek strength in numbers. This will help galvanize the organized labor movement, leading to increasing activism, strikes, and violent clashes aimed at protecting jobs and boosting compensation. Alternatively, some firms may have a hard time finding workers with appropriate skill sets because of limits on immigration, education-spending shortfalls, and migratory shifts stemming from resource and economic troubles.

Marketing will prove especially problematic when governments, businesses, and individuals are aggressively cutting back on spending and are reorienting their lives to a low-key, more frugal existence. Most customers will be intensely focused on price. But they will also demand high quality and durability, extensive service and support, and assurances that offerings don't exacerbate environmental concerns. While familiarity and a history of delivering on promises will be of some value, established brands won't necessarily have an edge. In many cases, large and well-known purveyors of such goods and services stand to lose out as globalization wanes. Locally based firms may also gain from customer worries about buying tainted or shoddy goods from other locales as well as the halo effect associated with their hiring practices.

Economic and logistical realities will also make it difficult for companies to expand their range of offerings or seek to satisfy a variety of tastes through endless permutations of established brands. At the same time, the end of consumerism and a shift away from conspicuous consumption will reinforce a tendency toward less rather than more. That will make it harder for businesses to differentiate their goods and services, except through head-to-head competition based on price, sale terms, availability, or support.

Threats to Security

There's no doubt that security-related issues will become a key focus of attention for almost all businesses in the troubled times ahead. The specter of rising crime, growing social unrest, infrastructure failure, terrorism, and geopolitical conflict will boost the need for exhaustive risk analysis, emergency planning, and emergency notification systems in the event that something goes wrong—which it invariably will. Changing times will also require tighter screening of people and packages to protect staff members, premises, and equipment. To stop internal fraud and theft, employers will need to adopt a level of pre- and post-employment due diligence that is exhaustively thorough.

Apart from the more mundane threats stemming from power failures and difficulties sourcing necessary parts and equipment, networks and technology will also be exposed to increasing cyber terrorism, electronic espionage, and other unwelcome intrusions. As noted previously, some nations have been particularly aggressive in their efforts to gain commercial advantage by breaking into information systems and stealing proprietary data. But not all such efforts will be aimed at gathering intelligence. In an April 2008 article ("Hackers Warn High Street Chains"), for example, *BBC News* detailed a warning from "elite hackers" who claimed that retail store chains in the United Kingdom would be "the next victims of cyber terrorism" and that "criminals could use the kind of tactics which crippled Estonia's government and some firms" in 2007.

Owners, managers, and employees can expect these and other threats, including many that are not yet known, to make their lives far more difficult than they have been during the era of peace and prosperity. The fact that the pressures will come from any number of directions will only worsen matters. On the one hand, resource-related constraints, rising interest rates and risk premiums, fragmented markets and fading economies of scale, higher taxes, and geopolitical instability will drive up costs. On the other hand, the fallout from changing spending habits, unraveling imbalances, economic deterioration, protectionism, and years of profligate spending and borrowing will weigh on revenues. All of this is set to occur at a time when official government tallies reveal that margins and profits are at unsustainable multi-decade highs.

Still, "tough times" doesn't necessarily mean "tough luck" in terms of prospects for growth. In any economy, some markets and sectors invariably gain in comparison to others. Products and services that boost efficiency and allow individuals, communities, and countries to become more self-sufficient will likely find at least some favor. So will products and processes that can increase output of food, water, and energy in a sustainable manner. Businesses that figure out ways to transform waste products into valuable commodities or that come up with economical alternatives in the areas of transportation, heating and cooling, and sanitation also stand to benefit. Sadly, the biggest winners of all may well be those firms that can provide security and ways for customers to protect themselves against an ever-growing array of threats.

Chapter 8

Small Fortunes

I think it was a long step forward in my trading education when I realized at last that when old Mr. Partridge kept on telling the other customers, "Well, you know this is a bull market!" he really meant to tell them that the big money was not in the individual fluctuations but in the main movements—that is, not in reading the tape but in sizing up the entire market and its trend.

—"Larry Livingston" in *Reminiscences of a Stock Operator*

Wall Street was a much different place when *Reminiscences of a Stock Operator* was first published more than 80 years ago. Yet the often-reprinted book remains a staple reference for traders and investors. Most historians believe the first-person account of the experiences of the fictional character Livingston, written by journalist Edwin Lefèvre, was actually a biography—or perhaps, an edited autobiography—of stock speculator Jesse Livermore, who made (and lost) several fortunes during the early part of the twentieth century. Throughout the book, the charismatic protagonist serves up insights that have proved timeless. Indeed, today's investors might view his assertion that "the game does not change and neither does human nature" as ironic—but spot on.

One pearl of wisdom provides an apt warning for the treacherous times ahead: "Among the hazards of speculation the happening of the unexpected—I might even say of the unexpectable—ranks high." While the statement seems obvious on its face, up until recent years, at least, investors had become somewhat inured to a pattern where the trend of rising share prices and falling bond yields has been only intermittently interrupted by corrections, crashes, and upheavals. But many developments, most notably the transition to a new global order, suggest the impetus behind a long-running bull market—and one of history's most benign investing environments—is fading fast.

To be sure, there are good reasons why investors—in the United States and elsewhere—have stuck with optimistic, longer-term outlooks. For one thing, despite serious hiccups along the way—including the crash of 1987 and the bursting of the dot-com bubble at the turn of the millennium—markets have regularly bounced back and pushed higher, sometimes quickly, over the course of the past two and a half decades. The broad fundamentals have also been supportive. American economic and military might and the fall of communism have engendered worldwide stability and unprecedented growth. Globalization and technology have encouraged individuals, businesses, and countries to work together, focusing productive energies and allowing them to tap a worldwide marketplace of billions. Central bankers and politicians have repeatedly greased the wheels of fiscal and monetary policy to forestall any backsliding.

Now, though, the pillars of prosperity are crumbling. Signs point, for example, to a dramatic transition from a stable and familiar unipolar world to one in which various interests are aggressively competing for influence and control. In the wake of the leadership vacuum, many emerging powers, including China and Russia, will assert their authority across countries and continents, in an attempt to don the imperialist mantle left behind as a broken United States slides into isolationism and economic decay. Iran and Venezuela, increasingly emboldened by popular support for their swaggering anti-Americanism and their willingness to take the lead on strategic matters, will look to further capitalize on resource advantages and press forward with efforts to dominate regional agendas.

Under the circumstances, it shouldn't be a surprise when those who have gained the upper hand try to reshape things. Many will shake off the yoke of a Western-dominated economic, political, and social framework. They will abandon globalization and the aggressive Western-sponsored push for unfettered free trade. They will propose agendas, rules, standards, and mechanisms that mainly serve their own interests. Those who harbor anger and resentments about past wrongs will look to set matters straight, perhaps through economic retribution or, increasingly, armed conflict. However things play out, one thing seems clear. A global changing of the guard signals the onset of an investing environment that is far more uncertain, volatile, and danger-ous than what most people have been used to before now.

Further compounding matters is the fact that the United States' once undisputed position at the top of the economic heap is seri-ously at risk. To be sure, it will likely be some time before nations such as China and India, which accounted for 10 percent and 4.3 percent of global output, respectively, catch up to and move past the United States, with its 23 percent share of global gross domestic product based on 2007 World Bank data ("World Bank Study Says 12 Economies Account for More Than Two-Thirds of World's Output"). Yet the economic downturn that arguably began in the middle of the cur-rent decade—following years of waste and profligacy, a record-setting buildup of public and private debt, a hollowing out of the nation's industrial base, and the worst collapse in housing prices since the Great Depression—sets the stage for a crippling contraction that will dim the U.S.—and global—outlook for years to come.

Still, while the United States will be the main loser, it won't be alone. The rest of the world will also be wracked by what is likely to be a long and debilitating malaise. In recent years, optimistic analysts have argued that relative economic gains in developing nations, especially over the past decade, would insulate—decouple—their economies from American travails. It is true that standards of living have risen sharply in many formerly agrarian and subsistence-based nations. That raises the prospect that growth could eventually become self-sustaining, as export-oriented businesses turn inward to satisfy a structural rise in domestic demand.

However, there's little evidence to suggest that even the world's second largest economy has reached that point—yet. Indeed, policy makers in China and elsewhere have warned in recent years that faltering U.S. growth would have serious and far-reaching repercussions.

An Array of Negative Undercurrents

Numerous undercurrents will play a role in undermining the long-running economic boom. A prolonged and messy unwinding of myriad excesses and cross-border imbalances will trigger heavy losses and constant upheaval in equity and bond markets, causing long-term structural damage to important financing mechanisms. Along with the slow-motion meltdown in U.S. real estate prices, property busts in Europe, Asia, and Australia will lead to a devastating wealth contraction that saps confidence and slashes overall consumption for years, if not decades. Commercial and investment banks will continue to suffer the consequences of past sins and the bursting of history's biggest credit bubble. Because of ongoing balance-sheet woes and funding difficulties, most will be in no position—or mood—to help reinvigorate growth through an appreciable increase in lending.

Advanced and developing nations alike will witness mounting calls for tariffs, quotas, preferences, and other trade and investment restrictions that favor domestic businesses at the expense of those based elsewhere. Such efforts will dampen already diminishing cross-border commerce and undercut global prosperity. Protectionist stirrings and hostility toward neoliberal ideals will spread quickly from country to country and region to region. Labor strife and heightened social unrest—especially in populous countries like China, which has relied on export-oriented approaches to keep its economy humming—will also weigh on activity. Ultimately, these and other developments will lead to cascading losses, surging unemployment, soaring bankruptcies, and souring sentiment. They will also contaminate markets and financial systems that have long greased the wheels of business and industry with productivity-enhancing capital.

A deteriorating global economy will further dim the outlook for the U.S. dollar, already suffering the consequences of the country's sagging geopolitical and economic fortunes. Oil-rich countries like Saudi Arabia, for example, which has to a great extent maintained structural links to and large portfolios of the currency for strategic purposes, will have much less incentive to do so when the U.S. protective umbrella is in tatters. China and other export-driven nations will also lose their appetite for the currency, especially as faltering growth abroad spurs the need for increasing public spending at home. Whether these and other large state holders of greenbacks reduce future accumulations, reallocate funds elsewhere, or dump what they have, the results will be largely the same: a weaker dollar, and increasing turbulence and uncertainty.

But governments won't be the only ones fanning the flames of currency instability. Many private-sector operators will also abandon the dollar. Waning global trade and the prospect that key commodities will be priced in yuan, rubles, and other currencies will reduce the need to acquire and hold greenbacks for transactional purposes. Individual and institutional investors with portfolio allocations that are over-weight dollar-denominated assets, reflecting the relative importance of the American economy to that of the rest of the world, will naturally adjust holdings as the U.S. star fades. Those who've accumulated the American currency because of its legacy as a store of value and a universally accepted medium of exchange will be forced to reconsider. Some will simply be motivated by the sound of a thundering herd heading for the exits. All of a sudden, an anchor of stability will have become a suffocating lead weight.

Other threats to prosperity and stability center on resource constraints. Evidence of ongoing depletion and the difficulties of discovering and developing new and existing sources of supply, adverse demographic trends, the dramatic price spikes of recent years, and the pattern of rising per-capita consumption rates in developing countries all point to the fact that the era of cheap and abundant energy, food, water, and other essential commodities is over. In the United States and other economically advanced nations, decades of relatively low prices have encouraged wasteful behavior and dangerous overdependence. More recently, rapid expansion in the developing world has sparked widespread calls for a greater share of the pie. The result: not enough of what everybody needs and wants to go around.

This mismatch will cause problems on any number of fronts. Take trade, for example. Spurred on by the lure of cheap foreign labor, vast improvements in communications and technology, and globalization's unifying impetus, businesses around the world have created intricate supply chains that are thousands of miles long. However, these arrangements depend on transportation networks and logistical facilities that consume extraordinary quantities of fossil fuels. As competition for energy to meet more pressing needs heats up, cross-border commerce will bear the brunt of any shortfalls. Growing conflicts between haves and have-nots—and rival haves—will also boost the geopolitical temperature, further undermining integrative efforts. Together with the continuing struggle for global influence, increasing social instability, and aggressive resource nationalism, it makes for an explosively divisive mix. Over time, such pressures could easily lead to supply lines being cut, markets being closed, resource-dependent infrastructure being shut down, and businesses being left high and dry.

It goes without saying that the growing likelihood of nationalizations and expropriations will pose a serious threat to energy, mining, and other resource-related companies, especially those operating in regions that are already notoriously unstable. But such threats won't necessarily be limited in terms of scope, location, or origin. Rising nationalism and diminished fears of an American—or Western—counterresponse will embolden governments around the world to seize the local units of foreign-owned firms in a variety of industries, including technology and aerospace. Meanwhile, those doing the taking might not be the usual suspects. Egged on by populists and nationalists and by public hysteria, large-consumer nations—including the United States—may well decide that difficult times justify an unprecedented response. Interestingly, less than half of those surveyed in a June 2008 Rasmussen poll were against nationalizing the oil industry ("Just 47 Percent Oppose Nationalizing Oil Industry").

Not Just Resources

Although resource-related strains will serve as regular catalysts for upheaval, other stresses will also set off eruptions and conflicts. Worsening economic conditions, for example, will spawn protests and full-scale riots by the unemployed and the impoverished. Nationalism and xenophobia will engender random attacks on foreigners and mob-on-mob violence. Ethnic, cultural, and religious schisms will provoke tense standoffs that suddenly escalate into civil conflicts. Competition among powerful geopolitical rivals will lead to war. Not all of the schisms will turn bloody, of course. The combination of economic, political, and social woes will lead to other, less violent splits, though outcomes may be just as disturbing. To be sure, unwieldy regional groupings, including the EU and NAFTA, will be especially at risk of falling apart as conditions deteriorate. Yet political units of all shapes and sizes will also be undermined by separatist and secessionist pressures, especially in traditionally volatile regions like Africa and South America. Whatever the case, all of it makes for a much riskier outlook as far as growth, returns, and preservation of capital are concerned.

Along with heightened geopolitical instability, hostile economic circumstances, and continuing dollar woes, other pressures will also drive risk spreads higher. The appetite for U.S. stocks, bonds, and other investments won't be hurt just by antipathy toward the currency. Demand will also be undermined by the broader trend of investors around the world seeking to repatriate funds back home, out of choice or necessity. The impetus will come from many directions. Heightened protectionism, including controls on cross-border capital flows, will play a role. So will finacial difficulties that spawn conversions of assets into cash to make up for shortfalls. Preference shifts stemming from rising nationalism, policies and political pressures that encourage local and regional investing and spending, and the powerful influence of state-run funds will also inhibit the flow of funds into the world's largest market.

Some will argue that bad news for the United States must be good news for others, especially emerging powers like China, which will be aided still further by its substantial holding of reserves. While that may be true in some respects, it won't necessarily apply on an absolute basis. No doubt China's currency will eventually strengthen relative to others, which, in theory, represents a substantial opportunity. But the Asian nation will also be buffeted by many treacherous crosswinds, including a loss of competitiveness in and an overreliance on export markets, rising social unrest as jobless totals soar, the devastating fallout from years of environmental degradation, and the bursting of an extraordinary and unsustainable investment bubble. Protectionist pressures and other threats originating from all sides could make it difficult, if not impossible, for foreigners to invest in or get their money out of the country or the currency.

Similar concerns will apply in the case of investments targeted, say, at countries that benefit from substantial resource wealth. Oil-rich nations like Saudi Arabia, Qatar, and United Arab Emirates, which have, up until recent years, maintained dollar pegs, may see their respective currencies rise in value as economic and political developments force established links to be broken. But that doesn't take away from other factors that will undermine growth, financial returns, and social conditions in those countries. Aside from the fact that widespread economic weakness will exert significant downward pressure on revenues in the near term—opening up a potentially destabilizing gap between income and spending—many producers are based in volatile regions, have weak or corrupt governments, and are committed to spending and investment habits that sow the seeds of future instability. In addition, no small number already suffer from domestic ills that will become much more relevant as geopolitical conditions worsen.

Opportunity Knocks?

That is not to say there won't be ways to make money under certain circumstances. But even then, the dynamics of a changing world order heighten the risk that an unexpected development could trigger substantial losses. Canada, for example, seems to offer great promise as an investment destination. With its relatively stable history and political structure (though, as elsewhere, that is subject to change), rich deposits of hydrocarbons and other commodities, access to water, and arable land for farming, the country would seem to have a lot going for it. Yet its proximity to an increasingly assertive Russia, deep economic ties to a foundering United States, the transportation and logistical costs associated with its sprawling land mass, and secessionist pressures in Quebec may more than offset those advantages.

Other countries with significant natural resource wealth, including Brazil, New Zealand, Thailand, and Vietnam, also seem like they could be attractive havens for long-term investment. But again, the downside risks are not inconsequential. In fact, while these and other countries may well be the beneficiaries of a seminal shift that favors producers over consumers, their advantages also make them tempting targets for aggressive interlopers and internal factions looking to gain the upper hand in a broad-based scramble for power. Aside from that, any calculation needs to take into account other important factors, including geographic location and weather patterns, economic maturity and financial assets, political systems, and self-defense capabilities. Disadvantages in some areas might prove overwhelming in an increasingly hostile world.

More broadly speaking, other developments, including demographic trends, also darken the outlook for many asset classes. In the United States, Japan, Russia, and most countries in Europe, populations are aging, some at much faster rates than others. This has several implications. For one thing, it suggests that productive capacity in these countries will wane; real estate, stocks, and other financial assets will increasingly be sold or exchanged for safer alternatives; and social costs will rise, whether they are affordable or not. In the United States, where savings rates have been too low for too long, retirement-related portfolios could be liquidated en masse as a matter of survival. There will also be intense pressure for higher taxes, increased borrowing, and inflationary money creation. Needless to say, all of this has negative implications for profits, economies, markets—and investment returns.

Gender imbalances in China and India, as well as large and growing aggregations in various parts of the world of poor, uneducated, and unsettled populations—many originating from Muslim countries—represent another threat to growth and stability. In some cases, the disparities will trigger dissension and political uncertainty. In others, they will spawn violent clashes and armed conflict, both within and across borders. Either way, the fallout is likely to be economically debilitating, with the ripple effects felt globally. While firms that produce weapons or provide security services might prosper under such circumstances, they will likely prove to be notable exceptions. Of course, that is aside from knowing which particular companies might fare better than others amid changing geopolitical realities.

The trend of large-scale government involvement in the private sector, already burgeoning in the developing world, will gain a strong foothold in traditional free-market-oriented countries, especially as deteriorating economic conditions leave businesses in vital industries at risk of failure. Meanwhile, geopolitical strains, growing protectionist and isolationist sentiments, and the challenges of operating over long distances will, as noted previously, slash the economy-of-scale advantages that large private-sector enterprises, especially publicly traded multinational corporations, have enjoyed during the globalization era. The exceptions will be those firms—like Russia's Gazprom, for instance—that have substantial financial, economic, and political backing from the state.

The expansion of the Russo-Chinese model will alter market dynamics in a variety of ways. By definition, public-sector overseers tend to have different motives than traditional stakeholders when it comes to investment and commercial decision making. Instead of focusing solely or primarily on boosting investment returns, state-dominated firms are inclined to take strategic concerns, populist pressures, and the desires of powerful local interests into account. Corruption, favoritism, and bureaucratic risk aversion can factor in as well. Distortions may also arise because certain industries—natural resources, defense, and financial services, for example—are given preference over less strategically important sectors.

Authoritarian governments in thriving developing-world countries have long demonstrated a preference for secrecy, selective dissemination, dissembling, and backroom dealing. While it is foolish to assume that such goings-on don't also occur in other settings, especially when they revolve around efforts to secure some sort of competitive advantage, unelected regimes have no real incentive to be open and honest about what they are up to. They carefully control the flow of information and tend not to address issues that might raise questions, cause disruptions, or undermine their grip on power. For obvious reasons, they are unwilling to tip their hand about strategic intentions. Undoubtedly, this can make it very difficult to accurately assess economic, investment, and market conditions.

Attitudes like these invariably feed through and influence governance, communications, and other policies at state-dominated companies in those countries. Typically, such enterprises are less transparent and more aggressive than comparable private-sector operators. While they might not want to be seen, for political reasons at least, as riding roughshod over workers' rights or environmental concerns in home markets, those issues seem to matter much less when it comes to their machinations elsewhere, especially when their efforts are aligned with national interests. Indeed, as the global temperature heats up, emerging powers will undoubtedly make the most of all of the economic weapons they have at their disposal. Aside from having state-run companies do their bidding, they will tap other financial firepower, including large pools of capital held as reserves or in sovereign wealth funds (SWFs). Resources might be used to try to acquire foreign-owned firms in key industries or to support existing and prospective allies. Alternatively, the goal might be to destabilize or destroy economies and financial systems of rivals by reallocating or dumping holdings of bonds and other assets of the intended target. Needless to say, the fallout could be devastatingly far-reaching.

Even when they are looked at in narrower terms, these and other unsettling developments will serve to inflict considerable damage on the undercarriage of existing financial market mechanisms. As risk aversion grows; as economic conditions sour; as banks, brokers, and other critical institutions continue to suffer the consequences of a bursting credit bubble; and as public and private investors around the world seek to repatriate funds and rein in their horns, trading conditions will naturally become more challenging. Liquidity will diminish, day-to-day volatility will increase, the ebb and flow of prices will be much more confusing and irregular than now, and some trading arenas will unravel or disappear from view.

Searching for Safety

A disorderly unwinding of global imbalances, turbulence in financial markets, and a wrenching contraction in the U.S. and other economies will stir a natural preference for the safe and the familiar. Heightened geopolitical uncertainty, resource-related constraints, and growing protectionism will undermine faith in globalization. Both developments will augment a shift toward regionalization and localization of economic activity and investment flows. Consequently, business cycles and market movements will be disjointed and hard to decipher. Commercial and investment decision making, meanwhile, will increasingly be swayed by political interests, cultural differences and other idiosyncracies, and the luck of geography. Sectors that are favored in one region will be shunned in others. Traditional fundamentals may matter less than the question of which firms or industries will benefit from favoritism and government largesse. In some countries, activity will come to be dominated by a few large state-controlled firms. In others, the economic universe will be comprised of a large and ever-changing array of smaller enterprises. Globally, relative comparisons will become somewhat meaningless.

Investor expectations, risk tolerances, time horizons, and asset class preferences will also vary according to location. In locales where geopolitical threats, social instability, and economic circumstances naturally boost day-to-day volatility and uncertainty about the outlook, there will likely be greater interest in short-term speculation and sectors with inherent strategic advantages. In regions where populations are aging rapidly, structural relationships between asset classes may diverge, with equities losing out to fixed-income markets. Demand for Islamic investment products will continue to expand in those areas where Muslim populations are large or increasing. According to "The Islamic Funds and Investments Report," Shariah-compliant investable assets in Gulf Cooperation Council countries and the Far East had already reached $267 billion in the spring of 2008.

Certainly, there has been widespread and growing interest in international diversification in recent decades. Yet developments already cited, along with numerous others, indicate that that the risks associated with investing or even simply keeping money abroad will be far greater than in the past. As globalization wanes, many countries will be less than concerned about protecting foreigners' rights, interests, and investments. The shift away from a Western-dominated framework will see the introduction of arbitrary rules and standards favoring local and regional operators. Governments in many parts of the world will attempt to manipulate data and markets to the advantage of domestic investors. Locals may also be afforded a great deal of leeway when it comes to insider trading and taking advantage of outsiders.

Other factors will further heighten the risks associated with venturing overseas. There's little doubt, for instance, that dismal economic conditions, turbulent financial markets, trade and resource-related disruptions, abrupt government policy changes, and unexpected political shocks will force many companies and countries into default or bankruptcy. More worrisome, however, is the prospect that geopolitical and domestic strife (cyber wars; local, regional, and global cross-border conflicts; civil unrest, revolutions, and abrupt changes of the guard); capital controls; limits on cash withdrawals and currency convertibility; hyperinflationary economic policies; and any number of other developments could easily lead to a sudden and total wipeout. The funds may not even be gone in a literal sense; they may simply be inaccessible for an indefinite period of time.

Of course, that doesn't mean the domestic investing environment—speaking from the point of view of U.S. investors—will be any less onerous. Deepening economic malaise; restrictions on trade, capital, and travel; and repeated supply-chain disruptions will blow a hole in many business models. A growing number of firms will be forced to aggressively retrench or be driven to the wall. The seemingly relentless fallout from the collapsing credit bubble, unraveling cross-border imbalances, and upheaval in markets will also provoke ongoing failures of banks, brokers, and other financial institutions. That, in turn, will undermine essential payment and settlement mechanisms and trigger periodic systemic crises. The risks of being in the wrong place at the wrong time will be formidable.

Economic woes and deteriorating public finances will also provoke all sorts of ill-considered and ill-conceived efforts to turn back the tide. In countries around the world, policy makers will try various approaches, including boosting tax rates, cutting services, and shifting costs onto businesses and individuals. Once things get bad enough, however, they will turn to other, more destructive approaches. These might include cranking up the government printing presses, thereby triggering a hyperinflationary spiral; mandating forced conversions of savings and investments into government bonds; and nationalizing or expropriating businesses. Amid the fallout from unrelenting economic pressures, waning global influence, and a widespread loss of faith in its currency, odds are that the United States will have little choice but to resort to some and probably all of these measures. For American investors, it will be the worst of all worlds.

The Biggest Loser

Over the next decade, in fact, there are likely to be few winners among the various asset classes. U.S. equities—as well as shares listed in other countries—face some of the strongest headwinds, especially given that valuations in recent years have not only been above long-term averages, but have also been far removed from the troughs seen during more turbulent times. The trailing price-earnings (P/E) ratio for the S&P 500 index, for example, a popular gauge calculated by dividing the price of the benchmark index by the earnings of its constituent members during the prior 12 months, hovered around 21 in the summer of 2008, nearly 50 percent above its long-term average and almost three times as high as the lows recorded during the Great Depression, World War II, and the late 1970s, when oil-shock-induced inflation was running rampant. Even after the plunge in prices that occurred in the fall of 2008, the market's P/E ratio only just touched neutral territory.

Bear in mind, too, that the current measure of P/E is calculated on the basis of the most recent pattern of earnings. Even ignoring the argument that a plethora of unfolding developments darkens the outlook for most, if not all, businesses in the years ahead, government statistics reveal that U.S. corporate margins and profits stood at multidecade highs relative to overall output of goods and services at the end of 2007. Yet history has shown that, even in normal circumstances, profits tend to revert to longer-term averages over the course of time, largely because high returns attract growing competition, spur worker demands for increased wages and benefits, and stimulate efforts by governments to capture a proportionately larger share of the fruits of growth for public coffers.

Another established method of assessing whether share prices are cheap or expensive is to compare current dividend yields with past averages. Admittedly, this approach has not worked well during the era of sharply declining interest rates. The fact that stock yields have loosely tracked those available in fixed-income markets makes sense at one level, of course, given that investors and managers tend to take both measures into account when determining outlooks, allocations, and strategies. Nevertheless, a comparison with historical trends is eye-opening. At its fall 2008 nadir of around 3.5 percent, calculated on the basis of dividends paid out during the prior four quarters, the S&P 500 was yielding fractionally less than its average over 80 years. Moreover, that value was only one-quarter to one-half the highest dividend yields recorded during the worst moments of earlier hard times.

Of course, this analysis doesn't even take into account the fact that an expanding array of firms will be bleeding buckets of red ink or be driven out of business. Nor does it factor in a broader structural shift that favors smaller companies, domestic firms with locational or strategic advantages, and businesses involved in certain sectors, including those tailored to the realities of a resource-constrained age. The benchmark S&P 500 index, for instance, is comprised of 500 of the largest companies in the United States, with energy and materials-sector firms accounting for less than a fifth of overall weightings. Meanwhile, data from the Bureau of Economic Analysis indicates that American firms derived around 25 percent of their earnings from foreign markets over a recent five-year span. While a weaker dollar could lend some support in this regard, the countervailing forces—including tightening trade restrictions around the globe—will likely matter more.

Also weighing on share prices, as well as those of other investments, will be relentless supply pressures and structural shifts that reduce overall demand for risky assets. After years in which tax policies, aggressive monetary stimulation, and a steady influx of foreign investment helped foster an addictive dependence on borrowed money, financial firms, in particular, along with many other businesses in the United States and elsewhere, will be repeatedly driven to try to raise capital to bolster balance sheets in an increasingly hostile operating environment. Meanwhile, ongoing economic deterioration will not only spur efforts to fund household shortfalls through asset liquidations, but will also cause increasingly risk-averse investors to raise precautionary cash or shift allocations in favor of seemingly safer options.

Some might argue—perhaps convincingly—that equities stand to benefit in a hyperinflationary environment like that which has been seen most recently in the African nation of Zimbabwe. Generally speaking, when the value of a nation's currency is depreciating rapidly because the government has cranked up the monetary printing presses, whatever isn't spent on necessities or invested in hard assets often has nowhere else to go but the stock market, especially in economies where cross border capital flows are tightly controlled. Nonetheless, the broad array of negatives, including heightened geopolitical instability,√ faltering growth a disorderly unwinding of large cross-border imbalances, a surge in defaults and bankruptcies, and malfunctioning markets, suggests the risks of investing in equities could far outweigh the prospective rewards in this kind of scenario.

Another Casualty

Of course, a hyperinflationary environment is the worst possible time to own instruments that offer fixed payouts. However, circumstances don't even have to get that bad: A slower rate of depreciation in the value of a currency can also decimate bond portfolios. Even assuming that inflation concerns remain somewhat moot, the fixed-income √ sector will still be a dangerous place to invest in the years ahead. That is despite the ostensibly bullish combination of a weakening economy and a heightened preference for safety.

For one thing, there is a big difference between how corporate bonds, for example, perform during a garden-variety downturn as opposed to a more calamitous contraction. While the notion of receiving a steady stream of income is alluring, surging defaults and bankruptcies create the risk of serious loss of principal. The bursting credit bubble and the global orgy of borrowing that has taken place over many decades has created tremendous risk of persistent and cascading failures of overleveraged individuals, companies, and governments around the world. At the same time, an era of excessive reliance on credit has fostered an addiction that will see continuing desperate attempts to borrow money, sometimes regardless of terms. Odds are it won't just be those in the lower strata who are looking to tap loan sharks offering financing at exorbitant rates. And while equity-market woes will draw some funds into the fixed-income arena, pressures stemming from forced liquidations and voluntary cash raising will nonetheless weigh on prices.

The outlook isn't that much better for government-issued debt. Under normal circumstances, there is a greater likelihood of getting repaid by a public-sector borrower—especially one that can print what it owes. But the times ahead will be anything but normal. In the

United States, in particular, the nation's loss of status and the dollar's waning fortunes will heighten worries about credit risk and undermine demand for U.S. government securities. Indeed, Abigail Moses of *Bloomberg* reported in March 2008 that trading in certain derivative products indicated "the risk of losses on U.S. Treasury notes exceeded German bunds [government bonds] for the first time ever" amid concerns over the bursting credit bubble. Meanwhile, with strategic, economic, and other incentives gone, large state holders, including the Chinese, Japanese, and Mideast oil producers, will increasingly turn sellers. Governments in the United States and abroad will also be scrambling to fill gaps caused by crashing revenues and a crush of domestic spending needs, including those related to security and infrastructure. With respect to overall supply and demand, the picture will be ugly.

Needless to say, equities won't benefit from rising yields. But neither will real estate, at least in the near term, though the outlook for this particular asset class is somewhat more convoluted. Much depends on what type of property is involved and at what stage of the cycle various countries and economies are in. Housing, commercial, and industrial properties are likely to remain in the doldrums the longest. Arable land, properties that contain deposits of natural resources or have access to waterways and railroads, and those that provide a measure of self-sufficiency or protection against hostile natural or geopolitical elements will have the edge, at least in relative terms. The risk, of course, is that the more attractive an investment is, the more likely it will be that others will come along and try to grab it for themselves.

Over time, occasionally fast-changing developments will alter the dynamic for different segments of the property market. In locations where serious inflation has taken hold, real estate will likely be seen as a hedge. Conflicts and confrontations in some regions will boost the relative attractiveness of holdings in more secure locales. Supply disruptions or demand surges—in connection, perhaps, with natural disasters, terrorist attacks, or the onset of war—could spark a desperate scramble for resource-rich properties, even those that might have dubious value under ordinary circumstances. Bear in mind, however, that real estate has always had a unique appeal, in good times and bad. It is a symbol of power and influence, especially where there's a sense that it might also have strategic value. So it shouldn't be surprising to see some governments ignoring laws or rewriting rules in ways that reduce or diminish what has often been seen as an inalienable right. Under the circumstances, ownership might not necessarily convey the same benefits going forward as in the past. In some respects, the factors that will make cross-border investing more treacherous will also have to be taken into account when property is involved, regardless of where it is situated.

The Promise of Commodities

Given the broader fundamentals surrounding the issue of resource constraints, along with other unfolding developments, commodities seem to offer the best all-around prospect for making money and preserving wealth in the years ahead, though there are a number of important caveats. No doubt many state and nonstate interests—including criminal enterprises—will be aggressively vying for control of key resources and wellsprings of supply. All sorts of pressures, including geopolitical power plays, ongoing economic strains, and mounting social instability, will drive these efforts. While such intensity is a necessary ingredient for prices to move higher, it also lays the groundwork for thuggery, economic hardball, and outright theft. In other words, while it might be a trader's dream to own something that others want, this might not necessarily be a position of strength in some circumstances.

What's more, while a number of long-term trends, including a structural shift upwards in developing-country per-capita consumption levels, have created something of a floor for energy, food, and water prices, other factors will also come into play. The combination of the sharp price run-ups in recent years and a far-reaching economic slowdown will likely serve to temper demand at one level, at least in the short run. The widespread social upheaval that took place when the prices of corn, rice, wheat, and other foodstuffs spiked to new highs in 2007 and 2008 will also spur efforts by policy makers to limit price increases or restrict overall consumption. Ultimately, such controls will prove ineffectual and short-lived. Nonetheless, they could temporarily have the desired effect.

Market structures, production dynamics, and logistical issues will be important considerations insofar as which commodities are worth focusing on. Arguably, potable water and the facilities necessary to treat

it may well offer the best prospects for price appreciation in the years
ahead. In a June 2008 article, for example, Ambrose Evans-Pritchard
of the *Telegraph* highlighted "a Goldman Sachs report [that] said water
was the 'petroleum for the next century,' offering huge rewards for
investors who know how to play the infrastructure boom." The World
Water Council has estimated that $4.5 trillion of water infrastructure
investment is needed by 2025 to develop sufficient sources to meet global needs (see "World Water Vision" by William J. Cosgrove and Frank
R. Rijsberman).

Practically speaking, however, the only way for most investors to
play this trend is to have a stake in firms that own treatment facilities
and distribution networks, or that manufacture relevant technology or
offer related services. That raises the question of risk-reward, because
of the dangers stemming from investing in large firms, those that are
not locally based, and equities as a whole, among others. The same also
holds true with respect to similarly promising industries, including conventional and alternative energy, agriculture, and infrastructure. Even in
those sectors that somehow manage to do well despite all the obstacles,
the fact that so many changes are afoot could easily mean that today's
best prospect is tomorrow's worst nightmare. An investor could be right
about the sector, but wrong about the stock.

At least some of these risks won't apply when it comes to investing
in precious metals. Traditionally, gold, silver, and platinum have been
valued not only for their cosmetic and industrial applications, but for
their rarity, durability, portability, and other inherent attributes. More
important, these commodities have been universally recognized as
stores of value and mediums of exchange—as money, in other words.
In days gone by, there might not have been much difference between
holding money in a convenient paper form or as silver coins and gold
bars. However, in the era of fiat currencies, the relationship between
the two broke down long ago. Most modern currencies, such as the
dollar, are no longer linked to hard assets like gold and silver. They are
merely promises—many of which will be broken—of the governments
that issued them.

For decades, the fact that there were no fixed constraints on the
issuance of fiat currency didn't seem to matter that much, to most people at least. Society seemed to flourish in the absence of a gold standard,

with the wheels greased by the credit-based money creation of central and commercial banks. Yet the benefits have been somewhat illusory. Over time, the prices of many goods and services have crept higher in relative terms as a growing supply of freshly minted currency debased that which was already in circulation. Those efforts have sowed the seeds of their own demise. With interest compounding, the result is that in many countries around the world, too many obligations have been created relative to the resources that are available to service them.

Changing Preferences

In an era of growing turbulence and uncertainty, where the political and economic landscape is being dramatically transformed, economic and financial preferences will change. Over time, more and more people will come to view precious metals as a haven against all kinds of threats, and, perhaps, the only way of storing wealth that has any hope of retaining its value. They will accumulate gold, silver, and platinum in all their forms. Skyrocketing demand will eventually drive the prices of these metals to levels that are dramatically higher than they are today. That will, in turn, boost the value of properties that are rich in precious metals and companies with the technology and know-how to get the stuff out of the ground.

However, it won't be an easy ride. Shares of mining companies, for example, may be an even riskier investment than other equities because of operational needs (including demand for energy), geopolitical instability, and the constant threat of expropriation. Otherwise, the deflationary one-two punch of a credit meltdown and a crumbling global economy will lead to continuing and large-scale liquidations of all types of assets, including precious metals, at least in the short run. For reasons already noted, storing and securing these commodities could become very costly and difficult to arrange. The fact that they have universal appeal means that powerful interests will be on the prowl to acquire these resources for themselves, by deception or force. Out of desperation or as a means of maintaining control during chaotic times, policy makers may try to restrict ownership of gold, silver, and platinum and confiscate outstanding supplies.

In the end, of course, investing in any asset—including precious metals—in any type of environment always entails some degree of risk. Even during the challenging times ahead, despite all the known obstacles, some investors may decide various options are worth considering. Those who accept the argument that share prices, for example, have nowhere to go but down could choose to make any number of bearish long-term bets, including selling stocks or stock-index futures short. They may even try to trade the invariable countertrend rallies along the way. Alternatively, those who recognize the compelling case for technologies that boost efficiency, alternative forms of energy and transportation, security services and products, or small businesses that can serve a valuable niche in a more localized world might consider the upside to be sufficiently great even if a great many things go wrong.

Regardless of whatever approach is taken, the key to success will be to keep the bigger picture in mind. As Lefèvre/Livermore—or "Livingston," if one prefers—noted more than 80 years ago, it's about "sizing up the entire market and its trend." In the dangerous years ahead, that will be more important than ever.

Chapter 9

The Power of One

"FEMA is not going to hesitate at all in this storm. We are not going to sit back and make this a bureaucratic process. We are going to move fast, we are going to move quick, and we are going to do whatever it takes to help disaster victims."

—MICHAEL BROWN, DIRECTOR, FEDERAL EMERGENCY
MANAGEMENT AGENCY

It was August 28, 2005, a day before the arrival of Hurricane Katrina, one of the deadliest storm systems ever to make landfall in the United States, when Michael Brown spoke those words. To many Americans, the fact that Washington, through the Federal Emergency Management Agency (FEMA)—a Department of Homeland Security agency tasked with disaster preparedness and response—stood ready to counter the impending threat to the U.S. Gulf coast was reassuring. After all, the federal government had vast resources at its disposal. Those in charge could call upon the services of various National Guard units and the military, if necessary. On top of that, FEMA had, in a 2001 report, identified a major hurricane hitting New Orleans as one of the three most likely disasters to strike the United States. To most rational observers, that meant the agency had had more than enough time to put an effective plan in place.

Unfortunately, Brown's reassurances came back to haunt the soon-to-be-ex-director of FEMA. Instead of a comprehensive and coherent crisis management strategy, there was confusion and uncertainty. Instead of a coordinated and well-oiled response, there was Keystone Cops–like chaos and bureaucratic paralysis. Instead of maintaining order and providing support to those in need, the government's slipshod handling of the situation facilitated periods of near anarchy, suffering, and despair. Faced with the challenge of having to cope on their own, people responded in various ways. Many who had been left stranded in the flood-ravaged New Orleans basin sought higher ground, hoping to ride things out until conditions improved. Others banded together in an effort to secure water and food, protect themselves from flood-related fallout, and seek a means of escape.

Some also succumbed to more primitive instincts, looting and rampaging and attacking others in the vicinity, to ensure they survived or otherwise came out ahead in the face of the onslaught. For these individuals, primal urges seemed to take over when electrical power, clean water, sanitation facilities, and basic infrastructure were no longer available; when access to sustenance seemed ever more in doubt; and when an unraveling of the established order signaled that what they were dealing with was a uniquely perilous time—where it was every man for himself. Indeed, it wasn't just the fallout from nature's dark forces or breakdowns in the established mechanisms of modern society that people were concerned about. They also worried about the threats posed by others.

Overall, developments set to take place in the years ahead will bring out the best and, increasingly, the worst in people—of all ages, backgrounds, and walks of life. Although some individuals naturally cope better with change than others do, history suggests that many are, to say the least, uncomfortable with the anxiety and sense of vulnerability that stems from dramatic upheaval. Minds work overtime and fight-or-flight instincts can easily take over, especially when familiar, everyday routines are turned upside down and the little matter of procuring life's necessities suddenly becomes a really big deal. Small insecurities can pile up and collide with larger worries, stirring confusion and doubt. People wonder how or even whether they will be able to cope. They fret about what will happen if they can't.

Those feelings will likely be pronounced in a country like the United States, where no small number of people once dreamed of streets paved with gold. Over the course of the past few decades, Americans have been conditioned to believe that they live in a place where food, water, and other essentials would remain relatively inexpensive and, barring an unusual hiccup, always available. Although gasoline, natural gas, and heating oil might cost more each year due to "inflation," most people have not really thought about what they would do if they could not obtain the fuel they needed to drive to town, the gas or oil required to heat their homes, and the electricity necessary to power lights, appliances, and the accoutrements of modern life. In sum, most have never really questioned the American dream.

But various developments are set to change all this. The issue of resource constraints—among other things—means people will have to reevaluate aspects of their lives that few would have even considered during the era of abundance. The prospect of rising prices for and reduced availability of some forms of energy, especially hydrocarbon-based fuels, will force Americans to learn, perhaps the hard way, that locational options, lifestyle choices, and living arrangements that once seemed straightforward have become a confusing jumble, with potentially onerous and maybe even life-threatening ramifications. Suddenly, a great many factors will have to be taken into account that didn't seem to matter too much before. People will have to make decisions about a future they have almost no familiarity with. Simply carrying on doing what their parents did might be the worst decision of all.

Where to Go, What to Do

Although it has always been a matter of importance for most people, making the correct choices about where and how to live will be even more of an imperative in a world where energy is in short supply. The great American pastime of hopping into the car and heading to the mall for shopping, a restaurant for a meal, or a theater for a bit of entertainment might be little more than a distant memory when there are fuel shortages and power outages, businesses are moving or shutting down, jobs have become scarce, the financial and logistical burdens of owning a car or a residence have become ever more difficult, roadways and other transportation infrastructure have deteriorated past the point of no return, and a safe arrival home is not necessarily guaranteed.

The changing dynamics of the energy market mean that many cities—though not all—will gain at the expense of suburbs, reversing a decades-old pattern. Communities with mass transit systems and navigable waterways will draw residents away from those without such attributes. Small villages and metropolises that are largely inaccessible other than by car will wither and die. Sprawling communities in the middle of nowhere will become ghost towns, as energy concerns force businesses, individuals, and families to head for greener—or at least, more accessible—pastures. Low-density areas with large homes will lose their egoistic appeal. Once-thriving suburbs will become havens for the poor and the downtrodden. Over time, many will be overrun by gangs and criminals, left to their own devices as falling tax revenues cause government services to contract or completely disappear.

Energy and economic concerns will leave many people with no choice but to head for populous areas where there are jobs and some prospects for growth, as well as businesses that can supply many, if not all, of their daily needs. These won't be the only factors influencing migratory patterns, however. Worries over access to other vital resources will favor locales that have built-in advantages, including arable land nearby, abundant supplies of water, alternative sources of power, and climates that are not unduly harsh, whether hot or cold. Paradoxically, places that seem like perfect havens or are already densely populated may lose their appeal amid a vast influx of immigrants from elsewhere. Needless to say, areas that are overly exposed to the threat of social and geopolitical instability won't have much going for them, either.

Such a calculus means that small to midsize cities adjacent to rail lines and rivers—which are not flood-prone, of course—will likely have an ongoing attraction in the difficult times ahead. By the same token, well-known metropolises could be risky places to settle down, owing to the fact that few are truly self-sustaining. Despite the presence, for example, of mass transit systems in many large cities, most are still relatively energy-dependent, with multistory buildings and infrastructures that require ample supplies of uninterrupted power to function properly—or at all. They also depend in large degree on water and foodstuffs brought in from other locales.

Aside from that, dense populations naturally stir up pressure-cooker-like stresses that stimulate crime and social unrest. In a deteriorating economic environment where public finances are increasingly under strain, many such threats will fester and feed upon themselves. More important, perhaps, the most populous regions will continue to be seen as natural targets for a growing global network of terrorists, extremists, and agents of rival powers looking to wreak havoc in the now fading superpower.

But such factors will be only a starting point when it comes to decisions about where to live. Other realities will be equally important, including the question of whether employment or entrepreneurial opportunities are available. In an environment where end demand is contracting, competition is intensifying, markets are in turmoil, outside funding is difficult—if not impossible—to come by, resource-related constraints have undermined traditional operating approaches, and access to vendors and customers is a major concern, the smaller number of firms that do manage to survive will either look to scale back the size of operations, relocate to areas where opportunities seem greatest, or reconsider their entire approach to doing business. Some industries will shrink dramatically or disappear altogether, including those that cater to high-end consumers or create products ill suited to a new, more sober age.

Consequently, Americans will have to reorient the pattern of their working lives if they want to get by. Instead of seeking nine-to-five jobs at large, well-known firms, they will be forced to target employers catering more directly to everyday needs. After years of commuting home after a day's work and kicking back to relax, many will find they no longer have that luxury. They will instead head off to a second job—or maybe a third—or press forward with other efforts that might help boost the amount of income coming in. Those who have spent years in an office, sitting in front of a computer or pushing paper around, will discover that they have to get their hands dirty doing other, much less comfortable tasks. Quite simply, it will be a world in which working hours are climbing, pay and benefits are falling, opportunities are disappearing, and growing anxiety about what each day will bring is a disheartening fact of life.

Many people will be forced to go into business for themselves. They will have to come up with creative ways to use their knowledge and talents to satisfy the needs of others. That in itself is not so unusual. Entrepreneurs and owner-managers have long played an important role in the American economy. In recent years, small businesses have accounted for more than 50 percent of U.S. nonfarm private gross domestic product (GDP) and have employed roughly half of all private-sector workers, according to Small Business Administration data. While these numbers are already significant, they will nonetheless rise sharply during a time when the advantages of scale no longer apply. Of course, not everyone is cut out for such endeavors, which typically require administrative, planning, and other capabilities that come naturally to some. Even so, the drawbacks may prove irrelevant. Creating a business that produces products or provides services may well be a necessity, not a choice.

Creating a Personal Roadmap

Decisions on where to live and how to manage require that certain steps be taken in advance—preferably, before things really start falling apart. That includes developing a plan of action. Steeling for a difficult future makes more sense than flying by the seat of the pants. Those who are not quite sure where they stand will need to lay it all out like a standard risk analysis, highlighting strengths, weaknesses, opportunities, and threats. The effort might also entail putting together an inventory of skills, resources, and relationships that could prove valuable in some way. As in all situations where the risks are high, information gathering, lateral thinking, and "What if?" questioning are essential. Proper preparation also means stepping up efforts to acquire knowledge and establish connections with others, aided by training and networking. All of this will have to be done, of course, with the full knowledge that things might not work out as planned.

The process will also demand an intense reassessment of lifestyle choices. People will have to come up with a list of priorities, as well as options that might be available if and when things go wrong. The broad-based economic and financial unraveling of recent years should have already driven home the fact that the formerly profligate will have to start living within their means. They will need to decide which things matter most and allocate resources accordingly. After being brain-washed into believing that everyone could have it all, Americans will have to decide just what they can do without. Few will have the luxury of acquiring something just because they can. Even if they are able to, changing times mean there won't be much to choose from, anyway.

Aside from the difficulties caused by shortages and breakdowns, many people will find that they are constantly being tested in other ways. For the most part, Americans have been accustomed to a financial system that has functioned reasonably well over time. However, deteriorating economic conditions, ongoing dollar woes, bank failures and payment-mechanism mishaps, persistent market upheavals, and rising personal, business, and public-sector defaults and bankruptcies mean that spendable cash may be in short supply—or not available at all. If and when that happens, people will have to scramble—maybe even beg, borrow, or steal—to get what they need for themselves and their families. Over time, barter arrangements, alternative financial instruments, and collective support networks may come to supplant modern payment mechanisms and the use of traditional currencies.

A smooth-functioning financial system won't be the only thing that Americans can no longer take for granted. Rising interest rates, sharply falling tax revenues, and incessant demands for increasing public spending stemming from security concerns, infrastructure failures, and an array of economic woes will turn Washington's already shaky finances into a shambles. The budgets of state and local governments will be in similarly bad shape. One result will be an ongoing decline in public services such as law enforcement and education. Another will be the shredding of various social and financial safety nets, including Social Security, Medicare, unemployment compensation, and other insurance-type programs. Aside from having to deal with a myriad of day-to-day challenges, people will have to make greater allowances for more devastating structural realities.

Where social services and other backstop arrangements are deficient or nonexistent, people often work hard at building up financial cushions. In places like China, for example, savings rates have traditionally been high, in part because there is inadequate state-backed or private-sector insurance coverage for health-related concerns. One key issue, of course, is the not so little matter of making enough money to cover regular outgoings—and then some. No doubt Americans will expend considerable time and effort trying to boost household income. But inflows can't be the only focus. Over the past few decades, many have chosen, for various reasons, to consume more and save less—often to the point where the money going out has far exceeded the amount coming in. However, as traditional support mechanisms evaporate, people will out of necessity be forced to turn that relationship around. They will have to figure out ways—like those with far lower per-capita incomes somehow manage to do—of holding on to more of what they earn.

To be sure, there will be countless roadblocks in the way of accumulating resources and boosting wealth. For some, the costs of constant upheaval will be a persistent drain on income and savings. Those who do manage to put something aside, meanwhile, will find that nest eggs are regularly exposed to a variety of threats. These include the failures of financial intermediaries, ill-conceived or ill-intentioned government policies, criminal activity, and geopolitical upheaval. But it won't just be investments—such as gold or silver—that are at risk. For practical and other reasons, people may also need to have cash or tradeable goods on hand, or occasionally to own physical and financial assets, which others will also have their eyes on. Given that, Americans will have to think long and hard about who they do business with and entrust their secrets to.

Blood Ties

Such warnings don't apply just in regard to commercial and financial ties. Family, social, and community relationships will likely assume a far greater degree of importance in a world of uncertainty, disruptions, and increasing danger. In the United States and elsewhere, there will almost certainly be a significant rise in the number of extended-family households, many with a growing number of adult children—and grandchildren—living at home. Such a development should not be seen as particularly surprising. In economically deficient and broken-down societies, for example, it is not uncommon for households to expand and people to rely heavily on family networks—grandparents, parents, and children, as well as in-laws and other relatives—for support and assistance.

Indeed, some cultures view large households as a powerful resource and financial backstop—much like a nest egg—because of the familiarity element and the value of the available labor. Moreover, during earlier, more uncertain times, when no one could really be sure which outsiders could be trusted—before there were electronic communications networks and credit rating databases—blood ties often played an important role in lubricating the wheels of commerce and industry. That said, the possibility that desperate times will lead to desperate acts means Americans will have to be just as diligent in their dealings with those they hold dear as with those they don't really know at all.

In the past, when governments have maintained a hands-off approach in regards to social services, or when budgetary pressures have served to open up a gap between private needs and public resources, charities, community groups, and individual volunteers have stepped in to fill the breach. In the United States, for example, philanthropic efforts can be traced all the way back to the 1600s, when the first group of Pilgrims arrived on the *Mayflower*. Going forward, harsh realities will undoubtedly spur a call for and a resurgence of privately funded altruism.

But things won't end there. When it comes to the kinds of essential services that governments have traditionally been responsible for, including public safety, it has not been all that rare to see citizens take matters into their own hands when official efforts fall short. Indeed, a growing number of neighborhoods, businesses, and communities in the United States are already paying for private security services. Such programs have been supplementing—and even supplanting—state-sponsored policing in some instances. As time goes on, that trend will only increase.

All signs indicate, as emphasized previously, that safety and security concerns will assume a far greater measure of importance in the future than they have in recent decades. The combination of mounting conflicts over food, water, arable land, and other vital resources; collapsing government spending; heightened age, race, gender, religion, and other divides;

and rising geopolitical instability means that more and more people will be forced to take aggressive steps to protect themselves, their loved ones, their livelihoods, and their wealth. Odds are that there will be more gated communities popping up around the United States. At that point, however, the walls and restricted entranceways won't be seen as status symbols, but as a means of keeping out those who constitute a threat. The proliferation of barriers will also spawn unintended consequences: hardening differences, hindering cooperation, and heightening anxiety.

The changing dynamics of energy markets, crumbling government finances, infrastructure breakdowns, and security concerns will likely also engender a big shift in the way that children are educated. Busing or carpooling students to schools that may be many miles away will no longer be seen as economical or practical, especially in areas where populations and tax revenues are falling sharply. At the same time, rising crime rates, heightened social unrest, and growing ethnic, religious, and cultural schisms in other, more populated areas will spur parents to seek out safer alternatives. The result will almost certainly be a growing preference for homeschooling and small, neighborhood-based teaching facilities, resembling, perhaps, the traditional one-room schoolhouses that once dotted the landscape.

Modern health care systems will be undermined and dismantled by many of the same forces. Hospitals, clinics, and stand-alone offices, starved of cash, will fall apart or shut their doors. Those who have long paid most of the bills—governments, businesses, and private insurers—will press forward with efforts to shift the burdens elsewhere or simply turn off the tap. Meanwhile, amid a shrinking supply of services, medications, and providers, demand will take off, boosted by the afflictions of aging populations, infrastructure breakdowns that damage water treatment systems and waterways, an epidemic of epidemics, and the fallout from heightened violence and cross-border conflicts. Ringing 911—assuming the phone works—might not lead to an emergency response; on the contrary, the call might not get answered at all. Many Americans will discover that there is no professional assistance available to them. They will have to reach out to amateur practitioners nearby or come up with ways to heal themselves.

Overall, many aspects of society will revert back to a time when lifestyles, services, and patterns of behavior were far different from what people have become accustomed to. Economic realities, of course, will play a major role in the transition. More Americans will be walking, riding bicycles, traveling by boat, and getting around in vehicles that are cheap and nonpolluting—and unable to go very far. There will be increasing interest in locally sourced produce and livestock, grown and raised in individual gardens and minifarms, or collected through the efforts of cooperatives and communities. People will find they must become more efficient and self-sufficient in terms of energy and other resource needs. They will recycle rainwater, use heat from the sun, replace lighting, plug leaks, and brainstorm creative ways to get the most out of what they already have. They will also change their diets, altering the quantities and kinds of food they eat.

Not So Idyllic

Of course, these shifts won't be as idyllic as some might think. There will be little opportunity for leisure pursuits when so many more hours of a day are spent trying to earn a living, traveling from one place to another, growing and finding food, recycling resources and fixing equipment, educating children and managing households, and taking whatever steps are necessary to protect life and property from hostile elements. As time falls short, emotions will run high. Personal and professional relationships will also be buffeted by conflicting crosswinds. The urge to be allied against threats and uncertainty will draw people closer together, while the strains of resource concerns, social instability, and geopolitical conflict will drive them apart. Stress, anger, tiredness, and fear will make for a combustible mix that can explode without warning. Many will turn to religion and spirituality for answers. Others will look for whatever means of escape they can find.

Early on, many Americans will place great faith in the power of technology to overcome the challenges they face. But such optimism assumes, in part, that the electricity needed to power systems and devices will be available and affordable; that the energy, materials, and facilities necessary to create the products that can make things happen will be accessible; and, finally, that the designers, parts makers, and technicians who help keep systems up and running can do so in future.

Otherwise, while it is a good bet that the Internet will continue to exist in some form or other, the entire network will be exposed to constant economic, technological, and geopolitical stresses that will likely devalue its usefulness over time. Among other things, declining user fees or the abrupt failure of firms that maintain its backbone could lead to frequent and extended outages.

Communications networks will also be a focal point for competing interests as they vie for dominance in the wake of a changing world order. Terrorists and extremists will look to use the Internet as a medium for spreading their message and interacting with like-minded individuals based elsewhere. Governments will try to increase their repressive control through surveillance, censorship, and the development of subsystems that are inaccessible to outsiders.

All of this will be but a backdrop to an array of perilous geopolitical crosscurrents. Regions, countries, cities, and communities will be shaken and split apart by protests and clashes, rebellions and revolutionary stirrings, acts of terrorism, and full-scale war. At the same time, various governments and groups will step up efforts to squelch dissent, forcibly maintain order, and increase the amount of resources under their direct control.

These won't be the only threats to health and safety. Many individuals will also be affected by the fallout from various systemic breakdowns. Among the dangers are famines and droughts; food-, water-, and airborne diseases; building and infrastructure collapses; and toxic spills and industrial accidents that cause life-threatening changes to the surrounding environment. Along with all the other steps they must take, Americans will need to make sure they come up with emergency strategies, escape routes, and exit plans in case the worst comes to pass. It's worth keeping in mind, however, that for most people, moving to another country—or even to another part of a suddenly divided nation—could prove extraordinarily difficult in the face of moves to lock down borders and restrict the free flow of goods, capital, and people.

In reality, Americans may also have to think about protecting themselves in other, more aggressive ways. For example, in the wake of the economic collapse that took place in Argentina in 2001—which impoverished many individuals and families and led to complete breakdown in a host of essential services—many people took matters into their own hands. They began walking around with handguns and other weapons for protection, and they banded together in groups to ensure their own safety. Like those who, in the dark days after Hurricane Katrina, decided that it was each and every man for himself, no small number of Americans will find that the question of their own survival leads them to a similar conclusion.

Conclusion

Many find fault with pessimistic visions of the future. They believe that human creativity and resourcefulness, the painful lessons of the past, and a relentlessly optimistic human spirit will help us move past and build on whatever troubles might be thrown in our path. Others note the fact that no matter what mankind has been through—civil wars and global conflicts, depressions and hyperinflations, natural and man-made disasters—the bad times have always come to an end and better times have invariably followed. A few even maintain, à la Newton's first law of motion, that because conditions have generally been good for so long, things are bound to carry on that way.

Arguably, the eruptions that have in recent times rocked markets and upended economies around the globe have exposed the foolhardiness of this last view, which seems to reflect the common human foible of extrapolating the past well into the future. Such was the logic that took hold not long before Hurricane Katrina slammed into New Orleans: It hadn't happened yet, so it wouldn't happen then. If anything, the abrupt reversal of fortune that occurred in 2007 and 2008 indicates that the risks are greatest when conditions are best. Given that, logic would suggest that the past half-century of unprecedented peace and prosperity has laid the groundwork for a dramatic pendulum swing back in the opposite direction.

And while it is true that Americans—and many, many others, for that matter—have weathered countless storms and tragedies, it doesn't mean that those who suffered through the hard times were not wracked with pain or left without scars. To individuals caught up in the Civil War, when a bloody schism over slavery and states' rights nearly tore the nation apart, or those dragged through the mud of the Great Depression, when economic collapse left millions of people destitute and in despair, Nietzscheian reassurances—"What does not destroy me, makes me stronger"—might seem like a cruel joke. Whatever supposed benefits might derive from such circumstances are certainly not appreciated while they are going on.

Most people would agree, in fact, that those who were around 80 years ago, or seven decades before that, would have welcomed some sort of insight into the unfolding upheavals, as well as knowledge of the steps they could or should take to steel themselves. No one knows precisely what the future holds, of course. Indeed, there have been many false alarms raised through the years, often by thoughtful and knowledgeable individuals. Even so, a look back in time indicates that when a true sea change is in the air, numerous warning signs are apparent beforehand, especially to those who are willing to open their eyes and assess the facts in the cold light of day.

Based on developments so far, it seems clear—to those who are paying attention, at least—that the world is on the cusp of one of those seminal moments: a time when, to paraphrase strategist, investor, and author Barton Biggs, mankind is set to endure yet another "episode of great wealth destruction." Look around: All of a sudden, social moods, political rhetoric, and geopolitical relations are becoming heated and unsettled—a notable change. Financial and other stresses that seemed manageable or even inconsequential only a few years back have burst out into the open, spawning turbulence and rivers of red ink. Meanwhile, nobody seems to be in charge, while many falsely claim to have all the answers.

Like the other great spasms in our history, the one that now seems to be unfolding is unlikely to be narrow in scope, shallow in depth, or short-lived in duration. In fact, the myriad strains that have built up over the course of the past several decades will continue to break loose in a seemingly endless sequence, careening into one another like a long line of cascading dominos. Tensions and imbalances that have been repeatedly ignored or otherwise kept under wraps will swell up and split open, triggering far-reaching economic, social, political, and geopolitical disturbances that spur further eruptions.

Under the circumstances, there will be no room for wishful thinking or for keeping the faith in individuals, organizations, systems, and structures that essentially brought us to this point. Instead, people will have to evaluate circumstances as realistically as possible and figure out for themselves what their options are—as individuals, owners and managers, and investors. They will need to marshal inner strengths and external resources, and garner the support of friends and family. Everything that they have taken for granted up until now will have to be looked at in a totally new light. Failure to take matters seriously could mean just that—serious failure.

Admittedly, it's hard to challenge the optimists' assumption that, at *some* point down the road, the strains and uncertainties will ease or disappear completely from view, or that major schisms and disruptions will close up or quiet down, excesses and dislocations will be resolved or unwound, and ashes left over from the many troubles that had come to pass will have enriched the roots of a return to better times. People will adjust lifestyles, approaches, and attitudes to a new scheme of things. Mankind will be ready, once again, to move forward, toward better times for all.

Until then, however, Americans will need to be extremely vigilant and ready for action. They will have to absorb the insights on these pages and take whatever steps are necessary to ensure they manage to get through the troubled times unscathed. They will have to acquire as much knowledge as they can about what is going on, set out a viable plan, adjust habits and attitudes, and focus on doing the kinds of things that will be required in order to survive—and, it is hoped, thrive—in a dark and dangerous world. Only then will they be ready for that hoped-for moment: when a light at the end of the tunnel suddenly appears.

Bibliography

Abbas, Mohammed. "Gulf Plans Revaluation Talks in Days: Bahrain." Reuters, December 8, 2007.

Abboud, Leila. "Let It Flow." *Wall Street Journal*, October 6, 2008.

Abboud, Leila, and John Biers. "Business Goes on an Energy Diet." *Wall Street Journal*, August 27, 2007.

Abdelhadi, Magdi. "Muslim Call to Adopt Mecca Time." *BBC News*, April 21, 2008.

Abdurasulov, Abdujalil. "Kazakhstan's Scary Uranium Ambitions." *BusinessWeek*, April 9, 2008.

Abelson, Alan. "Wolf at the Door." *Barron's*, January 7, 2008.

"About Decoupling." *Sudden Debt*, January 7, 2008. http://suddendebt.blogspot. com/2008/01/about-decoupling.html (accessed January 7, 2008).

"ACLU Suggests U.S. May Be Spying on Three Other Financial Services." *Raw Story*, July 19, 2006. www.rawstory.com/news/2006/ACLU_suggests_US_ may_be_spying_0719.html (accessed July 20, 2006).

"Active Conflicts by Region 1989–2006." Uppsala Conflict Data Program, Uppsala University. N.d. www.pcr.uu.se/research/UCDP/graphs/reg_year89. gif (accessed March 29, 2008).

Adams, Bob. "A New Life in Panama." *Barron's*, September 24, 2007.

Aeppel, Timothy. "Stung by Soaring Transport Costs, Factories Bring Jobs Home Again." *Wall Street Journal*, June 13, 2008.

185

Aizenman, N. C. "Islamic Finance Gains Momentum in US." *Gulf News*, May 19, 2008.

Akbar, Ali, and Nasser Karimi. "Putin Visits Iran, Sends Warning to U.S." Associated Press, October 16, 2007.

Akhavi, Khody. "U.S./Iran: Tough New Sanctions Could Backfire, Experts Warn." *Inter Press Service News Agency*, April 14, 2008.

Alexander, Paul. "Pakistan Could End Cooperation in War on Terror." Associated Press, September 13, 2008.

Ali, Irfan. "It's Not a War on Terror, But a War for Resources: Conference." *Daily Times* (Pakistan), September 12, 2008.

Ali, Tariq. "US Pushes Pakistan Towards the Brink." *Asia Times Online*, September 18, 2008. www.atimes.com/atimes/South_Asia/JI18Df01.html (accessed September 18, 2008).

Alison, Sebastian. "Georgie War Shows Russia 'Force to Be Reckoned With.'" *Bloomberg*, August 28, 2008.

Alison, Sebastian. "Putin Warns Energy-Dependent Russia of New Arms Race." *Bloomberg*, February 8, 2008.

Allam, Hannah. "Middle East Censors Seek to Limit Web Access." *McClatchy Newspapers*, December 24, 2007.

"American Power." *Economist*, June 28, 2007.

"Americans Dissatisfied with Political Sound Bites Are Turning to the Internet for a More Complete Picture, a New Study Finds." Associated Press, June 15, 2008.

"American Society of Civil Engineers Report Card for America's Infrastructure, 2005." www.asce.org/reportcard/2005/index.cfm (accessed September 29, 2006).

"America's New Trade Hypocrisy." *Korea Herald*, July 14, 2006.

"Amero Plot Real, Says Biz Columnist." *WorldNetDaily*, October 11, 2007.

Anderlini, Jamil. "China Eyes Overseas Land in Food Push." *Financial Times*, May 8, 2008.

Anderlini, Jamil. "Olympics Water Diversion Threatens Millions." *Financial Times*, February 26, 2008.

Anderson, Chris. "The Long Tail." *Wired*, June 2005. www.wired.com/wired/archive/12.10/tail_pr.html (accessed June 5, 2005).

Ang, Audra. "Chinese Security Forces Swarm Tibet." Associated Press, March 15, 2008.

Anonymous. "Zimbabwe: The Failures of a State." *Stanford Progressive*, June 2006.

"Antarctic Ice Shelf Disintegration Underscores a Warming World." National Snow and Ice Data Center, March 25, 2008. http://nsidc.org/news/press/20080325_Wilkins.html (accessed March 30, 2008).

"'Apocalyptic Scenario' If Egypt, Saudi Go Nuclear: Israel Minister." *Agence France-Presse*, November 9, 2007.

Appelbaum, Binyamin, and Lori Montgomery. "Citing Grave Financial Threats, Officials Ready Massive Rescue." *Washington Post*, September 19, 2008.

Apuzzo, Matt. "US: Immigrants May Be Held Indefinitely." Associated Press, November 13, 2006.

Arain, Suhail. "Low Supply Means It's the End of the Road for Cheap Oil." *Scotland on Sunday*, May 11, 2008.

"Archbishop of Canterbury: 'U.S. Is Worse than the British Empire at Its Peak.'" *Press Association*, November 25, 2007.

Arends, Brett. "Jeremy Grantham: All the World's a Bubble." *TheStreet.com*, April 27, 2007.

Arostegui, Martin. "South America on Brink of War." *Washington Times*, March 3, 2008.

"An Arrogant Approach: The Danger of Unilateralism—for the United States and the World." *Newsweek*, December 14, 2007.

Aron, Leon. "Russia's Next Target Could Be Ukraine." *Wall Street Journal*, September 10, 2008.

"As Big a Shock as the Russians Launching Sputnik." *Daily Mail* (UK), November 13, 2007.

Ash, Timothy Garton. "China, Russia and the New World Disorder." *Los Angeles Times*, September 11, 2008.

"Asia and the World Economy: The Alternative Engine." *Economist*, October 19, 2006.

"Asset-Backed Insecurity." *Economist*, January 17, 2008.

Assis, Claudia. "Emerging Markets Beckon." *Barron's*, December 24, 2007.

Athavaley, Anjali. "Sewer to Spigot: Recycled Water." *Wall Street Journal*, May 15, 2008.

"Australia: What to Do, What to Do about Our Energy Situation?" *Oil Drum*, May 15, 2008. www.theoildrum.com/node/3988 (accessed May 16, 2008).

Authers, John. "The Short View: Oil Burden." *Financial Times*, May 29, 2008.

Aversa, Jeannine. "Bernanke: Baby Boomers Will Strain U.S." Associated Press, October 4, 2006.

Ayres, Chris. "Scientists Find Bugs That Eat Waste and Excrete Petrol." *Times* (London), June 14, 2008.

"Baby Boom and Bust." *Economist*, May 11, 2008.

"Baby Boom, Baby Bust." *Bearwatch*, November 22, 2007. http://theylaughedatnoah. blogspot.com/2007/11/baby-boom-baby-bust.html (accessed November 24, 2007).

Baer, Robert. "How Iran Has Bush over a Barrel." *Time*, June 11, 2008.

"Bain Backs Out of 3Com Deal." *Bloomberg*, March 20, 2008.

Bajak, Frank. "Latin American Nations Edge Away from U.S." Associated Press, October 19, 2008.

Bajoria, Jayshree. "Nationalism in China." *Newsweek*, April 24, 2008.

Baker, Rodger. "China, the Olympics and the Visa Mystery." *Stratfor*, July 29, 2008. www.stratfor.com/weekly/china_olympics_and_visa_mystery (accessed July 30, 2008).

Baldwin, Richard. "The WTO Tipping Point." *Vox*, July 1, 2008. www.voxeu.org/index.php?q=node/1345 (accessed July 2, 2008).

Ball, Jeffrey. "U.N. Effort to Curtail Emissions in Turmoil." *Wall Street Journal*, April 12, 2008.

Baltimore, Chris. "U.S. Has Few Options as Oil Nations Tighten Grip." *Reuters*, June 6, 2008.

Barta, Patrick. "Asia's Slowdown Tests Key Support of Global Growth." *Wall Street Journal*, September 19, 2008.

Bartlett, Duncan. "Russia's Energy Giant Flexes Its Muscles." *BBC News*, February 24, 2008.

Batson, Andrew. "China Eco-Watchdog Gets Teeth." *Wall Street Journal*, December 18, 2007.

Batson, Andrew, and Shai Oster. "China's Power Woes Threaten Growth." *Wall Street Journal*, August 12, 2008.

Baute, Nicole. "The End of Travel." *Toronto Star*, August 2, 2008.

Bayh, Evan. "Time for Sovereign Wealth Rules." *Wall Street Journal*, February 13, 2008.

Beattie, Alan. "World Trade Decelerates Almost to Standstill, Says Study." *Financial Times*, March 20, 2008.

Beattie, Alan. "World Trade Talks Collapse in Acrimony." *Financial Times*, June 21, 2007.

Bedwell, Helena, and Denis Maternovsky. "Georgian Breakaway Region Seeks UN Recognition, Citing Kosovo." *Bloomberg*, March 5, 2008.

Beeby, Rosslyn. "Population Bomb 'Ticks Louder than Climate.'" *Canberra Times*, July 22, 2008.

"Beijing Air Pollution 'as Bad as It Can Get' Official Says." *Agence France-Presse*, December 27, 2007.

"Beijing May Be Running Out of Water." *RedOrbit News*, June 28, 2008. www.redorbit.com/news/science/1454685/beijing_may_be_running_out_of_water/index.html (accessed July 7, 2008).

Bellman, Eric, and Jackie Range. "Shortage of Laborers Plagues India." *Wall Street Journal*, May 1, 2008.

Belton, Catherine. "Copy China and Invest Abroad, Says Medvedev." *Financial Times*, January 31, 2008.

Benjamin, Matthew. "Paulson Plan May Push U.S. Debt to Post-WWII Levels." *Bloomberg*, September 23, 2008.

Benjamin, Matthew, and Mark Drajem. "Free-Trade Era May Be Nearing End amid Food, Growth Concerns." *Bloomberg*, June 13, 2008.

Bennett, Drake. "The Amero Conspiracy." *Boston Globe*, November 25, 2007.

Benoit, Bertrand. "US 'Will Lose Financial Superpower Status.'" *Financial Times*, September 25, 2008.

Berger, Knute. "The Future of 'Nowhere.'" *Crosscut.com*, August 18, 2008. www.crosscut.com/business-technology/16796/The+future+of+'nowhere'/ (accessed August 18, 2008).

Bergsten, C. Fred. "The Democrats' Dangerous Trade Games." *Wall Street Journal*, May 20, 2008.

Berman, Dennis K. "Russians Are Coming, Wallets in Hand." *Wall Street Journal*, July 22, 2008.

Bernstein, Jared, and Josh Bivens. "The Pain of Globalization." *Guardian* (UK), November 8, 2007.

Bernstein, Nina. "Italian's Detention Illustrates Dangers Foreign Visitors Face." *New York Times*, May 14, 2008.

Berry, Lauren. "Wind Appears on the Verge of Becoming a Power Player." *Charlotte Observer*, June 26, 2008.

Beste, Ralf, Cordula Meyer, and Christopher Schult. "Israeli Ministers Mull Plans for Military Strike against Iran." *Spiegel Online*, June 16, 2008. www.spiegel.de/international/world/0,1518,druck-559925,00.html (accessed June 18, 2008).

Bhadrakumar, M. K. "Russia and Turkey Tango in the Black Sea." *Asia Times Online*, September 12, 2008. www.atimes.com/atimes/Central_Asia/JI12Ag01.html (accessed September 15, 2008).

"The Big Sort." *Economist*, June 19, 2008.

"Biofuels Nothing Short of Disaster: Environmentalists to Blame as Emissions Worsen, World's Poor Starve." *Edmonton Journal*, April 13, 2008.

Birch, Douglas, and Mansur Mirovalev. "New 'Great Game' for Central Asia Riches." Associated Press, December 15, 2007.

Birchall, Jonathan, and Elizabeth Rigby. "Oil Costs Force P&G to Rethink Its Supply Network." *Financial Times*, June 26, 2008.

Black, Richard. "'No Sun Link' to Climate Change." *BBC News*, April 3, 2008.

Blagov, Sergei. "Thorns in the Rosy China-Russia Relationship." *Asia Times Online*, August 15, 2007. www.atimes.com/atimes/Central_Asia/IH15Ag01.html (accessed August 15, 2007).

Blakely, Rhys. "CEO Murdered by Mob of Sacked Indian Workers." *Times* (London), September 23, 2008.

Blas, Javier, and Daniel Ten Kate. "Jump in Rice Price Fuels Fears of Unrest." *Financial Times*, March 27, 2008.

Blas, Javier. "Fear of Unrest Mounts as Hunger Spreads." *Financial Times*, April 3, 2008.

Bluestein, Greg. "No Backup If Atlanta's Faucets Run Dry." Associated Press, October 19, 2007.

Blustein, Paul. "Fissures Deep and Wide Shatter World Trade Talks." *Seattle Times*, July 5, 2006.

Bodansky, Yossef. *Chechen Jihad: Al Qaeda's Training Ground and the Next Wave of Terror.* New York: HarperCollins, 2007.

Bohlen, Celestine. "Europe Struggles to Reconcile Free Speech, Muslim Sensibilities." *Bloomberg*, March 24, 2008.

"Bolivia on the Brink." *Washington Post*, September 16, 2008.

Bortin, Meg. "Global Poll Shows Wide Distrust of United States." *International Herald Tribune*, June 27, 2007.

Boswell, Randy. "U.S. Shifts Arctic Foreign Policy." *Canwest News Service*, August 9, 2008.

Bowring, Philip. "Beware an Angry China." *International Herald Tribune*, April 8, 2008.

"BP Statistical Review of World Energy 2007." BP p.l.c., June 2007.

Brabeck-Letmathe, Peter. "Global Drying." *Wall Street Journal*, June 13, 2008.

Bradley, Donald. "High Gas Prices Threaten to Drain Small Towns' Populations." *Kansas City Star*, June 28, 2008.

Bradsher, Keith. "Asia Rethinks American Investments amid Market Upheaval." *New York Times*, September 18, 2008.

Bradsher, Keith. "A Drought in Australia, a Global Shortage of Rice." *New York Times*, April 17, 2008.

Bradsher, Keith. "High Rice Cost Creating Fears of Asia Unrest." *New York Times*, March 29, 2008.

Bradsher, Keith. "Hoarding Nations Drive Food Costs Ever Higher." *New York Times*, June 20, 2008.

Bradsher, Keith. "Trucks at Heart of China's Diesel Problems." *International Herald Tribune*, December 8, 2007.

Bradsher, Keith, and David Barboza. "Pollution from Chinese Coal Casts a Global Shadow." *New York Times*, June 11, 2006.

Bradsher, Keith, and Andrew Martin. "Shortages Threaten Farmers' Key Tool: Fertilizer." *New York Times*, April 30, 2008.

"Brazil's Courts, Military Question Amazon Policy." *Associated Press*, August 4, 2008.

Brecher, Gary. "How Birthrate Is Turning Modern Conventional Warfare on Its Head." *AlterNet*, May 26, 2008. www.alternet.org/module/printversion/86451 (accessed May 26, 2008).

Brimelow, Peter, and Edwin S.. Rubenstein. "The Cost of Soaring Public and Private Debt Levels." *MarketWatch*, May 29, 2008.

Brinsley, John, and Kevin Carmichael. "Foreigners Sold Record $69.3 Billion in U.S. Assets." *Bloomberg*, October 16, 2007.

Brooks, Rosa. "Hey U.S., Welcome to the Third World!" *Los Angeles Times*, September 18, 2008.

Brown, Jeffrey J. "Is a Net Oil Export Hurricane Hitting the U.S. Gulf Coast?" *Oil Drum*, June 2, 2008. www.theoildrum.com/node/4092 (accessed June 2, 2008).

Brown, Jeffrey J., and Samuel Foucher. "A Quantitative Assessment of Future Net Oil Exports by the Top Five Net Oil Exporters." *Energy Bulletin*, January 7, 2008.

Brown, Matthew. "U.A.E. Decides to Maintain Dollar Peg after Review." *Bloomberg*, January 3, 2008.

Brown, Stephen P.A., Raghav Virmani, and Richard Alm. "Economic Letter— Insights from the Federal Reserve Bank of Dallas." *Federal Reserve Bank of Dallas*, May 2008. http://dallasfed.org/research/eclett/2008/e10805.html (accessed May 30, 2008).

Browne, Andrew. "China's Reserves Near Milestone, Underscoring Its Financial Clout." *Wall Street Journal*, October 17, 2006.

Brunnstrom, David. "U.S. Concerned by Russian Arms Sales to Iran, Syria." *Reuters*, March 21, 2007.

Brunwasser, Mathew, and Judy Dempsey. "Pipeline Cements Russia's Hold on Europe's Gas Supply." *New York Times*, January 19, 2008.

"Brussels Worried as Poll Shows 'No' Vote Ahead in Ireland." *Agence France-Presse*, June 6, 2008.

Bryanski, Gleb. "Russia's Kudrin Says WTO Entry Talks Near End." *Reuters*, March 25, 2008.

Bryner, Jeanna. "Humans Crave Violence Just Like Sex." *LiveScience*, January 17, 2008.

Buchanan, Patrick J. "Blowback from Bear-Baiting." *Yahoo! News*, August 15, 2008.

Buchanan, Patrick J. "Liquidating the Empire." *Antiwar.com*, October 14, 2008: www.antiwar.com/pat/?articleid=13588 (accessed October 14, 2008).

Buchanan, Patrick J. "Subprime Nation." *Real Clear Politics*, January 15, 2008. www.realclearpolitics.com/articles/2008/01/subprime_nation.html (accessed April 19, 2008).

Buchanan, Patrick J. "This Is How Empires End." *Antiwar.com*, July 20, 2007. www.antiwar.com/pat/?articleid=11319 (accessed July 21, 2007).

Buchanan, Patrick J. "The Party's Over." *Yahoo! News*, September 19, 2008.

Buchanan, Patrick J. "The Way Our World Ends." *WorldNetDaily*, May 2, 2008.

Buckley, Chris. "China Paper Urges New Currency Order after 'Financial Tsunami.'" Reuters, September 17, 2008.

Buckley, Chris. "China Says Father of Bird Flu Victim Also Infected." Reuters, December 7, 2007.

Buckley, Neil, and Catherine Belton. "Putin Calls for New Financial World Order." *Financial Times*, June 10, 2007.

Buckley, Neil, and Stefan Wagstyl. "Putin Calls for Response to U.S. 'Threat.'" *Financial Times*, July 25, 2007.

Burgess, Christopher. "Nation States' Espionage and Counterespionage." *CSO*, April 21, 2008.

Burton, John. "Asean Aims for Single Market by 2015." *Financial Times*, August 22, 2006.

Burton, Jonathan. "Diversifying Risk Gets Harder as Assets Move in Sync." *Investor's Business Daily*, April 10, 2006.

Callick, Rowan. "China Warns U.S. to Keep Out of Taiwan." *Australian*, December 6, 2007.

Callimachi, Rukmini. "Muslim Nations: Defame Islam, Get Sued?" Associated Press, March 14, 2008.

Caplan, Bryan. "The CNN Model of Violent Conflict." *EconLog*, April 28, 2008. http://econlog.econlib.org/archives/2008/04/the_cnn_model_o.html (accessed April 29, 2008).

Carew, Rick. "China's Sovereign Wealth Fund Forges Strategy, Hunts for Staff." *Wall Street Journal*, November 20, 2007.

Carey, Theresa W., and Kathy Yakal. "Scaling Hubbert's Peak." *Barron's*, May 2, 2004.

Carmichael, Kevin. "The End of the American Order." *Globe and Mail* (Canada), October 4, 2008.

Carney, John. "The Rise of Sovereign Funds: Good for the US, Bad for the World?" *Dealbreaker*, December 10, 2007. www.dealbreaker.com/2007/12/the_rise_of_sovereign_funds_go.php (accessed December 10, 2007).

Carpenter, Susan. "As Gas Prices Climb, So Do Scooter Sales." *Los Angeles Times*, June 28, 2008.

Carroll, Joe. "Brazil Oil Finds May End Reliance on Middle East, Zeihan Says." *Bloomberg*, April 24, 2008.

Casarini, Nicola. "Asia's Space Tigers Bare Their Teeth." *Asia Times*, November 9, 2007.

Casey, Doug. "Central Banks Looking to Exit the Dollar." *Safehaven*, July 28, 2006. www.safehaven.com/showarticle.cfm?id=5616&pv=1 (accessed July 29, 2006).

Cassidy, Robert. "The Failed Expectations of U.S. Trade Policy." *Foreign Policy in Focus*, June 4, 2008. www.fpif.org/fpiftxt/5274 (accessed June 5, 2008).

Castle, Stephen. "China Emerges as Major Player in Global Trade Talks." *New York Times*, July 29, 2008.

Cattaneo, Claudia. "New Power Brokers Packing Lock, Stock, and $100 Barrels." *Financial Post* (Canada), January 4, 2008.

Cha, Adriana Eunjung. "As China's Losses Mount, Confidence Turns to Fear." *Washington Post*, November 4, 2008.

Cha, Ariana Eunjung. "Rising Grain Prices Panic Developing World." *Washington Post*, April 4, 2008.

Cha, Ariana Eunjung. "Telecom Firm in China Sets Sights on U.S. Market: Ownership, Tactics Raise Security Issues." *Washington Post*, January 6, 2008.

Chaker, Anne Marie. "The Vegetable Patch Takes Root." *Wall Street Journal*, June 5, 2008.

Chakrabortty, Aditya. "Secret Report: Biofuel Caused Food Crisis." *Guardian* (UK), July 4, 2008.

Champion, Marc. "Ahmadinejad Adviser Says Iran Could Supply Nuclear Fuel Bank." *Wall Street Journal*, January 27, 2008.

Champion, Marc, and Charles Forelle. "Europe in Turmoil after Irish Vote." *Wall Street Journal*, June 14, 2008.

Chao, Loretta. "China Food-Safety Chief Resigns in Dairy Scandal." *Wall Street Journal*, September 23, 2008.

Chapa, Jorge. "Paint on Solar Power!" *Inhabitat.com*, March 24, 2008. www.inhabi-tat.com/2008/03/24/solar-power-without-a-solar-panel/ (accessed March 26, 2008).

Chapman, David. "Looking Down the Road." *Safehaven*, June 25, 2006. www.safehaven.com/showarticle.cfm?id=5436&pv=1 (accessed June 26, 2006).

Chapman, James. "David Cameron: I'll Tear Up the EU Treaty Even If It Has Been Signed." *Daily Mail* (UK), December 30, 2007.

Charbonneau, Louis. "Inequality in Major U.S. Cities Rivals Africa: U.N." Reuters, October 23, 2008.

"Chavez: Pull Reserves from U.S." Associated Press, January 26, 2008.

"Chavez Threatens to Halt Oil Exports to Europe." *ABC News* (Australia), June 20, 2008.

"Chavez Threatens to Stop Shipping Oil to U.S." Associated Press, February 10, 2008.

"Chavez Wants Reserves Moved from US." *Press TV*, July 2, 2008.

Chazan, Guy. "Cold Comfort: Arctic Is Oil Hot Spot." *Wall Street Journal*, July 24, 2008.

Chazan, Guy, and Benoit Faucon. "War Threatens Key Pipeline for Crude Oil." *Wall Street Journal*, August 12, 2008.

Chazan, Guy, and Neil King Jr. "Russian Oil Slump Stirs Supply Jitters." *Wall Street Journal*, April 15, 2008.

Chen, Kathy. "Amid Tension with U.S., China Faces Protectionist Surge at Home." *Wall Street Journal*, March 31, 2006.

Chen, Shu-Ching Jean. "Consumers in China Deal with Inflation Their Own Way." *Forbes*, November 15, 2007.

Chen, Vivien lo, and Thomas Keene. "Economist Stiglitz Says Iraq War Costs May Reach $5 Trillion." *Bloomberg*, March 1, 2008.

"China Alone Increased Worldwide CO2 Pollution 2% Last Year." *Daily Green*, June 16, 2008.

"China Controlling More of U.S. Economy." Associated Press, December 21, 2007.

"China: Diversifying Its Markets." *Angry Bear*, April 24, 2007. http://angrybear.blogspot.com/2007/04/china-diversifying-its-markets.html (accessed February 17, 2008).

"China Holds Tons of U.S. Debt and They Have All the Vegetables." *Economic Disconnect*, May 29, 2008. http://economicdisconnect.blogspot.com/2008/05/china-holds-tons-of-us-debt-and-they.html (accessed May 30, 2008).

"China's Economic Muscle 'Shrinks.'" *BBC News*, December 17, 2007.

"China's Economy to Become World's Biggest in 2035: Study." *Agence France-Presse*, July 8, 2008.

"China's Forex Reserves Hit 1.8 Trillion Dollars: Report." *Agence France-Presse*, June 27, 2008.

"China Denouces Proposed US Arms Sales to Taiwan: State Media." *Agence France-Presse*, October 4, 2008.

"China May Cut Its Dollar Holdings—CICC." *China Daily*, September 12, 2008.

"China Surpasses U.S. as Top Carbon Polluter: Study." *Agence France-Presse*, April 16, 2008.

"China to Replace U.S. as No. 1 Japan Trading Partner." *Asia Times Online*, August 24, 2004. www.atimes.com/atimes/China/FH24Ad03.html (accessed August 24, 2004).

"China Warns of Countermeasures If U.S. Congress Passes Trade Bill." *Agence France-Presse*, June 12, 2007.

"China Warns U.S. May Set Off Arms Race." *China Daily*, May 6, 2007.

Chivers, C. J. "Russia Expands Support for Breakaway Regions in Georgia." *New York Times*, April 17, 2008.

"CIA: China's Military Could Get 'Adversarial.'" *World Tribune*, May 8, 2008.

Clendenning, Alan. "Brazil Oil Field May Hold 8B Barrels." Associated Press, November 8, 2007.

"Climate Change a New Factor in Global Tensions: EU." *Agence France-Presse*, March 7, 2008.

"Climate Skepticism: The Top 10." *BBC News*, November 12, 2007.

Clover, Charles. "Invasion's Idealogues: Ultra-Nationalists Join the Russian Mainstream." *Financial Times*, September 8, 2008.

Cohen, Ariel. "Domestic Factors Driving Russia's Foreign Policy." *Backgrounder*, November 19, 2007.

Cohen, Patricia. "Susan Jacoby: Bemoaning an America That Values Stupidity." *International Herald Tribune*, February 15, 2008.

Coker, Margaret. "U.N. Food Chief Warns on Buying Farms." *New York Times*, September 10, 2008.

Coleman, Nick. "Russia Abandons Key Cold War Arms Treaty." *Agence France-Presse*, November 16, 2007.

"Collapsing Cities." *EDRO*. N.d. http://edro.wordpress.com/collapsing-cities/ (accessed March 1, 2008).

Conason, Joe. "'Seven Countries in Five Years.'" *Salon*, October 12, 2007. www.salon.com/opinion/conason/2007/10/12/wesley_clark/print.html (accessed October 14, 2007).

"Conflicts by Region and Year 1946–2006." Uppsala Conflict Data Program, Uppsala University. N.d. www.pcr.uu.se/research/UCDP/graphs/reg_year46.pdf (accessed March 29, 2008).

Connor, Steve. "Exclusive: The Methane Time Bomb." *Independent* (UK), September 23, 2008.

Conway, Edmund. "Call to Relax Basel Banking Rules." *Telegraph* (UK), December 16, 2007.

Copeland, Larry. "Most State Workers in Utah Shifting to 4-Day Week." *USA Today*, June 30, 2008.

Cornwell, Rupert. "Whoever Wins the Presidency Will Most Likely Fail to Take on the Unholy Trinity of Arms Manufacturers, the Pentagon, and Congress." *Independent* (UK), February 10, 2008.

Cornwell, Susan. "Anti-Semitism on Rise Globally: State Department." Reuters, May 14, 2008.

Corsi, Jerome R. "Bush Pushes Controversial SPP agenda: Meeting with Mexican, Canadian Leaders at 4th Annual Summit." *WorldNetDaily*, April 22, 2008.

Corsi, Jerome R. "Iran Launches Its 1st Space Rocket." *WorldNetDaily*, February 4, 2008.

Corsi, Jerome R. "New Data: Maybe Oil Isn't from Dead Dinos; Saturn Moon Has More Hydrocarbons than All of Earth's Known Reserves." *WorldNetDaily*, February 15, 2008.

Corsi, Jerome R. "North American Union: The Dream 'Is Dead.'" *WorldNetDaily*, August 4, 2008.

Cosgrove, William J., and Frank R. Rijsberman. "World Water Vision." World Water Council, 2000. www.worldwatercouncil.org/index.php?id=961&L=0%22onfo (accessed January 7, 2008).

Coughlin, Con. "If Pakistan Goes Bust, the Taliban Will Rule the Roost There as Well." *Telegraph* (UK), October 10, 2008.

"Country Energy Profiles." Energy Information Administration. N.d. http://tonto. eia.doe.gov/country/index.cfm (accessed October 11, 2008).

Coy, Peter. "The Slump: It's a Guy Thing." *Business Week*, May 22, 2008.

"The Cracks Are Showing." *Economist*, June 26, 2008.

Crenson, Matt. "GAO Chief Warns Economic Disaster Looms." Associated Press, October 28, 2006.

Creswell, Julie, and Ben White. "Wall Street, R.I.P.: The End of an Era, Even at Goldman." *New York Times*, September 28, 2008.

Cribb, Julian. "Tackling the Global Food Challenge." *ScienceAlert*, September 4, 2008. www.sciencealert.com.au/opinions/20080309–17885.html (accessed September 4, 2008).

"Crime in the United States 2006." United States Department of Justice, Federal Bureau of Investigation, September 2007. www.fbi.gov/ucr/cius2006/ (accessed March 29, 2008).

Crook, Clive. "The End of the American Exception." *Atlantic*, March 5, 2008.

Cui, Carolyn, and James T. Areddy. "The World Melts for Gold." *Wall Street Journal*, January 19, 2008.

Cullotta, Karen Ann. "As Gas Prices Rise, Teenagers' Cruising Declines." *New York Times*, June 29, 2008.

Cummins, Chip, and Peter Lattman. "Mideast and China Return to Scene with Investments in Financial Firms." *Wall Street Journal*, October 17, 2008.

"Currency Unions." *Financial Times*, December 27, 2007.

"Current and Historical Sector Weightings of the S&P 500." *Bespoke Investment Group*, April 24, 2008.

Daily, Matt, and Alonso Soto. "Experts Ask Ecuador Court to Fine Chevron $7–$16 Bn." Reuters, April 2, 2008.

Dancy, Joseph. "Grain Markets Panic Buying, Export Controls, and Food Riots." *Market Oracle* (UK), May 18, 2008. www.marketoracle.co.uk/Article4743.html (accessed May 18, 2008).

Daniel, Frank Jack, and Arshad Mohammed. "US, Venezuela to Escalate Crisis." Reuters, September 12, 2008.

Das, Satyajit. "'We Interrupt Regular Programming to Announce That the United States of America Has Defaulted . . . ' Part 2." *Eurointelligence*, July 24, 2007. www.eurointelligence.com/article.581+M563d02ed27c.0.html (accessed July 24, 2008).

Davidson, Paul. "Coal Plant Test Capturing Carbon Dioxide." *USA Today*, February 26, 2008.

Davis, Bob. "Financial Troubles Humble U.S." *Wall Street Journal*, September 29, 2008.

Davis, Bob. "IMF Fuels Critics of Globalization." *Wall Street Journal*, October 16, 2007.

Davis, Bob. "Rise of Nationalism Frays Global Ties." *Wall Street Journal*, April 28, 2008.

Davis, Bob. "Wanted: SWFs' Money Sans Politics." *Wall Street Journal*, December 20, 2007.

De Aenlle, Conrad. "Gold, Again, Becomes a Shield against the Unknown." *New York Times*, September 23, 2007.

"Deaths Reported in Tibet Protests." *BBC News*, March 15, 2008.

"Debt Facts." Concord Coalition, March 12, 2008. www.fiscalwakeuptour.com/issues/feddebt/debt-facts.html (accessed October 12, 2008).

Debusmann, Bernd. "Fading Superpower, Rising Rivals: Bernd Debusmann." Reuters, August 27, 2008.

"The Decline in America's Reputation: Why?" Subcommittee on International Organizations, Human Rights and Oversight of the House Committee on Foreign Affairs, June 11, 2008.

De Córdoba, José, and Jay Solomon. "Chávez Aided Colombia Rebels, Captured Computer Files Show." *Wall Street Journal*, May 9, 2008.

"The Decoupling Debate." *Economist*, March 6, 2008.

DeMoura, Helena. "Four Bolivian Regions Declare Autonomy from Government." *CNN*, December 15, 2007.

Dempsey, Judy. "Despite Crisis, Germany Sees Russia as Land of Opportunity." *New York Times,* October 25, 2008.

Dempsey, Judy. "Report Calls for a Radical Overhaul of NATO." *International Herald Tribune*, January 31, 2008.

Dempsey, Judy. "Russia Signs Central Asian Pipeline Deal." *International Herald Tribune*, December 20, 2007.

Deutsch, Claudia H. "A Threat So Big, Academics Try Collaboration." *New York Times*, December 25, 2007.

Diamond, Jared. *Collapse: How Societies Choose to Fail or Succeed*. New York: Viking, 2004.

Diamond, Jared. "What's Your Consumption Factor?" *New York Times*, January 2, 2008.

Dickie, Mure. "Beijing Defends Sovereign Funds." *Financial Times*, January 7, 2008.

Dillon, Sam. "Survey Finds Teenagers Ignorant on Basic History and Literature Questions." *New York Times*, February 27, 2008.

Dimbleby, Jonathan. "Russia: A Totalitarian Regime in Thrall to a Tsar Who's Creating the New Fascist Empire." *Daily Mail* (UK), May 17, 2008.

Dittrick, Paula. "OTC: Nuclear, Tidal Energy to Supplement Fossil Fuels." *Oil & Gas Journal*, May 9, 2008. www.ogj.com/articles/article_display.cfm?ARTICLE_ID=328358&p=7 (accessed May 12, 2008)

"Dollar Losing Clout around the World." Associated Press, March 13, 2008.

Dombey, Daniel. "America Faces a Diplomatic Penalty as the Dollar Dwindles." *Financial Times*, December 27, 2007.

Dombey, Daniel, and Stanley Pignal. "Europeans See U.S. as Threat to Peace." *Financial Times*, July 1, 2007.

"Doubts Grow on Russia's WTO Plans." *BBC News*, August 26, 2008.

Dougherty, Carter, and Katrin Bennhold. "For Europe's Middle-Class, Stagnant Wages Stunt Lifestyle." *New York Times*, May 1, 2008.

Dowd, Maureen. "Red, White and Blue Tag Sale." *New York Times*, January 20, 2008.

Downie, Andrew. "Is Latin America Heading for an Arms Race?" *Christian Science Monitor*, January 16, 2008.

"Downward Mobility." *New York Times*, August 30, 2006.

Dreazen, Yochi J. "Military Networks Increasingly Are Under Attack." *Wall Street Journal*, March 12, 2008.

Dreazen, Yochi J. "Russia–U.S. Shift in Power Balance May Mold Summit." *Wall Street Journal*, July 10, 2006.

Dreazen, Yochi J. "U.S. Says New Find Shows Iran Still Sends Arms to Iraq." *Wall Street Journal*, April 25, 2008.

Dreazen, Yochi J., and Philip Shishkin. "Growing Concern: Terrorist Havens in 'Failed States.'" *Wall Street Journal*, September 13, 2006.

Drew, Jill. "China Reports Military Budget of $59 Billion: Sharp Buildup Raises Concern in U.S. over Intentions, 'Opacity.'" *Washington Post*, March 5, 2008.

Drohan, Madelaine. "The Great Doha Trade Divide." *Globe and Mail* (Canada), July 25, 2008.

"Drug Cartels to Mexican Police: 'Join Us or Die.'" Associated Press, May 18, 2008.

Duchene, Lisa. "Are Water Wars in Our Future?" *Gantdaily.com*, June 8, 2008. www.gantdaily.com/print.php?a=2207 (accessed June 8, 2008).

Dugger, Ceilia W. "Toilets Underused to Fight Disease, U.N. Study Finds." *New York Times*, November 10, 2006.

Dujisin, Zoltán. "Europe: Going Nuclear Despite Warnings." *Inter Press Service News Agency*, May 24, 2008.

Dyer, Geoff. "China to Tighten Capital Controls in Clampdown on 'Hot Money.'" *Financial Times*, July 3, 2008.

Dyer, Geoff, and Andrew Balls. "China Signals Reserves Switch Away from Dollar." *Financial Times*, January 5, 2006.

Dyer, Gwynne. "The Real Reason for Vast U.S. Defense Bill." *New Zealand Herald*, February 13, 2008.

Dyer, Gwynne. "U.S. Dollar: No Longer the World's Currency?" *Gwynnedyer.com*, November 30, 2007. http://gwynnedyer.com/articles/Gwynne%20Dyer%20article_%20%20US%20Dollar.txt (accessed November 30, 2007).

Dyson, Tom. "Your Last Chance at the Secret African Supermarket." *Financial Sense*, July 12, 2006. www.financialsense.com/editorials/sjuggerud/2006/0712.html (accessed July 15, 2006).

"'East Asia Must Prepare for Possible Dollar Collapse.'" *Hindu*, March 29, 2006.

Eberstadt, Nicholas. "China's One-Child Mistake." *Wall Street Journal*, September 17, 2007.

Eckholm, Erik. "America's 'Near Poor' Are Increasingly at Economic Risk, Experts Say." *New York Times*, May 8, 2006.

Edlund, Lena, Hongbin Li, Junjian Yi, and Junsen Zhang. "More Men, More Crime: Evidence from China's One-Child Policy." *IZA*, December 2007. http://ftp.iza.org/dp3214.pdf.

"Eight Possibilities Heading into '08." *Investor's Business Daily*, January 2, 2008.

Eizenstat, Stuart E., and Michael C. Maibach. "Protect Our Heritage." *Wall Street Journal*, March 30, 2006.

ElBoghdady, Dina, and Allan Lengel. "Held Back by the House: Sinking Home Prices, Slow Sales Can Complicate Workers' Relocation Plans." *Washington Post*, June 14, 2008.

Elder, Miriam. "Russia Threatens to Seize Swathe of Arctic." *Telegraph* (UK), September 17, 2008.

Elliott, Michael. "China Takes on the World." *Time*, January 11, 2007.

Ellsworth, Brian. "Chavez Says Food Prices 'Massacre' of World's Poor." Reuters, April 23, 2008.

Emshwiller, John R. "Federal Law Enforcement Helps to Tackle Expanding Gang Problem." *Wall Street Journal*, October 16, 2008.

"The End of Arrogance: America Loses Its Dominant Economic Role." *Spiegel Online*, September 30, 2008. www.spiegel.de/international/world/0,1518,581502,00 .html (accessed October 5, 2008).

"The End of Cheap Food." *Economist*, December 6, 2007.

"End of Cheap Labour Looms in China." Reuters, March 11, 2008.

"The End of Suburbia as We Know It?" *Bryant Park Project from NPR News*, June 19, 2008. www.npr.org/templates/story/story.php?storyId=91681112 (accessed June 20, 2008).

"End of US Era—Now China Calls the Tune." *Sydney Morning Herald*, October 13, 2008.

"Energy Conservation." *Wikipedia*, June 21, 2008. http://en.wikipedia.org/wiki/ Energy_conservation (accessed June 25, 2008).

"Energy Race between India and China." *AsiaNews*, March 31, 2008. www. asianews.it/index.php?1=en&art=11896&size=A (accessed March 31, 2008).

Engdahl, F. William. "Russia Georgia War—Washington Risks Nuclear War by Miscalculation." *Market Oracle*, August 11, 2008. www.marketoracle.co.uk/ Article5834.html (accessed August 12, 2008).

England, Andrew. "Saudis to Launch $5.3bn Sovereign Fund." *Financial Times*, April 28, 2008.

Enrich, David, Randall Smith, and Damian Paletta. "Citigroup, Merrill Seek More Foreign Capital: Moves, Foreshadowing Further Write-Downs, Raise Regulatory Issues." *Wall Street Journal*, January 10, 2008.

Epstein, Rafael. "UN Chief Warns of Civil Unrest amid World Food Shortage." *ABC News* (Australia), April 30, 2008.

Espo, David. "McCain Calls for Building 45 New Nuclear Reactors." Associated Press, June 18, 2008.

"Ethnic Violence Intensifies in India's Assam State." *Wall Street Journal*, October 6, 2008.

"EU Leaders Sign Landmark Treaty." *BBC News*, December 13, 2007.

Evans–Pritchard, Ambrose. "Asian Countries Begin to Burst the Oil Bubble." *Telegraph* (UK), May 30, 2008.

Evans–Pritchard, Ambrose. "Authorities Lose Patience with Collapsing Dollar." *Telegraph* (UK), April 18, 2008.

Evans–Pritchard, Ambrose. "BIS Warns of Great Depression Dangers from Credit Spree." *Telegraph* (UK), June 25, 2007.

Evans–Pritchard, Ambrose. "China Threatens 'Nuclear Option' of Dollar Sales." *Telegraph* (UK), August 10, 2007.

Evans–Pritchard, Ambrose. "EMU Is More Unworkable Than Ever." *Telegraph* (UK), May 8, 2008.

Evans–Pritchard, Ambrose. "Euro at Risk from Europe's Economic Storm." *Telegraph* (UK), January 1, 2008.

Evans–Pritchard, Ambrose. "Europe's Deep Rift Exposed over ECB's Interest Rate Policy." *Telegraph* (UK), June 11, 2008.

Evans–Pritchard, Ambrose. "Fatwa Against the Dollar?" *Telegraph* (UK), December 17, 2007.

Evans–Pritchard, Ambrose. "Fears of a Commodity Crash Grow." *Telegraph* (UK), March 5, 2008.

Evans–Pritchard, Ambrose. "Financial Crisis: Countries at Risk of Bankruptcy from Pakistan to Baltics." *Telegraph* (UK), October 10, 2008.

Evans–Pritchard, Ambrose. "Financial Crisis: Who Is Going to Bail Out the Euro." *Telegraph* (UK), October 8, 2008.

Evans–Pritchard, Ambrose. "Foreign Investors Veto Fed Rescue." *Telegraph* (UK), March 17, 2008.

Evans–Pritchard, Ambrose. "Global Free Market for Food and Energy Faces Biggest Threat in Decades." *Telegraph* (UK), May 10, 2008.

Evans–Pritchard, Ambrose. "Morgan Stanley Warns of 'Catastrophic Event' as ECB Fights Federal Reserve." *Telegraph* (UK), June 17, 2008.

Evans–Pritchard, Ambrose. "Russia May Cut Off Oil Flow to the West." *Telegraph* (UK), August 29, 2008.

Evans–Pritchard, Ambrose. "Water Crisis to Be Biggest World Risk." *Telegraph* (UK), June 5, 2008.

Evans–Pritchard, Ambrose. "Why Break-Up of Faltering Euro Could Be the Way Ahead." *Telegraph* (UK), September 18, 2006.

Evenett, Simon. "Trade Frictions with China: Do Western Policymakers Have an End Game?" *Vox*, December 17, 2007. www.voxeu.org/index.php?q=node/798 (accessed December 18, 2007).

"The Failed States Index 2007." *Foreign Policy*, July/August 2007.

Faiola, Anthony. "Dollar's Fall Is Felt around the Globe." *Washington Post*, December 24, 2007.

Faiola, Anthony. "The End of American Capitalism." *Washington Post*, October 10, 2008.

Fairclough, Gordon. "China-Product Scare Hits Home, Too." *Wall Street Journal*, July 20, 2007.

Fairclough, Gordon, and Loretta Chao. "Pentagon Feels Chill Set in with China as Beijing Reacts to U.S.-Taiwan Deal." *Wall Street Journal*, October 8, 2008.

Fallows, James. "The $1.4 Trillion Question." *Atlantic Monthly*, January/February 2008.

Fam, Mariam. "Food Prices Hit Subsidy Plans." *Wall Street Journal*, March 4, 2008.

Fan Jianqing. "Taking One's Own Road of Economic Development." *People's Daily Online*, February 18, 2008. http://english.peopledaily.com.cn/90001/6356066.html (accessed March 3, 2008).

Faries, Bill. "Bolivia Seizes Transredes Gas Pipeline from Sell, Ashmore." *Bloomberg*, June 2, 2008.

Farmani, Hiedeh. "Iran Warns on Nuclear Cooperation, Rattles Saber over Gulf." *Middle East Times*, September 17, 2008.

Farrar, Lara. "Is America's Suburban Dream Collapsing into a Nightmare?" *CNN*, June 16, 2008.

Faulconbridge, Guy. "Russia Says It Must Stake Claim to Arctic Resources." Reuters, September 12, 2008.

Faulconbridge, Guy. "Russia Signs Europe Arms Pact Suspension into Law." Reuters, November 30, 2007.

"FBI: Violent Crime Inches Higher in U.S." Associated Press, June 4, 2007.

"Fed-Up Families Turn to Barbed Wire, Shotguns to Police Neighborhood." *Local6.com*, July 1, 2008. www.local6.com/print/16756820/detail.html (accessed July 2, 2008).

Feffer, John. "Hidden Asia Pacific Arms Race: Six Countries Talk Peace While Preparing for War." *Japan Focus*, March 19, 2008. http://japanfocus.org/products/topdf/2704 (accessed April 3, 2008).

Felix, Robert. "U.S. Food Riots Much Closer Than You Think." *Rense.com*, October 23, 2007. www.rense.com/general78/riots.htm (accessed October 27, 2007).

Ferguson, Niall. "Empire Falls." *Vanity Fair*, October 2006.

Ferguson, Niall. "The Great Dying: A Memo to Market Dinosaurs." *Financial Times*, December 13, 2007.

Ferguson, Niall. "An Ottoman Warning for Indebted America." *Financial Times*, January 1, 2008.

Ferguson, Niall. "Trading on Commodities." *Wall Street Journal*, December 19, 2006.

Fialka, John. "Energy Independence: A Dry Hole?" *Wall Street Journal*, July 5, 2006.

Fields, Gary. "Murder Spike Poses Quandary." *Wall Street Journal*, May 6, 2008.

Findley, Paul. "The High Cost of Subservience to Israel." *Crimes and Corruption of the New World Order News*, June 8, 2007. http://mparent-2.blogspot.com/2007/06/high-cost-of-subservience-to-israel.html (accessed June 12, 2007).

Fireman, Ken. "Gates Says U.S., Russia 'Agree to Disagree' on Arms Sales." *Bloomberg*, October 13, 2007.

Fitzgerald, Alison, and Mark Drajem. "Free Trade in Food Is 'on the Ropes' amid Shortages, Price Rise." *Bloomberg*, June 19, 2008.

Flakus, Greg. "Mexico Wages Bloody War with Drug Cartels." *VOA News*, May 21, 2008.

Flandez, Raymund, and Kelly K. Spors. "Tackling the Energy Monster." *Wall Street Journal*, June 16, 2008.

Flint, Robert. "Asian Currencies Headed Up." *Barron's*, January 14, 2008.

"Food Prices on the Rise Worldwide." *CNN Money*, March 25, 2008.

"Food Safety Worries Change Buying Habits, Poll Finds." Associated Press, July 18, 2008.

"Food Shortages: Oil, Globalization, Mechanization." *Angry Bear*, July 9, 2008. http://angrybear.blogspot.com/2008/07/food-shortages-oil-globalization.html (accessed July 9, 2008).

Ford, Peter. "Behind Bad Baby Milk, an Ethical Gap in China's Business." *Christian Science Monitor*, September 17, 2008.

"Foreign Portfolio Holdings of U.S. Securities," Department of the Treasury, Federal Reserve Bank of New York, May 2007.

Forelle, Charles. "Irish Ire May Stall Treaty Overhauling How EU Works." *Wall Street Journal*, May 22, 2008.

"For Sale: West's Deadly Nuclear Secrets." *Sunday Times* (London), January 6, 2008.

"France's EU Presidency to Focus on Immigration." *Deutsche Presse-Agentur*, June 6, 2008.

Francis, David. "Dependence on Russian Gas Worries Some—but Not All—European Countries." *Christian Science Monitor*, March 6, 2008.

Freedman, Jennifer M. "U.S. May Face Penalty of $4 Billion over Cotton Trade." *Bloomberg*, June 2, 2008.

Freeland, Chrystia. "The New Age of Authoritarianism." *Financial Times*, August 11, 2008.

French, Howard W. "Wave of Mixed Signals as U.S. Ship Is Snubbed." *International Herald Tribune*, December 7, 2007.

Friedli, Douglas. "U.S. Woes Grow as Sudan Warns Bank to Stay Away from Weakening Dollar." *Scotsman* (UK), December 30, 2007.

Friedman, George. "The Medvedev Doctrine and American Strategy." *Stratfor*, September 2, 2008. www.stratfor.com/weekly/medvedev_doctrine_and_american_strategy (accessed September 5, 2008).

Friedman, George. "The Real World Order." *Stratfor*, August 18, 2008. http://www.stratfor.com/weekly/real_world_order (accessed August 19, 2008).

Friedman, George. "The Russo-Georgian War and the Balance of Power." *Stratfor*, August 12, 2008. www.stratfor.com/weekly/russo_georgian_war_and_balance_power (accessed August 13, 2008).

Friedman, George. "2008 and the Return of the Nation-State." Stratfor, Ovtober 27, 2008. www.stratfor.com/weekly/2008/027_2008_and_return_nation_state (accessed October 28, 2008).

Friedman, Thomas L. "Imbalances of Power." *New York Times*, May 21, 2008.

Friedman, Thomas L. "The New Cold War." *New York Times*, May 14, 2008.

Frolov, Vladimir. "The Coming Conflict in the Arctic: Russia and U.S. to Square Off over Arctic Energy Reserves." *Global Research*, July 17, 2007. www.globalresearch.ca/index.php?context=va&aid=6344 (accessed July 17, 2007).

"Frontline: The Storm." *Public Broadcasting Service*, November 24, 2005. www.pbs.org/wgbh/pages/frontline/storm/etc/script.html (accessed July 4, 2008).

Gaffen, David. "More Talk of Abandoning Dollar Pegs." *Market Beat*, March 12, 2008. http://blogs.wsj.com/marketbeat/2008/03/12/more-talk-of-abandoning-dollar-pegs/ (accessed March 12, 2008).

Gale, Jason. "Flu Pandemic May Cost World Economy Up to $3 Trillion." *Bloomberg*, October 17, 2008.

Gardner, Claire. "MTV Gen's 'Black Holes of History' Blamed on Hollywood." *Scotsman* (UK), December 11, 2003.

Garnham, Peter. "Russian Reserve Switch Boosts Yen." *Financial Times*, October 16, 2006.

"Gas Prices Encourage Telecommuting." Associated Press, June 6, 2008.

"Gates Warns of the Limits of US Military Power." *Agency France-Presse*, September 29, 2008.

Gaynor, Tim. "Illegal Immigrants 'Self Deport' as Woes Mount." Reuters, December 24, 2007.

"Georgia Pulls out of Air Defense Treaty with Russia." *RIA Novosti*, May 5, 2008.

Gerencher, Kristen. "Americans Down on the U.S. Health-Care System." *MarketWatch*, July 13, 2008.

Gertz, Bill. "Several Arrested in Chinese Spy Sweep." *Washington Times*, February 11, 2008.

"Getting to Know Islamic Banking." *International Political Economy Zone*, February 27, 2008. http://ipezone.blogspot.com/2008/02/getting-to-know-islamic-banking.html (accessed March 1, 2008).

Ghattas, Kim. "Poll Shows Arabs' Dislike for US." *BBC News*, April 15, 2008.

Ghosh, Pallab. "Climate Set for 'Sudden Shifts.'" *BBC News*, April 2, 2008.

Gibson, Eloise. "Homemade Power Banishes the Bills." *New Zealand Herald*, May 19, 2008.

Gilbert, Mark. "Italy Backslides to Pre-Euro Economic Malfeasance." *Bloomberg*, January 17, 2008.

Gilbert, Mark. "There's Nothing Sacrosanct about U.S. AAA Rating." *Bloomberg*, July 17, 2008.

Gioia, Dana. "The Impoverishment of American Culture." *Wall Street Journal*, July 19, 2007.

Girard, Keith. "On Energy, It's the Gulpers vs. the Sippers." *New York Times*, August 3, 2007.

"Give Up Now? Citi Sees 'Terminal Decline' for Banks' Modern Business Models." *FT Alphaville*, January 9, 2008. http://ftalphaville.ft.com/blog/2008/01/09/10032/give-up-now-citi-sees-terminal-decline-for-banks-modern-business-models/ (accessed January 9, 2008).

"Global Economy: GDP for 2004 and 2005 (Current US$)." *GeoHive*. www.xist.org/earth/ec_gdp1.aspx (accessed January 7, 2008).

"The Global Housing Boom: In Come the Waves." *Economist*, June 16, 2005.

"Globalization: Threat or Opportunity?" International Monetary Fund, April 12, 2000. www.imf.org/external/np/exr/ib/2000/041200to.htm (accessed May 4, 2008).

"Global Population at a Glance: 2002 and Beyond." U.S. Department of Commerce, U.S. Census Bureau, March 2004.

Gold, Russell, and Ann Davis. "Oil Officials See Limit Looming on Production." *Wall Street Journal*, November 19, 2007.

Gongloff, Mark. "Tumult Tests Allure of U.S. to Foreigners." *Wall Street Journal*, September 19, 2008.

Gongloff, Mark. "Will Bailout Spur Inflation? Hedge That Bet." *Wall Street Journal*, September 23, 2008.

Goode, Erica, and Riyadh Mohammed. "Iraq Signs Oil Deal with China Worth Up to $3 Billion." *New York Times*, August 29, 2008.

Goodman, Peter S. "The Dollar's Dominance Called into Question." *International Herald Tribune*, May 11, 2008.

Goodman, Peter S. "Fuel Prices Shift Math for Life in Far Suburbs." *New York Times*, June 25, 2008.

Goodman, Peter S. "Is America Too Big to Fail?" *International Herald Tribune*, July 20, 2008.

Goodman, Peter S., and Louise Story. "Overseas Investors Buy Aggressively in U.S." *New York Times*, January 20, 2008.

Goodspeed, Peter. "Russia Maneuvers into U.S. Backyard." *National Post* (Canada), September 17, 2008.

"Gorbachev Says British Leadership Panders to the United States." *RIA Novosti*, July 27, 2007.

Gordon, Michael P., and Eric Schmitt. "U.S. Says Exercise by Israel Seemed Directed at Iran." *International Herald Tribune*, June 20, 2008.

Gorman, Siobhan. "Georgia States Computers Hit by Counterattack." *Wall Street Journal*, August 12, 2008.

Gourlay, Chris, Jonathan Calvert, and Joe Lauria. "FBI Denies File Exposing Nuclear Secrets Theft." *Sunday Times* (London), January 20, 2008.

Graham, Stephen. "Official: Pakistan Should Reconsider Its Ties to US." Associated Press, June 12, 2008.

Gray, John. "Power, Corruption and Lies." *Observer* (UK), September 28, 2008.

"(Greed & Fear) Flirting with Armageddon." *FT Alphaville*, January 18, 2008. http://ftalphaville.ft.com/blog/2008/01/18/10287/greed-fear-flirting-with-armageddon/ (accessed January 18, 2008).

Green, Matthew, and Catherine Belton. "Gazprom Plans Africa Gas Grab." *Financial Times*, January 4, 2008.

"Greenland's Ice Cap Melting Faster than Expected: Experts." *Agence France-Presse*, September 22, 2008.

"Greenpeace Founder Now Backs Nuclear Power." *Idaho Statesman*, April 24, 2008.

Greenwald, Glenn. "The Bipartisan Consensus on U.S. Military Spending." *Salon*, January 2, 2008.

Greenwald, Glenn. "Rice: Military Power Is 'Not the Way to Deal in the 21st Century." *Salon*, August 19, 2008.

Grice, Andrew. "China the Victor as Europe Fails to Secure Trade Deal with Africa." *Independent* (UK), December 10, 2007.

Grimmett, Richard F. "Conventional Arms Transfers to Developing Nations, 1997–2004." Library of Congress, Congressional Research Service, August 29, 2005.

Gronquist, Kristina M. "The Myth of U.S. Cultural, Religious, Political, and Social Superiority." *Information Clearing House*, April 25, 2005. www.information-clearinghouse.info/article8657.htm (accessed April 9, 2008).

Gros, Daniel. "Watch the Price of Carbon!" *Vox*, December 21, 2007. www.voxeu.org/index.php?q=taxonomy/term/620 (accessed December 22, 2007).

Grusky, Sara. "The Corporate Takeover of Water in Ecuador." *AlterNet*, November 9, 2007. www.alternet.org/environment/67451/ (accessed November 12, 2007).

Guerrera, Francesco. "Americans Lose Faith in Citi and Merrill." *Financial Times*, January 22, 2008.

"Guess What Iran's Nuclear Plans Have Sparked?" *WorldNetDaily*, May 27, 2008.

Gutterman, Steve. "Putin Says Ties with Latin America a Top Priority." Associated Press, September 25, 2008.

Gutterman, Steve. "Russia, Venezuela Sign Oil and Gas Deals." Associated Press, September 26, 2008.

Guha, Krishna. "The World's Currency Could Be a U.S. Problem." *Financial Times*, November 9, 2007.

Gulyas, Carol. "Seven Ways to Save Energy by Saving Water." *CleanTechnica*, June 15, 2008. http://cleantechnica.com/2008/06/15/seven-ways-to-save-energy-by-saving-water/ (accessed June 16, 2008).

Gupte, Pranay. "Singapore's Quiet Giant." *Portfolio*, December 26, 2007.

Haass, Richard N. "The Age of Nonpolarity: What Will Follow U.S. Dominance." *Foreign Affairs*, May/June 2008.

Habel, Janette. "Latin America Breaks Free of the U.S." *Le Monde Diplomatique*, January 2008. http://mondediplo.com/2008/01/05latinamerica (accessed January 7, 2008).

Hacker, Jacob S. *The Great Risk Shift*. New York: Oxford University Press, 2006.

Hacker, Jacob S. "The Privatization of Risk and the Growing Economic Insecurity of Americans." *SSRC*, February 14, 2006. http://privatizationofrisk.ssrc.org/Hacker/pf/ (accessed September 10, 2006).

"Hackers Warn High Street Chains." *BBC News*, April 25, 2008.

Hafezi, Parisa. "Iran to 'Hit Tel Aviv, U.S. Ships' If Attacked." Reuters, July 8, 2008.

Hafezi, Parisa. "Iran, Venezuela in 'Axis of Unity' against U.S." Reuters, July 2, 2007.

Hagens, Nate. "Relocalization: A Strategic Response to Climate Change and Peak Oil." *Oil Drum*, June 6, 2007. www.theoildrum.com/node/2598 (accessed June 20, 2008).

Haider, Zeeshan. "Pakistan Troops Fire Turns Back U.S. Helicopters." Reuters, September 15, 2008.

Halliday, Fred. "The Mysteries of the American Empire." *ZNet*, December 9, 2007. www.zmag.org/content/print_article.cfm?itemID=14467&sectionID=72 (accessed December 29, 2007).

Halligan, Liam. "Bet Your Bottom Dollar Tensions Will Follow." *Telegraph* (UK), December 5, 2007.

Halligan, Liam. "Financial Crisis: Default by the US Government Is No Longer Unthinkable." *Telegraph* (UK), September 21, 2008.

Halpin, Tony. "Russia Approves Hike in Defense Spending." *Times* (London), September 19, 2008.

Halpin, Tony. "Russia Engages in 'Gangland' Diplomacy as It Sends Warships to the Caribbean." *Times* (London), September 23, 2008.

Halpin, Tony, and Alexi Mostrous. "Russia Ratchets Up Tensions with Arms Sales to Iran and Venezuela.'" *Times* (London), September 19, 2008.

Halpin, Tony. "Russia 'Will Match West in New Arms Race.'" *Times* (London), February 8, 2008.

Hamlin, Kevin. "China May Spend $58 Billion to Aid Growth, Gong Says." *Bloomberg*, August 19, 2008.

Harding, Luke. "Putin, the Kremlin Power Struggle and the $40bn. Fortune." *Guardian* (UK), December 21, 2007.

Harrabin, Roger. "Living in a World without Waste." *BBC News*, July 11, 2008.

Harris, Robert. "Pirates of the Mediterranean." *New York Times*, September 30, 2006.

Hattingh, Shawn. "Liberalizing Food Trade to Death." *Monthly Review*, June 2008.

Hayward, Tony. "Let the Markets Solve the Energy Crisis." *Financial Times*, June 11, 2008.

Hearn, Kelly. "For Peru's Indians, Lawsuit against Big Oil Reflects a New Era." *Washington Post*, January 31, 2008.

Hebert, Josef. "Wind Energy Expected to Grow Dramatically." *Agence France-Presse*, May 12, 2008.

Heffer, Simon. "The Union of England and Scotland Is Over." *Telegraph* (UK), November 14, 2007.

Heinberg, Richard. "Coal in the United States." *Oil Drum*, May 29, 2008. www.theoildrum.com/node/4061 (accessed May 29, 2008).

Heintz, Jim. "Russia: Poland Risks Attack Because of U.S. Missiles." Associated Press, August 15, 2008.

Hellasious. "About Decoupling." *Sudden Debt*, January 7, 2008. http://suddendebt.blogspot.com/2008/01/about-decoupling.html (accessed July 1, 2008).

Helman, Christopher. "Strange Behavior." *Forbes*, May 19, 2008.

Helprin, Mark. "The Challenge from China." *Wall Street Journal*, May 13, 2008.

Hendrickson, David C. "The Curious Case of American Hegemony: Imperial Aspirations and National Decline." *World Policy Journal*, July 1, 2005.

Herbert, Bob. "Here Come the Millennials." *Spiegel Online*, May 13, 2008. www.spiegel.de/international/0,1518,druck-552873,00.html (accessed May 13, 2008).

Herd, D., M. Ward, and B. Seeger. "Included by Design: A National Strategy for Accessible Housing for All." *Australian Network for Universal Housing Design*, November 2003.

Herman, Arthur. "Russia and the New Axis of Evil." *Wall Street Journal*, August 29, 2008.

Hersh, Seymour M. "A Strike in the Dark: What Did Israel Bomb in Syria?" *New Yorker*, February 11, 2008.

Herskovitz, Jon. "Famine Fears for North Korea." Reuters, April 30, 2008.

Hickley, Matthew. "The Uninvited Guest: Chinese Sub Pops Up in Middle of U.S. Navy Exercise, Leaving Military Chiefs Red-Faced." *Daily Mail* (UK), November 13, 2007.

Hider, James. "Dimitri Medvedev Raises Specter of New Cold War." *Times* (London), August 26, 2008.

Higgins, Alexander G. "Iran Rejects Nuclear Inspections Unless Israel Allows Them." Associated Press, May 5, 2008.

Higgins, Andrew. "In Europe, God Is (Not) Dead." *Wall Street Journal*, July 14, 2007.

Hiro, Dilip. "America on the Downward Slope." *TomDispatch.com*, August 20, 2007. www.tomdispatch.com/post/174830 (accessed August 3, 2008).

Hiro, Dilip. *Blood of the Earth: The Battle for the World's Vanishing Oil Resources*. New York: Nation Books, 2007.

Hiro, Dilip. "A Nuclear-Free Mirage." *Uruknet.info*, February 8, 2008. www.uruknet.de/?p=m40970&hd=&size=1&1=e (accessed February 9, 2008).

Hirschberg, Peter. "Netanyahu: It's 1938 and Iran Is Germany; Ahmadinejad Is Preparing Another Holocaust." *Haaretz Daily Newspaper* (Israel), November 14, 2006.

Hirsh, Michael. "Target: Iran?" *Newsweek*, May 8, 2008. www.newsweek.com/id/136065 (accessed May 16, 2008).

Hitt, Greg. "China Focus May Stall Bush's Trade Plans." *Wall Street Journal*, December 31, 2007.

Hitt, Greg. "Mood Shift Against Free Trade Puts Republicans on Defensive." *Wall Street Journal*, October 31, 2008.

"The Hobbled Hegemon." *Economist,* June 28, 2007.

Hodson, Peter. "Global Shortage of Metals Looming." *Financial Post* (Canada), February 25, 2008.

Hoguet, George. "Market Insight: Sovereign Funds Should Be Watched with Caution." *Financial Times,* December 12, 2007.

Holthouse, David, and Mark Potok. "The Year in Hate: Active U.S. Hate Groups Rise to 888 in 2007." Southern Poverty Law Center, Spring 2008.

"Home Page of Robert J. Shiller: Online Data." Yale Department of Economics. N.d. www.econ.yale.edu/~shiller/data.htm (accessed October 15, 2008).

Homer-Dixon, Thomas. *The Upside of Down: Catastrophe, Creativity, and the Renewal of Civilization.* Washington, DC: Island Press, 2006.

"Honda Rolls Out New Zero-Emission Car." Associated Press, June 16, 2008.

Hooker, Jane, and Walt Bogdanich. "China: Tainted Drugs Tied to Maker of Abortion Pill." *New York Times,* January 31, 2008.

Hosseinian, Zahra, and Fredrik Dahl. "Iran Tests Missiles, Vows to Hit Back If Attacked." Reuters, July 9, 2008.

Hosseinian, Zahra, and Parisa Hafezi. "Iran Sees Nuclear Power This Time Next Year." Reuters, January 30, 2008.

Hotter, Andrea, and Matt Whittaker. "Gold May Regain Luster for World's Central Banks." *Wall Street Journal,* September 28, 2008.

Hotz, Robert Lee. "Huge Dust Plumes from China Cause Changes in Climate." *Wall Street Journal,* July 20, 2007.

Howley, Victoria. "Chinese Companies Continue on U.K. Shopping Spree." *MarketWatch,* April 21, 2008.

"How the Spooks Took Over the News." *Independent* (UK), February 11, 2008.

"How to Deal with a Falling Population." *Economist,* July 26, 2007.

"Huawei, 3-Com: The Year the Rat Began to Swallow the Python." *Angry Bear,* January 6, 2008. http://angrybear.blogspot.com/2008/01/huawei-3-com-year-rat-began-to-swallow.html (accessed January 6, 2008).

Hughes, John. "Major Casting Changes Forthcoming for the World Stage." *Christian Science Monitor,* February 14, 2007.

Humber, Yuriy. "Putin Beats Soviet Sword into Atomic Weapon for Generator Sales." *Bloomberg,* March 14, 2008.

Humphries, Conor. "Russia Test-Fires New-Generation Strategic Missile." *Agence France-Presse,* September 18, 2008.

"Hunt Launched for 'Dirty Bomb' Ingredients." *WorldNetDaily,* January 31, 2008.

Hussain, Zahid. "Doubts on Pakistan Grow amid Disunity." *Wall Street Journal*, May 14, 2008.

Hutchinson, Martin. "The Bear's Lair: The New Cold War Era." *Prudent Bear*, August 18, 2008. www.prudentbear.com/index.php/bearlairarchivedisplay?art_id=10099 (accessed August 24, 2008).

Hutchinson, Martin. "Creating a Great Depression." *Prudent Bear*, September 26, 2008. www.prudentbear.com/index.php/bearlairarchivedisplay?art_id=10123 (accessed October 7, 2008).

Hutchinson, Martin. "The Enronization of America." *Prudent Bear*, April 2, 2007. www.prudentbear.com/articles/show/1951 (accessed April 3, 2007).

Hutchinson, Martin. "Eroding Western Living Standards." *Prudent Bear*, January 7, 2008. www.prudentbear.com/index.php?view=article&catid=33:BearLair&id=4902:eroding-western-living-standards&tmpl=component&print=1&page= (accessed July 1, 2008).

Hutchinson, Martin. "The Future Won't Resemble the Past." *Prudent Bear*, December 10, 2006. www.prudentbear.com/index.php/bearlairarchivedisplay?art_id=7964 (accessed December 11, 2006).

Hutchinson, Martin. "Is Japan's Past Our Future?" *Prudent Bear*, July 17, 2006. www.prudentbear.com/index.php/bearlairarchivedisplay?art_id=7930 (accessed July 18, 2006).

Hutchinson, Martin. "A New Model for Nastiness." *Prudent Bear*, June 23, 2008. www.prudentbear.com/index.php/archive_menu?art_id=5090 (accessed June 27, 2008).

Hutton, Will. "Power, Corruption and Lies." *Guardian* (UK), January 8, 2007.

"IAEA: Iran to Upgrade Missile for Nuke Use." *CBS News*, September 16, 2008.

"IAEA: Tehran Is Withholding Information on Nuclear Arms." Associated Press, May 26, 2008.

Ikenberry, G. John. "The Rise of China and the Future of the West." *Foreign Affairs*, January/February 2008.

"Illiberal Capitalism." *Financial Times*, January 17, 2008.

"Individual Privacy under Threat in Europe and U.S., Report Says." Associated Press, December 20, 2007.

Institute for the Study of Labor. "More Men, More Crime: Evidence from China's One-Child Policy." *Docuticker*, December 26, 2007. www.docuticker.com/?p=18535 (accessed December 26, 2007).

"International Energy Agency Says 2050 Baseline Scenario Is for Oil Demand to Rise 70%—Equivalent to Five Times Today's Production of Saudi Arabia." *Finfacts*, June 6, 2008. www.finfacts.ie/irishfinancenews/International_4/article_1013826_printer.shtml (accessed June 6, 2008).

International Energy Outlook 2007; Chapter 5, "Coal." Energy Information Administration, May 2007. www.eia.doe.gov/oiaf/ieo/coal.html (accessed March 17, 2008).

"International Trade/Global Economy." *Polling Report*. www.pollingreport.com/trade.htm (accessed January 1, 2008).

"The Invasion of the Sovereign-Wealth Funds." *Economist*, January 17, 2008.

"Iran Declaring 'Economic Warfare.'" *WorldNetDaily*, November 16, 2006.

"Iran Dumps U.S. Dollar for Oil Trades." Associated Press, April 30, 2008.

"Iran in Talks with China to Store Strategic Reserves." *Gulf News*, June 11, 2007.

"Iran Not Seeking to Build Nuclear Weapons: Putin." *Agence France-Presse*, May 31, 2008.

"Iran Oil Bourse May Use Russian Ruble." *Press TV*, February 15, 2008.

"Iran Plans to Launch Two More Rockets into Space." *Agence France-Presse*, February 11, 2007.

"Iran, India to Sign Oil Deals." *Persian Journal*, March 20, 2008.

"Iran, Russia's Gazprom Sign Energy Cooperation Deal." *Agence France-Presse*, July 13, 2008.

"Iran Says Its Space Probe Sending Data to Earth." *Agence France-Presse*, February 17, 2008.

"Iran Says It Tests Advanced Centrifuges." Associated Press, April 8, 2008.

"Iran Starts Installing New Nuclear Centrifuges." *Agence France-Presse*, April 8, 2008.

"Iran to Seek Bids for 19 Atomic Power Plants: MP." Reuters, December 24, 2007.

"Iran Vows Not to Halt Its Nuclear Program Despite Pressure." Associated Press, May 4, 2008.

"Iran Withdraws $75 Billion from Europe: Report." Reuters, June 16, 2008.

Ironside, Kirsty. "Blame Both Sides in Russia-EU Energy Spat." *BusinessWeek*, November 9, 2007.

Irvine, Martha. "Wired-Weary Youth Seek Face Time." Associated Press, October 6, 2006.

Isachenkov, Vladimir. "China, Russia Condemn U.S. Missile Defense Plans." Associated Press, May 23, 2008.

"Is Mother Russia Nearing WTO Accession?" *International Political Economy Zone*, March 27, 2008. http://ipezone.blogspot.com/2008/03/is-mother-russia-nearing-wto-accession.html (accessed March 27, 2008).

"Israel Reaches Strategic Decision Not to Let Iran Go Nuclear." *Jerusalem Post*, August 29, 2008.

"Israeli Minister Says Alternatives to Attack on Iran Running Out." *Agence France-Presse*, June 6, 2008.

"Is the Party Over in China? Massive Unemployment Looms." *World Tribune*, February 15, 2008.

"Italy and Britain Eye Nuclear Power Potential." Reuters, July 13, 2008.

"It's All about Petrol." *Al-Ahram Weekly*, November 30, 2007.

"It's WWlll, and U.S. Is Out of Ideas." *New York Daily News*, July 9, 2006.

Jacobs, Karen. "New Focus on Customer Service as Economy Slows." Reuters, June 20, 2008.

Jacoby, Jeff. "The Coming Population Bust." *Boston Globe*, June 18, 2008.

Jacoby, Susan. "The Dumbing of America." *Washington Post*, February 17, 2008.

Jacques, Martin. "The Death of Doha Signals the Demise of Globalization." *Guardian* (UK), July 13, 2006.

Jahn, George. "Developing World's Role in Nuclear Renaissance Raises Safety Concerns." Associated Press, January 13, 2008.

Jahn, George. "Iran Says Any Attack Would Provoke Fierce Reaction." Associated Press, July 2, 2008.

James, Frank. "The 'Budget and Leadership Deficits.'" *Chicago Tribune*, August 21, 2006.

James, Harold. "The Euro's Success Could Also Be Its Downfall." *Financial Times*, May 18, 2008.

James, Ian. "Chavez Warns of War with Colombia." Associated Press, March 2, 2008.

Janardhan, Meena. "U.S. Could Trigger Deadly Middle East Arms Race." *AlterNet*, August 9, 2007. www.alternet.org/module/printversion/59218 (accessed April 3, 2008).

"Japan Accuses Russia in Airspace Row." *ABC News* (Australia), February 9, 2008.

"Japan Will Allow Military Use of Space." *Houston Chronicle*, May 24, 2008.

Jaques, Robert. "Boffins Turn Exhaust Fumes into Power." *VNUNet.com*, June 4, 2008. www.vnunet.com/vnunet/news/2218246/boffins-turn-exhaust-fumes (accessed June 7, 2008).

Jensen, Kristin, and Heidi Przybyla. "U.S. Race Begins in Search for 'Wise Policy' on Terror, Economy." *Bloomberg*, January 3, 2008.

Johnson, Chalmers. "How to Sink America." *TomDispatch.com*, January 22, 2008. www.tomdispatch.com/post/174884/chalmers_johnson_how_to_sink_america (accessed January 22, 2008).

Johnson, Chalmers. "A National Intelligence Estimate on the United States." *Information Clearing House*, January 17, 2007. www.informationclearinghouse.info/article16260.htm (accessed December 5, 2007).

Johnson, Chalmers. *Nemesis: The Last Days of the American Republic*. New York: Metropolitan Books, 2006.

Johnson, Keith. "Peak Oil: IEA Inches Toward Pessimists' Camp." *Wall Street Journal*; Environmental Capital, July 1, 2008. http://blogs.wsj.com/environmentalcapital/2008/07/01/peak-oil-iea-inches-toward-the-pessimists-camp/ (accessed July 2, 2008).

Johnson, Kevin. "FBI: Murder Drops 6.5% in Big Cities." *USA Today*, March 29, 2008.

Johnson, Steve. "Dollar Faces Punishment for U.S.'s Economic Imbalances." *Financial Times*, April 10, 2006.

"Join Nato and We'll Target Missiles at Kiev, Putin Warns Ukraine." *Guardian* (UK), February 12, 2008.

Jordan, Miriam. "Fewer Latino Migrants Send Money Home, Poll Says." *Wall Street Journal*, May 1, 2008.

Jordan, Miriam. "Now Boarding: Illegal Immigrants On One-Way Tickets Home." *Wall Street Journal*, October 17, 2008.

Jordan, Miriam, and Conor Dougherty. "Immigration Slows in Face of Economic Downturn." *Wall Street Journal*, September 23, 2008.

Jordan, Miriam. "In Immigrant Fight, Grass-Roots Groups Boost Their Clout." *Wall Street Journal*, September 28, 2006.

Jordan, Pav. "Bolivia's Richest Region Votes 'Yes' on Autonomy." Reuters, May 5, 2008.

Joshi, Jitendra. "'Benign Neglect' from U.S. as Dollar Dives." Associated Press, December 3, 2006.

Jung, Alexander, and Wieland Wagner. "Vietnam Is the New China: Globalization's Victors Hunt for the Next Low-Wage Country." *Spiegel Online*, May 14, 2008. www.spiegel.de/international/business/0,1518,druck-553301,00.html (accessed May 19, 2008).

"Just 47% Oppose Nationalizing Oil Industry." *Rasmussen Reports*, June 16, 2008. www.rasmussenreports.com/public_content/business/general_business/just_47_oppose_nationalizing_oil_industry (accessed June 17, 2008).

Kagan, Robert. "League of Dictators?" *Washington Post*, April 30, 2007.

Kagan, Robert. "Power Play." *Wall Street Journal*, August 30, 2008.

Kahn, Joseph. "China Courts Africa, Angling for Strategic Gains." *New York Times*, November 3, 2006.

Kahn, Joseph. "China Shows Assertiveness in Weapons Test." *New York Times*, January 20, 2007.

Kahn, Joseph, and Mark Landler. "China: China Grabs West's Smoke-Spewing Factories." *CorpWatch*, December 21, 2007. www.corpwatch.org/article.php?id=14862&printsafe=1 (accessed December 22, 2007).

Kanter, James. "Sweden Turning Sewage into a Gasoline Substitute." *International Herald Tribune*, May 27, 2008.

Karajan, Jason. "Dash for Cash." *CFO Europe*, July 8, 2008.

Karlin, Mark. "Is the American Empire on the Brink of Collapse?" *AlterNet*, March 24, 2007. www.alternet.org/module/printversion/49603 (accessed March 24, 2007).

Karoly, Lynn A., and Constantjin W.A. Panis. "The 21st Century at Work." Rand Corporation, 2004.

Kaufan, Jonathan, and Carol Hymowitz. "At the Barricades in the Gender Wars." *Wall Street Journal*, March 29, 2008.

Kaufman, Marc. "U.S. Finds It's Getting Crowded Out There." *Washington Post*, July 9, 2008.

Kaylan, Melik. "Welcome Back to the Great Game." *Wall Street Journal*, August 13, 2008.

Kedrosky, Paul. "Emerging Markets' Oil Appetite Exceeds U.S." *Infectious Greed*, April 22, 2008. http://paul.kedrosky.com/archives/2008/04/22/emerging_countr.html (accessed April 22, 2008).

Kedrosky, Paul. "Water, Oil and the Life and Death of Cities." *Infectious Greed*, July 2, 2008. http://paul.kedrosky.com/archives/2008/07/02/water_oil_and_t.html (accessed July 2, 2008).

Keeley, Graham. "After the Boomers, Meet the Children Dubbed 'Baby Losers.'" *Observer* (UK), May 11, 2008.

Keeling, Drew. "Why Legal Barriers Are Not Critical to Deterring Immigrants." *Vox*, May 12, 2008. www.voxeu.org/index.php?q=node/1129 (accessed May 13, 2008).

Kelleher, Elizabeth. "Trade Spurs Economic Growth among Poorest Countries." America.gov, January 10, 2008. www.america.gov/st/econ-english/2008/January/20080110172903berehellek0.8494684.html (accessed May 4, 2008).

Kempe, Frederick. "Thinking Global: Why Economists Worry about Who Holds Foreign Currency Reserves." *Wall Street Journal*, May 9, 2006.

Kennedy, Paul. *The Rise and Fall of the Great Powers*. New York: Random House, 1987.

Kerr, Simeon. "Doha Considers Dropping Dollar Peg." *Financial Times*, January 30, 2008.

Khalaf, Rhoula. "UAE Set to Launch Nuclear Programme." *Financial Times*, January 20, 2008.

Khalid, Matein. "The Coming Gas Supply Shock in the Gulf." *Khaleej Times* (United Arab Emirates), July 24, 2008.

Khalilzad, Zalmay. "Iran's Nuclear Threat." *Wall Street Journal*, March 4, 2008.

Khanna, Parag. *The Second World: Empires and Influence in the New Global Order.* New York: Random House, 2008.

Khanna, Parag. "These Are the New Middle Ages, Not a New Order." *Guardian* (UK), September 12, 2008.

Khanna, Parag. "Waving Goodbye to Hegemony." *New York Times*, January 27, 2008.

Khripunov, Igor. "Would-Be Nuclear Nations a Risk: Global Community Needs to Train, Follow Up on Countries That Are Novices in Generating Power from Atomic Fission." *Atlanta Journal Constitution*, March 31, 2008.

Kilbinger, Sara Seddon. "Investors, Seeking Roads to Riches, Turn to Infrastructure." *Wall Street Journal*, May 3, 2006.

Kim, Lucian, and Henry Meyer. "Putin Sees 'New Balance of Power' in World Economy." *Bloomberg*, June 10, 2007.

Kim, Kwang-Tae. "N Korea Vows to Boost 'War Deterrent.'" Associated Press, August 20, 2008.

Kinetz, Erika. "The Unexpected Winners in the Oil and Food Crunch." *Newsweek*, May 17, 2008.

King, Neil, Jr. "Anti-Americanism Is a Big Hit at U.N." *Wall Street Journal*, September 21, 2006.

King, Neil, Jr. "Global Oil-Supply Worries Fuel Debate in Saudi Arabia." *Wall Street Journal*, June 27, 2008.

King, Neil, Jr. "Senate Advances Foreign-Investment Legislation." *Wall Street Journal*, March 31, 2006.

King, Neil, Jr. "Stalled U.S.-India Talks Imperil Business Opening." *Wall Street Journal*, July 20, 2007.

King, Neil, Jr. "White House Sets Long View on Oil." *Wall Street Journal*, March 20, 2008.

King, Neil, Jr., and Peter Fritsch. "Energy Watchdog Warns of Oil-Production Crunch." *Wall Street Journal*, May 22, 2008.

Kissel, Mary. "Delhi Drama." *Wall Street Journal*, September 4, 2007.

"Kissinger Warns of Possible 'War of Civilizations.'" *Agence France-Presse*, September 13, 2006.

Klare, Michael T. *Blood and Oil: The Dangers and Consequences of America's Growing Dependence on Imported Petroleum.* New York: Metropolitan Books, 2004.

Klare, Michael T. "An Oil-Addicted Ex-Superpower." *Asia Times Online*, May 10, 2008. www.atimes.com/atimes/Global_Economy/JE10Dj05.html (accessed May 11, 2008).

Klare, Michael T. "The Post-Abundance Era." *Foreign Policy in Focus*, November 30, 2006. www.fpif.org/fpiftxt/3744. *Asia Times Online*, December 7, 2006. www

.atimes.com/atimes/global_economy/hl07dj03.html (accessed December 11, 2006).

Klein, Aaron. "Syria 'Intensely' Arming Itself." *WorldNetDaily*, March 9, 2008.

Klein, Naomi. "China's All-Seeing Eye." *Rolling Stone*, May 29, 2008.

Kleinman, Mark. "Qataris Poised to Snap Up $3bn Stake in Credit Suisse." *Telegraph* (UK), January 1, 2008.

Kopecki, Dawn. "Fannie Mae, Freddie Mac Fall as Paulson Takes Control." *Bloomberg*, September 8, 2008.

Kosich, Dorothy. "China Still Only World's No. 2 Gold Producer—But Aiming for the Top Spot." *Mineweb*, January 30, 2008. www.mineweb.com/mineweb/view/mineweb/en/page34?oid=45514$sn=Detail (accessed February 2, 2008).

"Kosovo Independence: 'End of Europe.'" *RIA Novosti*, February 16, 2008.

Kotlikoff, Laurence J. "Is the United States Bankrupt?" Federal Reserve Bank of St. Louis *Review*, July/August 2006.

Kramer, Andrew E. "Putin Wants New Economic 'Architecture.'" *International Herald Tribune*, June 10, 2007.

Kramer, Andrew E. "Russia: As Gazprom Goes, So Goes Russia." *New York Times*, May 11, 2008.

Kramer, Andrew E. "Russia Creates a $32 Billion Sovereign Wealth Fund." *New York Times*, February 1, 2008.

Kramer, Andrew E. "Russia Quietly Prepares to Switch Some Oil Trading from Dollars to Rubles." *International Herald Tribune*, February 25, 2008.

Krauss, Clifford. "Oil Demand Will Grow, Despite Prices, Report Says." *New York Times*, July 2, 2008.

Krauss, Clifford. "Oil-Rich Nations Use More Energy, Cutting Exports." *New York Times*, December 9, 2007.

Krauss, Melvyn. "Myth of U.S.-EU Economic Decoupling." *Japan Times*, November 21, 2007.

Krebs, Brian. "Washington Prepares for Cyber War Games." *Washington Post*, March 7, 2008.

Krugman, Paul. "Dealing with the Dragon." *New York Times*, January 4, 2008.

Krugman, Paul. "Grains Gone Wild." *New York Times*, April 7, 2008.

Krugman, Paul. "The Great Illusion." *New York Times*, August 15, 2008.

Krugman, Paul. "Katrina All the Time." *New York Times*, August 31, 2007.

Krugman, Paul. "The Oil Nonbubble." *New York Times*, May 12, 2008.

Krugman, Paul. "Trouble with Trade." *New York Times*, December 28, 2007.

Kudrin, Alexei. "Era of Empires Is Over for Global Bodies." *Financial Times*, September 30, 2007.

Kunstler, James Howard. *The Long Emergency: Surviving the Converging Catastrophes of the Twenty-First Century.* New York: Atlantic Monthly Press, 2005.

Kunstler, Jim. "The Agenda Restated." *Clusterfuck Nation by Jim Kunstler,* February 5, 2007. http://jameshowardkunstler.typepad.com/clusterfuck_nation/2007/02/the_agenda_rest.html (accessed February 19, 2007).

Kupchinsky, Roman. "Russia: Gas Export Plans Dependent on Central Asia." *Radio Free Europe/Radio Liberty,* March 28, 2006.

Kurlantzick, Joshua. "Charm Offensive: How China's Soft Power Is Transforming the World." Foreign Policy Research Institute, August 2007.

"Kuwait's KIA Looking at Asia Investment—Finmin." Reuters, July 17, 2008.

"Kyoto Will Be the Death of Them." *Angry Economist,* December 12, 2007. http://angry-economist.russnelson.com/kyoto.html (accessed December 14, 2007).

Ladd, Chris. "Algae Startups Confront Promise of Miracle Fuel with Big Summer." *Popular Mechanics,* May 29, 2008.

LaFranchi, Howard. "Iran's Pursuit of Nuclear Power Raises Alarms." *Christian Science Monitor,* February 27, 2007.

LaGesse, David. "Small Moves You Can Take at Home to Conserve: These Gadgets Save Power without Breaking the Bank." *U.S. News & World Report,* April 17, 2008.

Lague, David. "Russia and China Rethink Arms Deals." *International Herald Tribune,* March 2, 2008.

Lahart, Justin. "Businesses Scramble to Offset Rising Cost of Transportation." *Wall Street Journal,* June 30, 2008.

Lahart, Justin. "Fresh Capital Gives Economy a New Look." *Wall Street Journal,* December 27, 2007.

Lahart, Justin. "Maybe the Globe Isn't Immune to Slowing U.S.: Doubts Spread on View That Europe and Asia Will Pick Up the Slack." *Wall Street Journal,* November 28, 2007.

Lahart, Justin, Patrick Barta, and Andrew Batson. "New Limits to Growth Revive Malthusian Fears." *Wall Street Journal,* March 24, 2008.

Laing, Jonathan R. "What Could Go Wrong with China?" *Barron's,* July 31, 2006.

Laitner, Sarah, Ben Hall, and Jan Cienski. "Sarkozy Calls for EU Immigrant Crackdown." *Financial Times,* May 29, 2008.

Lancaster, Carol. "The Chinese Aid System." *Center for Global Development,* June 2007.

Landay, Jonathan S., and John Walcott. "Pentagon Institute Calls Iraq War 'a Major Debacle' with Outcome in Doubt." *McClatchy Washington Bureau,* April 17, 2008. www.mcclatchydc.com/100/story/34101.html (accessed April 18, 2008).

Landler, Mark. "Housing Woes in U.S. Spread Around Globe." *New York Times,* April 14, 2008.

Larsen, Peter Thai. "Payback Time." *Financial Times*, January 6, 2008.

"Latin Leftists Line Up Behind Politically Troubled Bolivia." *Agence France-Presse*, April 23, 2008.

Lauria, Joe. "The Coming War with Iran: It's About the Oil, Stupid." *Huffington Post*, April 14, 2008. www.huffingtonpost.com/joe-lauria/the-coming-war-with-iran_b_96428.html (accessed April 14, 2008).

Lavelle, Marianne. "Energy Costs Around Your House: Heating Is Still No. 1, but New Devices Add Electric Bills." *U.S. News & World Report*, April 17, 2008.

Lavelle, Marianne. "Putting Your Home on an Energy Diet." *U.S. News & World Report*, April 17, 2008.

Lavelle, Marianne. "Three Ways Businesses Can Save on Power." *U.S. News & World Report*, April 17, 2008.

Layton, Lyndsey. "Chemical Law Has Global Impact." *Washington Post*, June 12, 2008.

Ledeen, Michael. "Bush Paves Way for Martial Law." *NewsMax*, March 25, 2007.

Lee, Don. "China's Economic Boom Is Creating Growing Pains." *Los Angeles Times*, January 3, 2008.

Lee, Wee Sui. "Andy Xie Warns of China Crash." Reuters, April 30, 2007.

Lefèvre, Edwin. *Reminiscences of a Stock Operator*. Orig. pub. 1923; New York: John Wiley & Sons, 1994.

Leggett, Karby, Jay Solomon, and Neil King Jr. "Threat of Wider Mideast War Grows." *Wall Street Journal*, July 14, 2006.

Lendman, Stephen. "The War on Working Americans." Rense.com, August 29, 2007. http://rense.com/general78/neh.htm (accessed August 31, 2007).

Leonhardt, David. "A Diploma's Worth? Ask Her." *New York Times*, May 21, 2008.

Leow, Claire. "Indonesia Confirms Death of Boy from Bird Flu, 88th Fatality." *Bloomberg*, October 13, 2007.

Leppard, David. "U.S. Says It Has Right to Kidnap British Citizens." *Sunday Times* (London), December 2, 2007.

Leslie, Jacques. "China's Pollution Nightmare Is Now Everyone's Pollution Nightmare." *Christian Science Monitor*, March 19, 2008.

Lever, Rob. "China's Economy 40 Percent Smaller Than Estimated: Analyst." *Agence France-Presse*, November 15, 2007.

Lewis, Leo. "Japanese Treasure Hunters Race to Exploit Seabed Rocks for High-Tech Industries." *Times* (London), December 29, 2007.

Lim, Benjamin Kang. "Eye on Taiwan, Shanghai Plans Major Air Raid Drill." *Guardian* (UK), September 12, 2007.

Linn, Allison. "Business Trying to See into Future." *MSNBC*, June 8, 2007.

Liptak, Adam. "Unlike Others, U.S. Defends Freedom to Offend in Speech." *New York Times*, June 12, 2008.

"List of States with Nuclear Weapons." *Wikipedia*, March 19, 2008. http://en.wikipedia.org/wiki/List_of_states_with_nuclear_weapons (accessed March 20, 2008).

Liu, Henry C.K. "The Coming Trade War and Global Depression." *Henry C.K. Liu: Independent Critical Analysis and Commentary*, June 18, 2005. http://henryckl.ipower.com/page5.html (accessed January 8, 2008).

Liu, Henry C.K. "Friedman's Misplaced Monument." *Asia Times*, September 5, 2008.

"Living Dangerously." *Economist*, January 22, 2004.

"Living Simply Provides Economic Shelter." Associated Press, August 9, 2008.

Li Yanping. "China to Cap Energy, Utility Prices to Cool Inflation." *Bloomberg*, January 9, 2008.

Lloyd, Carol. "Is Suburbia Turning into Slumburbia?" *San Francisco Chronicle*, March 14, 2008.

Lobe, Jim. "*Foreign Policy* Increasingly Flows Through Pentagon." Antiwar.com, March 7, 2008. www.antiwar.com/lobe/?articleid=12478 (accessed August 3, 2008).

"Local or Global." *Angry Bear*, May 1, 2008. http://angrybear.blogspot.com/2008/05/local-or-global.html (accessed May 2, 2008).

Lohr, Steve. "Energy Use Can Be Cut by Efficiency, Survey Says." *New York Times*, November 29, 2006.

Lohr, Steve. "U.S. Has History of Intervention." *International Herald Tribune*, October 13, 2008.

"Looking at America." *New York Times*, December 31, 2007.

Lopez, Octavio Rivera. "More Mexicans Leaving U.S. under Duress." *Dallas Morning News*, July 5, 2008.

"Losing the American Dream." *Phoenix.com*, July 19, 2007. http://bostonphoenix.com/boston/news_features/documents/01701323.htm (accessed July 19, 2007).

Lovasz, Agnes, and Stanley White. "Dollar Slumps to Record on China's Plans to Diversify Reserves." *Bloomberg*, November 7, 2007.

Love, Brian. "'Old World' Economics Run into Triple Trouble—OECD." Reuters, June 4, 2008.

Lowe, Christian. "NATO Risks Georgia Rebels' Secession: Russia." Reuters, March 11, 2008.

Lubold, Gordon. "Record U.S. Defense Spending, but Future Budgets May Decline." *Christian Science Monitor*, February 6, 2008.

Lucas, Ryan. "Russia Criticizes U.S. 'Imperial Thinking.'" Associated Press, February 7, 2008.

Luce, Edward, and Krishna Guha. "Summers and Rubin to Highlight Lagging Wages." *Financial Times*, July 25, 2006.

Luhby, Tami. "Fed in AIG Rescue—$85B Loan." CNNMoney.com, September 17, 2008.

Luhnow, David. "How Brazil Broke Its Oil Habit: Government's Central Role May Prove Unpalatable to U.S." *Wall Street Journal*, February 6, 2006.

Luhnow, David. "Mexico Tries to Save Big, Fading Oil Field." *Dow Jones Newswire*, April 5, 2007.

"Lula: United South America to Shake Global Balance of Power." *Earth Times*, May 23, 2008. www.earthtimes.org/articles/show/207594,lula-united-%20south-america-to-shake-global-balance-of-power.html (accessed May 24, 2008).

Lutz, Catherine. "Bases, Empire, and Global Response." *Fellowship of Reconciliation*, Winter 2007.

Lynch, David J. "Law Enforcement Struggles to Combat Chinese Spying." *USA Today*, July 22, 2007.

Lynch, David J. "Some Would Like to Build a Wall around U.S. Economy." *USA Today*, March 15, 2006.

Lyons, John. "Bolivia's Morales Restarts Overhaul." *Wall Street Journal*, August 12, 2008.

Lyons, John. "Colombia Says FARC Sought to Make 'Dirty Bomb.'" *Wall Street Journal*, March 5, 2008.

MacDonald, Alistair. "Scottish Party's Stronger Hand Further Tests Brown." *Wall Street Journal*, August 13, 2008.

MacDonald, Fiona, and Matthew Brown. "Gulf States May End Dollar Pegs, Kuwait Minister Says." *Bloomberg*, May 1, 2008.

"Major Sovereign Wealth Funds in Asia and the Gulf." *Times* (London), December 27, 2007.

Malone, Andrew. "How China's Taking Over Africa, and Why the West Should Be VERY Worried." *Daily Mail* (UK), July 18, 2008.

Mandel, Michael. "Multinationals: Are They Good for America?" *BusinessWeek*, February 28, 2008.

"Manufacturers Need Educated and Skilled Workforce to Compete in Global Economy." *Industry Week*, April 24, 2008.

"Mapping the Global Future: Report of the National Intelligence Council's 2020 Project." National Intelligence Council, December 2004. www.dni.gov/nic/NIC_2020_project.html (accessed November 17, 2007).

Maranjian, Selena. "Are Your Ready for Disaster?" *Motley Fool*, March 29, 2006.

Margolis, Eric. "Another 'Red Scare.'" *Crimes and Corruption of the New World Order News*, March 9, 2008. http://7777–2.blogspot.com/2008/03/another-red-scare.html (accessed October 3, 2008).

Marsh, Peter. "China to Overtake U.S. as Largest Manufacturer." *Financial Times*, August 10, 2008.

Marshall, Will. "Let's Pop the Deficit Bubble." *Wall Street Journal*, May 2, 2008.

Martin, Andrew. "The Mideast Facing a Choice between Crops and Water." *New York Times*, July 21, 2008.

Mauldin, John. "Do Trade Deficits Matter?" *Thoughts from the Frontline Weekly Newsletter*, May 12, 2006. www.frontlinethoughts.com/article.asp?id=mwo051206 (accessed May 13, 2006).

Mauldin, William, and Maria Kolesnikova. "Norilsk Rises as Russian Billionaires Propose Merger." *Bloomberg*, May 29, 2008.

Mayer, Isabelle Linden. "Iranian Budget Shift to Euros Causes Little Damage to Dollar." *Wall Street Journal*, December 19, 2006.

Mayerowitz, Scott, and Jennifer Parker. "Bush, Paulson: Financial Market Bailout Could Cost Taxpayers Hundreds of Billions." *ABC News*, September 19, 2008.

McCutcheon, Chuck. "Experts Warn U.S. Is Coming Apart at the Seams." *Seattle Times*, August 26, 2006.

McCutcheon, Chuck. "Internet Fuels Hunger for Information: Anti-Secrecy Activists Urge More Openness." *Newhouse News Service*, March 13, 2005.

McDonnell, Patrick J. "Bolivia Imposes Martial Law on Northern Province." *Los Angeles Times*, September 13, 2008.

McGreal, Chris. "Chinese Aid to Africa May Do More Harm than Good, Warns Benn." *Guardian* (UK), February 8, 2007.

McKeeby, David. "Terrorism Report Highlights Global Challenge." America. gov, April 30, 2007. www.america.gov/st/washfile-english/2007/April/20070425112825idybeekcm0.2628443.html (accessed April 1, 2008).

McKenna, Barrie. "Dead End for Free Trade." *Globe and Mail* (Canada), May 17, 2008.

McKibben, Bill. "Civilization's Last Chance." *Los Angeles Times*, May 11, 2008.

McKinnon, John D. "NATO Countries Endorse U.S. Missile-Defense System." *Wall Street Journal*, April 3, 2008.

McKinnon, Ronald, and Steve H. Hanke. "A Rescue Plan for the Dollar." *Wall Street Journal*, December 27, 2007.

McMullen, Alia. "Forget Oil, the New Global Crisis Is Food." *Financial Post* (Canada), January 4, 2008.

McNally, Terrence. "Is the Deadly Crash of Our Civilization Inevitable?" *AlterNet*, February 13, 2007. www.alternet.org/module/printversion/47963 (accessed February 15, 2007).

McSmith, Andy. "The Dollar's Decline: From Symbol of Hegemony to Shunned Currency." *Independent* (UK), November 17, 2007.

McWilliams, Gary, and David Kesmodel. "As Food Prices Rise, Shoppers Stock Up." *Wall Street Journal*, May 1, 2008.

Mead, Walter Russell. "The Great Fall of China." *Los Angeles Times*, December 30, 2007.

Mearns, Euan. "Why Oil Costs over $120 per Barrel." *Oil Drum*, May 20, 2008. www.theoildrum.com/node/4007 (accessed May 28, 2008).

"Medvedev Warns West against Applying Sanctions." Associated Press, September 15, 2008.

Mellor, William, and Le-Min Lim. "China Drills Where Others Dare Not Seek Oil." *International Herald Tribune*, October 2, 2006.

"Mexican Cartels 'Threaten State.'" *BBC News*, July 14, 2008.

"Mexican Company Predicts End of Oil." *Prensa Latina*, July 27, 2007.

"Mexican Oil Output Could Drop by One Third." *Daily Green*, January 2, 2008. www.thedailygreen.com/environmental-news/latest/mexico-oil-47010204 (accessed January 3, 2008).

Meyer, Henry, and Ryan Chilcote. "Putin Says 'War Has Started,' Georgia Claims Invasion." *Bloomberg*, August 8, 2008.

Michael, Clarence. "Greenback Vulnerable to Reshuffle of Gulf State Coffers." *Business Times* (Asia), April 7, 2006.

Milken, Michael. "A Boomer Bust?" *BusinessWeek*, April 26, 2006.

Millard, Peter, and David Luhnow. "Mexico's Plan to Open Oil Market May Not Solve Production Woes." *Wall Street Journal*, May 29, 2008.

Miller, John W. "Global Trade Talks Fail as New Giants Flex Muscle." *Wall Street Journal*, July 30, 2008.

Miller, Leslie. "Foreign Companies Buy U.S. Roads, Bridges." Associated Press, July 15, 2006.

Miller, Rich. "Crisis Exposes Flaws in U.S. Economy, Tarnishes Image." *Bloomberg*, September 18, 2008.

Miller, Rich. "World May Be Lucky to Get Worst Recession Since 1983." *Bloomberg*, October 13, 2008.

Milmo, Cahal. "2008: The Year a New Superpower Is Born." *Independent* (UK), January 1, 2008.

Milne, Seumas. "Georgie Is the Graveyard of America's Unipolar World." *Guardian* (UK), August 28, 2008.

Minyan, Peter. "The Courage to Choose." *Minyanville*, December 26, 2007. www.minyanville.com/articles/index/a/15340 (accessed December 28, 2007).

Mitra, Sramana. "The Coming Death of Indian Outsourcing." *Forbes*, February 29, 2008.

Moffett, Matt. "Brazil Joins Front Rank of New Economic Powers." *Wall Street Journal* Online, May 13, 2008. http://online.wsj.com/article_print/SB121063846832986909.html (accessed May 13, 2008).

Mollenkamp, Carrick, Susanne Craig, Serena Ng and Aaron Lucchetti. "Crisis on Wall street as Lehman Totters, Merrill Is Sold, AIG Seeks to Raise Cash." *Wall Street Journal*, September 15, 2008.

"The Monsters Are Due on Maple Street." *Wikipedia*. N.d. http://en.wikipedia.org/wiki/Monsters_Are_Due_on_Maple_Street (accessed May 22, 2008).

Morales, Alex. "Scientists Adjust 'Doomsday Clock' as Threat Grows." *Bloomberg*, January 17, 2008.

Morgenson, Gretchen. "The Peril That Trails an Oil Shock." *New York Times*, August 22, 2004.

Morley, Robert. "Sidebar: History Says Dollar Is Doomed." *Trumpet*, February 2007.

Mortished, Carl. "Already We Have Riots, Hoarding, Panic: The Sign of Things to Come?" *Times* (London), March 7, 2008.

Mortished, Carl. "Gulf States May Soon Need Coal Imports to Keep the Lights On." *Times* (London), May 19, 2008.

Mortished, Carl. "Oil Price Crisis Threatens to Reverse Globalization." *Times* (London), June 11, 2008.

"Moscow Sends Warning to Intl. Forces." *B92*, April 11, 2008. www.b92.net/eng/news/politics-article.php?yyyy=2008&mm=04&dd=11&nav_id=49297 (accessed April 11, 2008).

Moseley, Staff General Michael. "USAF Strategic Posture Unchanged after Russian Bomber Flights." *U.S. Air Force AIM Points*, February 21, 2008. http://aimpoints.hq.af.mil/display.cfm?id=24230&printer=yes (accessed March 1, 2008).

Moses, Abigail. "U.S. Treasuries Riskier than German Debt, Default Swaps Show." *Bloomberg*, March 11, 2008.

Mouawad, Jad. "Rising Demand for Oil Provokes New Energy Crisis." *New York Times*, November 9, 2007.

Moyers, Bill. "Bill Moyers Journal." *Public Broadcasting Service*, February 15, 2008. www.pbs.org/moyers/journal/02152008/watch2.html (accessed March 1, 2008).

Muenchau, Wolfgang. "Dollar's Last Lap as the Only Anchor Currency." *Eurointelligence*, November 27, 2007. www.eurointelligence.com/article.581+M534fefbd657.0.html (accessed November 27, 2007).

Mui, Ylan Q. "Grads Boomerang Back Home—Lessons Continue." *Houston Chronicle*, September 10, 2006.

Mukasey, Michael B. "Remarks Prepared for Delivery by Attorney General Michael B. Mukasey on International Organized Crime at the Center for Strategic and International Studies." April 23, 2008. www.usdoj.gov/ag/speeches/2008/ag_speech_080423.html (accessed April 25, 2008).

Mukherjee, Andy. "Water Threatens Urbanization, Prosperity." *Bloomberg*, December 4, 2007.

Murphy, Dan. "Middle East Racing to Nuclear Power." *Christian Science Monitor*, November 1, 2007.

Murray, Danielle. "Oil and Food: A Rising Security Challenge." *Mindfully.org*, May 9, 2005. www.mindfully.org/Food/2005/Oil-Food-Security9may05.htm (accessed March 21, 2008).

"Muslims More Numerous than Catholics:Vatican." Reuters, March 30, 2008.

"Muslims Tell Christians: Make Peace with Us or Survival of World Is at Stake." *Evening Standard* (UK), October 11, 2007.

"NAFTA at Fourteen: Historic Mexico–USA Showdown Looms." *Frontera NorteSur*, December 24, 2007. http://mexidata.info/id1662.html (accessed December 24, 2007).

Nakashima, Ellen, and Steven Mufson. "Hackers Have Attacked Foreign Utilities, CIA Analyst Says." *Washington Post*, January 19, 2008.

Nasseri, Ladane, and Thomas Penny. "Israel May Attack Iran This Year, Pentagon Official Tells ABC." *Bloomberg*, July 1, 2008.

Navarro, Peter. "Sovereign Wealth Funds: China's Potent Economic Weapon." *Christian Science Monitor*, February 8, 2008.

Neuger, James G. "Irish Referendum May Doom EU Dream for United States of Europe." *Bloomberg*, June 8, 2008.

Neuger, James G., and Simon Kennedy. "Taj Mahal Won't Accept Bush Dollars as India Laments Lost Value." *Bloomberg*, December 19, 2007.

Nery, Natuza. "Brazil Says It Won't Tolerate Overthrow in Bolivia." September 11, 2008.

"New Survey: 82 Percent of Americans Think Health Care System Needs Major Overhaul." Commonwealth Fund, August 7, 2008. www.commonwealthfund.org/newsroom/newsroom_show.htm?doc_id=698592 (accessed August 7, 2008).

"The Next Step for World Trade." *New York Times*, August 2, 2008.

Nimr, Suleiman, and Wissam Keyrouz. "Gulf Summit Opens with Warning of Regional Explosion." *Agence France-Presse*, December 9, 2006.

"Nitrogen Pollution Harming Ecosystems and Contributing to Global Warming." *Mongabay.com*, May 15, 2008. http://news.mongabay.com/2008/0515-nitrogen. html (accessed May 27, 2008).

Novak, Candice. "Can Wal-Mart Do 'Local'?" *U.S. News & World Report*, July 24, 2008.

"Nuclear Missiles Parade across Red Square." *Agence France-Presse*, May 9, 2008.

Nussbaum, Bruce. "What's Really on the Davos Agenda." *BusinessWeek*, January 18, 2008.

Nussbaum, Roger. "Stuff." *Random Roger's Big Picture*, November 26, 2007. http://randomroger.blogspot.com/2007/11/stuff.html (accessed November 27, 2007).

Nye, Joseph. "Day One at Davos and the Low Ebb of American Soft Power." *Huffington Post*, January 24, 2007. www.huffingtonpost.com/joseph-nye/day-one-at-davos-and-the-_b_39536.html (accessed March 1, 2008).

Nyquist, J. R. "The Advantage of the Nation State." *Financial Sense; Global Analysis with J. R. Nyquist*, December 28, 2007. www.financialsense.com/stormwatch/geo/pastanalysis/2007/1228.html (accessed December 28, 2007).

Nyquist, J. R. "Alien Minds." *Financial Sense; Global Analysis with J. R. Nyquist*, January 18, 2008. www.financialsense.com/stormwatch/geo/postanalysis/2008/0118. html (accessed January 19, 2008).

Nyquist, J. R. "Buchanan's Day of Reckoning, Part III." *Financial Sense; Global Analysis with J. R. Nyquist*, May 2, 2008. www.financialsense.com/stormwatch/geo/pastanalysis/2008/0502.html (accessed May 2, 2008).

Nyquist, J. R. "The Cold War Never Ended." *Financial Sense; Global Analysis with J. R. Nyquist*, February 1, 2008. www.financialsense.com/stormwatch/geo/pastanalysis/2008/0201.html (accessed February 2, 2008).

Nyquist, J. R. "The Danger Is Not Fully Appreciated." *Financial Sense; Global Analysis with J. R. Nyquist*, September 12, 2008. www.financialsense.com/stormwatch/geo/pastanalysis/2008/0912.html (accessed September 12, 2008).

Nyquist, J. R. "A Dangerous Passage." *Financial Sense; Global Analysis with J. R. Nyquist*, May 16, 2008. www.financialsense.com/stormwatch/geo/pastanalysis/2008/0516.html (accessed May 16, 2008).

Nyquist, J. R. "The Downward Trend Is Unstoppable." *Financial Sense; Global Analysis with J. R. Nyquist*, October 26, 2007. www.financialsense.com/stormwatch/geo/pastanalysis/2007/1026.html (accessed October 26, 2007).

Nyquist, J. R. "The Enemy's Scheme of Attack." *Financial Sense; Global Analysis with J. R. Nyquist*, June 27, 2008. www.financialsense.com/stormwatch/geo/analysis.html (accessed June 28, 2008).

Nyquist, J. R. "Russia's Concept for Dominating Europe." *Financial Sense; Global Analysis with J. R. Nyquist*, September 12, 2008. www.financialsense.com/stormwatch/geo/pastanalysis/2008/0815.html (accessed August 18, 2008).

Nyquist, J. R. "Russia's Undeniable War Preparations." *Financial Sense; Global Analysis with J. R. Nyquist*, August 24, 2007. www.financialsense.com/stormwatch/geo/pastanalysis/2007/0824.html (accessed August 27, 2007).

Nyquist, J. R. "Strategic Relationships." *Financial Sense; Global Analysis with J. R. Nyquist*, March 7, 2008. www.financialsense.com/stormwatch/geo/pastanalysis/2008/0307.html (accessed March 8, 2008).

Nyquist, J. R. "Years of Crisis Ahead." *Financial Sense; Global Analysis with J. R. Nyquist*, April 1, 2008. www.financialsense.com/stormwatch/geo/pastanalysis/2008/0104.html (accessed April 1, 2008).

"Obama's Image Slips, His Lead over Clinton Disappears; Public Support for Free Trade Declines." Pew Research Center, May 1, 2008.

O'Hehir, Andrew. "American Empire, Going, Going . . ." *Salon*, November 19, 2007.

Ohlemacher, Stephen. "World Population to Hit 7 Billion in 2012." Associated Press, June 19, 2008.

"Oil Crisis Triggers Fevered Scramble for the World's Seabed." *Telegraph* (UK), May 27, 2008.

O'Keefe, Brian. "Here Comes $500 Oil." *Fortune*, September 22, 2008.

Olive, David. "'Be the Change You Wish to See.'" *Toronto Star*, November 25, 2007.

Onaran, Yalman, and Chia-Peck Wong. "Merrill Lynch to Get $6.2 Billion from Temasek, Davis." *Bloomberg*, December 24, 2007.

Onstad, Eric. "Arabian Warren Buffett to Inject Billions into Africa." Reuters, December 19, 2007.

"OPEC Considers Dumping U.S. Dollar." *Press TV*, February 15, 2008.

"Open-Door Policy." *Wall Street Journal*, March 30, 2006.

"Operation Wetback." *Wikipedia*, April 21, 2008. http://en.wikipedia.org/wiki/Operation_Wetback (accessed May 13, 2008).

Orszag, Peter. "Issues in Climate Change." Congressional Budget Office, November 16, 2007.

Osborn, Andrew. "Russia Sets Pipeline Deal With China." *Wall Street Journal*, October 29, 2008.

"Overview of the Law Enforcement Strategy to Combat International Organized Crime." U.S. Department of Justice, April 17, 2008. www.justice.gov/ag/speeches/2008/ioc-strategy-public-overview.pdf (accessed April 18, 2008).

Pae, Peter. "Small-Town America: The New Bangalore?" *Los Angeles Times*, November 11, 2007.

Page, Jeremy. "Giants Meet to Counter U.S. Power." *Times* (London), February 15, 2007.

Pagnamenta, Robin. "Former President Bush Energy Adviser Says Oil Is Running Out." *Times* (London), July 2, 2008.

Painter, James. "Bolivia Poll Sparks Crisis Fears." *BBC News*, April 30, 2008.

Pan, Esther. "China, Africa, and Oil." Council on Foreign Relations, January 26, 2007.

Panzner, Michael J. *Financial Armageddon: Protecting Your Future from Four Impending Catastrophes*. New York: Kaplan Publishing, 2007.

Parussini, Gabriele, and Roman Kessler. "French, German Strikes Threaten Economic Plans." *Wall Street Journal*, November 15, 2007.

Passariello, Christina. "Logistics Are in Vogue with Designers." *Wall Street Journal*, June 27, 2008.

Pasztor, Andy. "Europeans Explore Expanding Their Space Efforts." *Wall Street Journal*, July 19, 2008.

Patton, Zach. "Tennessee and Georgia Put Up Their Dukes." *Governing.com*, February 27, 2008. http://governing.typepad.com/13thfloor/2008/02/tennessee-and-g.html (accessed March 1, 2008).

Pazarbaşioğlu, Ceyla, Mangal Goswami, and Jack Ree. "The Changing Face of Investors." International Monetary Fund, March 2007. www.imf.org/external/pubs/ft/fandd/2007/03/pazar.htm (accessed January 7, 2008).

"Peak Oil." *Wikipedia*, March 10, 2008. http://en.wikipedia.org/wiki/Peak_oil (accessed March 10, 2008).

Pelton, Tom. "The Coming Black Plague?" *Baltimore Sun*, July 20, 2008.

"The Pension Era, R.I.P." *Wall Street Journal*, August 4, 2006.

Pentland, William. "The Water-Industrial Complex." *Forbes*, May 14, 2008.

Perry, Joellen. "Strong Euro Splits Europe." *Wall Street Journal*, July 19, 2007.

Perry, Joellen, and Liz Rappaport. "Investors Raise Their Bets on Defaults in EU Countries." *Wall Street Journal*, October 31, 2008.

"Peru Mine Protesters Seize Police." *AiVit News*, June 17, 2008. http://news.aivit.com/2008/06/17/Peru_mine_protesters_seize_police/ (accessed June 17, 2008).

Pesek, William. "Asia's 'Euro' Is Short on Trust, Political Will." *Bloomberg*, May 8, 2008.

Pesek, William. "Girl Power May Be Just the Thing for Asian GDP." *Bloomberg*, March 12, 2008.

Peterson, Jonathan. "Struggle Awaits Half of Retirees." *Chicago Tribune*, June 18, 2006.

Peterson, Scott. "How Iran Would Retaliate If It Comes to War." *Christian Science Monitor*, June 20, 2008.

Pettis, Michael. "Demographic Projections and Trade Implications." *Michael Pettis: My Blog*, May 13, 2008. http://piaohaoreport.sampasite.com/china-financial-markets/blog/Demographic-projections-and-trad.htm (accessed May 13, 2008).

"PISA 2006: Science Competencies for Tomorrow's World." Organization for Economic Cooperation and Development, December 2007. www.oecd.org/document/2/0,3343,en_32252351_32236191_39718850_1_1_1_1,00.html (accessed January 7, 2008).

Plender, John. "Insight: Credit Squeeze Could Be Harbinger of a Chinese Crash." *Financial Times*, October 23, 2007.

Plender, John. "Insight: The Pitfalls of Financial Globalization Grow Clearer." *Financial Times*, November 20, 2007.

"PNAC Founder Predicts US–China War." *Presscue*, January 17, 2008. http://press-cue.com/node/41651 (accessed April 4, 2008).

"The Politics of Ports." *Wall Street Journal*, October 5, 2006.

Pollard, Dave. "In the Year 2045." *How to Save the World*, February 9, 2005. http://blogs.salon.com/0002007/2005/02/09.html (accessed July 2, 2006).

Pollard, Dave. "What to Expect When the Dollar Collapses." *How to Save the World*, May 15, 2006. http://blogs.salon.com/0002007/2006/05/15.html (accessed July 2, 2006).

Pomfret, James. "China Opens Hong Kong to U.S. Carrier." Reuters, November 22, 2007.

Poovey, Bill. "Secessionists Meeting in Tennessee." Associated Press, October 3, 2007.

Popkin, Joel, and Kathryn Kobe. "U.S. Manufacturing Innovation at Risk." Manufacturing Institute and Council of Manufacturing Associations, February 2006.

Porteous, Bruce. "A World without USA & Britain." *American Wars*, November 27, 2006. http://americanwars.blogspot.com/2006/11/world-without-usa-britain-by-bruce.html (accessed November 28, 2006).

Porter, Eduardo. "Study Finds Wealth Inequality Is Widening Worldwide." *New York Times*, December 6, 2006.

Postman, David. "Gingrich Says It's World War III." *Seattle Times*, July 15, 2006.

"A Post-Oil Future." *Reformer.com*, June 10, 2008. http://reformer.com/editorials/ci_9537173 (accessed June 10, 2008).

Pressley, James. "Bigg's Tips for Rich: Expect War, Study Blitz, Mind Markets." *Bloomberg*, January 30, 2008.

Pressley, James. "Zakaria Defies Doomsayers, Snags Obama in 'Post-American World.'" *Bloomberg*, May 23, 2008.

Preston, Julia. "Fewer Latino Immigrants in U.S. Sending Money Home." *International Herald Tribune*, April 30, 2008.

Price, David. "Energy and Human Evolution." *Energy Bulletin*, January 7, 2005. www.energybulletin.net/print.php?id=3917 (accessed August 10, 2007).

Price, Laura. "Morales Threatens to Nationalize Bolivia's Oil Fields, EFE Says." *Bloomberg*, May 19, 2008.

Primakov, Yeveny. "Russia to Independently Pursue Its National Interests." *RUVR, The Voice of Russia Broadcasting Company*, June 25, 2007. www.ruvr.ru/main.php?lng=eng&q=12868&cid=80&p=25.06.2007 (accessed June 28, 2007).

"Privacy and Human Rights 2006." *Privacy International*, December 18, 2007. www.privacyinternational.org/article.shtml?cmd[347]=x-347–559458 (accessed January 1, 2008).

"Profiting from Obscurity." *Economist*, May 5, 2005.

Pronina, Lyubov. "Chavez to Order $2 Billion of Russian Arms, Kommersant Reports." *Bloomberg*, May 12, 2008.

Pronina, Lyubov. "Medvedev Says Arctic Is Russian 'Resource Base' in 21st Century." *Bloomberg*, September 17, 2008.

"Protectionist U.S. Risks Losing Economic Leadership in Asia: Official." *Agence France-Presse*, July 8, 2008.

"Putin, Chavez Discuss Nuclear, Military Cooperation." *RIA Novosti*, September 26, 2008.

"Putin's Arctic Invasion: Russia Lays Claim to the North Pole—and All Its Gas, Oil, and Diamonds." *Daily Mail* (UK), June 29, 2007.

Rabinowitz, Gavin. "Indians, Chinese Jostling for Power." *NWA News*, June 8, 2008.

Racanelli, Vito J. "The Day of the Locust." *Barron's*, January 14, 2008.

Rachman, Gideon. "The Political Threats to Globalization." *Financial Times*, April 7, 2008.

Rachman, Gideon. "Q&A: Illiberal Capitalism." *Gideon Rachman's Blog*, January 22, 2008. http://blogs.ft.com/rachmanblog/2008/01/qa-illiberal-cahtml/ (accessed January 25, 2008).

Raids, Roma. "Italy Cracks Down on Illegal Immigrants." *Spiegel Online*, May 16, 2008. www.spiegel.de/international/europe/0,1518,druck-553753,00.html (accessed May 19, 2008).

Ramstad, Evan. "North Korea Backpedals on Nuclear Pact in Defiance of U.S." *Wall Street Journal*, August 27, 2008.

Randall, Maya Jackson. "U.S. May Clarify Scrutiny of Foreign Investments." *Wall Street Journal*, April 22, 2008.

Rauchway, Eric. "America's Hypocritical Impulse to Remake the World." *New Republic*, August 22, 2007.

"Realistic Rewards." *Economist*, August 19, 2004.

Redfern, Martin. "Antarctic Glaciers Surge to Ocean." *BBC News*, March 1, 2008.

Regalado, Antonio. "Brazilian Mining Titan Takes on Global Giants." *Wall Street Journal*, April 25, 2008.

Reid, Tim. "Arctic Cold War as U.S. Sends a Ship to Claim Riches under the Ocean." *Times* (London), August 13, 2008.

Reinhart, Carmen M., and Kenneth S. Rogoff. "Is the U.S. Sub-Prime Financial Crisis So Different? An International Historical Comparison." *NBER Working Paper* No. 13761, January 2008.

"Relative Size of U.S. Military Spending, 1940–2003." *Truth and Politics*. N.d. www.truthandpolitics.org/military-relative-size.php (accessed February 18, 2008).

"Relying on the Kindness of Strangers: Foreign Purchases of U.S. Treasury Debt." *U.S. Congress Joint Economic Committee—Economic Policy Brief*, November 2006.

Renton, Alex. "How the World's Oceans Are Running Out of Fish." *Guardian* (UK), May 11, 2008.

"Replace Capitalism with Islamic Financial System Cleric." *Agence France Presse*, October 12, 2008.

"Report: Muslim Leaders Want Mecca to Be Center of World Time Zones." *Fox News*, April 21, 2008.

"The Return of Nuclear Power." *Financial Times*, March 25, 2008.

Reynolds, James. "China's Elderly Care Conundrum." *BBC News*, August 23, 2007.

"Rich World's Consumerism May Cause African Famines, Experts Warn." *Agence France-Presse*, July 1, 2007.

Richter, Mathilde. "German Firms Pull Out as Chinese Fluff Teddy Production." *Agence France-Presse*, July 5, 2008.

Rieff, David. "Fading Superpower?" *Los Angeles Times*, September 9, 2007.

Rincon, Paul. "Nuclear's CO2 Cost 'Will Climb.'" *BBC News*, April 30, 2008.

"Riots, Instability Spread as Food Prices Skyrocket." *CNN*, April 14, 2008.

"The Rise of Nationalism." *Bangkok Post*, July 5, 2008.

"Rising Powers: The Changing Geopolitical Landscape." National Intelligence Council, December 2004.

Ritholtz, Barry L. "China on Course to Overtake U.S. Economy." *Big Picture*, February 11, 2005. http://bigpicture.typepad.com/comments/2005/02/china_on_course.html (accessed November 17, 2007).

Roach, Stephen S. "America's Inflated Asset Prices Must Fall." *Financial Times*, January 7, 2008.

Roach, Stephen S. "The Great Unraveling." Morgan Stanley, March 16, 2007.

Roach, Stephen S. "You Can Almost Hear It Pop." *New York Times*, December 16, 2007.

Robb, Greg. "Echoes of Iraq in Bush Handling of Mortgage Crisis." *MarketWatch*, September 23, 2008.

Roberts, Paul. "World Oil." *National Geographic*, May 16, 2008.

Roberts, Paul Craig. "American Hegemony Is Not Guaranteed." *Baltimore Chronicle & Sentinel*, April 14, 2008.

Roberts, Paul Craig. "How Empires Fall." *Counterpunch*, May 13, 2008. www.counterpunch.org/roberts05132008.html (accessed May 14, 2008).

Roberts, Paul Craig. "How Offsourcing Undermines America: Losing the Economy to Mythology." *Counterpunch*, June 11, 2007. www.counterpunch.org/roberts06112007.html (accessed June 12, 2007).

Roberts, Paul Craig. "Official Lies, Dogma and Unaccountable Power: The New Dark Age." *Counterpunch*, December 30, 2006. www.counterpunch.org/roberts12302006.html (accessed January 1, 2007).

Roberts, Paul Craig. "Offshoring Interests and Economic Dogma." *Counterpunch*, December 13, 2007. www.counterpunch.org/roberts12132007.html (accessed December 14, 2007).

Roberts, Paul Craig. "Supermodel Spurns the Dollar." *Counterpunch*, November 7, 2007. www.counterpunch.org/roberts11072007.html (accessed November 9, 2007).

Roberts, Paul Craig. "The Truth Comes Out about Offshoring." *V Dare*, June 12, 2007. www.vdare.com/roberts/070612_offshoring.htm (accessed August 23, 2007).

Roberts, Paul Craig. "Where Bush's New Cold War Is Headed: The Hegemony of the Cockroach." *Counterpunch*, August 13, 2007. www.counterpunch.org/roberts08132007.html (accessed August 15, 2007).

Roberts, Paul Craig. "Why No American President Will Stand Up to Israel." *Counterpunch*, November 14, 2007. www.counterpunch.org/roberts11142007.html (accessed November 14, 2007).

Robinson, Simon. "Notes on a Divided World." *Time*, April 26, 2007.

Roche, David. "The Global Money Machine." *Wall Street Journal*, December 14, 2007.

Roche, David. "Insight: Commodities Swamped in Rush to Safety." *Financial Times*, March 17, 2008.

Rodrik, Dani. "The *NYT* Doesn't Get It on Trade." *Dani Rodrik's Weblog*, December 23, 2007. http://rodrik.typepad.com/dani_rodriks_weblog/2007/12/the-nyt-doesnt.html (accessed December 23, 2007).

Roeder, Philip G. *Where Nation-States Come From: Institutional Change in the Age of Nationalism*. Princeton, NJ: Princeton University Press, 2007.

Rogers, David. "House Passes Border-Fence Bill, Changes to Rules on Earmarks." *Wall Street Journal*, September 15, 2006.

Rogers, Iain. "Banks Turned Markets into 'Monster': German President." Reuters, May 14, 2008.

Rogoff, Kenneth. "China May Yet Be Economy to Lose Sleep Over." *Financial Times*, February 4, 2008.

Rogoff, Kenneth. "Has the Moment Come to Replace the U.S. Dollar?" *Daily Star* (Lebanon), April 7, 2008.

Rogoff, Kenneth. "Turning a Blind Eye." *Guardian* (UK), December 4, 2006.

Rohter, Larry. "Shipping Costs Start to Crimp Globalization." *New York Times*, August 3, 2008.

Romero, Simon. "Venezuelan Leader Seizes Greater Economic Power." *New York Times*, May 18, 2008.

Rosenbloom, Stephanie. "Solution, or Mess? A Milk Jug for a Green Earth." *New York Times*, June 30, 2008.

Rosenkrantz, Holly. "Bush Urges Passage of Trade Accords with Latin American Nations." *Bloomberg*, October 13, 2007.

Rosenthal, Elisabeth. "In Spain, Water Is a New Battleground." *New York Times*, June 3, 2008.

Ross, John. "Return of the Gunboat." *Counterpunch*, July 29, 2008.

Roth, Alex. "After the Bubble, Ghost Towns across America." *Wall Street Journal*, August 2, 2008.

Roubini, Nouriel. "*Bloomberg*: Wealth Funds Are This Year's Davos 'It Girl' . . . But Next Year It May Be the Emerging Market Multinationals." *RGE Monitor; Nouriel Roubini's Global EconoMonitor*, February 4, 2008. www.rgemonitor.com/roubini-monitor/241828/bloomberg_wealth_funds_are_this_years_davos_it_girlbut_next_year_it_may_be_the_emerging_market_multinationals (accessed February 5, 2008).

Roubini, Nouriel. "Comrades Bush, Paulson and Bernanke Welcome You to the USSRA (United Socialist State Republic of America)." *RGE Monitor; Nouriel*

Roubini's Global EconoMonitor, September 9, 2008. www.rgemonitor.com/ roubini-monitor/253529/comrades_bush_paulson_and_bernanke_welcome_ you_to_the_ussra_united_socialist_state_republic_of_america (accessed September 10, 2008).

Roubini, Nouriel. "The Decline of the American Empire." *RGE Monitor; Nouriel Roubini's Global EconoMonitor*, August 13, 2008. www.rgemonitor.com/roubini-monitor/253323/the_decline_of_the_american_empire (accessed August 13, 2008).

Roubini, Nouriel. "Recoupling Rather than Decoupling: The Forthcoming Contagion to China, East Asia and Emerging Markets." *RGE Monitor; Nouriel Roubini's Global EconoMonitor*, November 23, 2007. www.rgemonitor.com/ blog/roubini/228535 (accessed November 23, 2007).

Roubini, Nouriel. "The World Is at Risk of a Global Systemic Financial Meltdown and a Severe Global Depression." *RGE Monitor; Nouriel Roubini's Global EconoMonitor*, October 9, 2008. www.rgemonitor.com/roubini-moni-tor/253973/the_world_is_at_severe_risk_of_a_global_systemic_financial_ meltdown_and_a_severe_global_depression (accessed October 10, 2008).

Rubin, Trudy. "U.S. Loses Its Status as Economic World Power." *Newsday*, January 31, 2008.

Rufus, Anneli. "Apocalypse in the Oceans." *AlterNet*, May 30, 2008. www.alternet. org/story/86789/ (accessed June 2, 2008).

Russell, Ben. "Water Will Be Source of War Unless World Acts Now, Warns Minister." *Independent* (UK), March 22, 2008.

Russell, Ben. "World Warned over Killer Flu Pandemic." *Independent* (UK), July 21, 2008.

"Russia & CIS: U.S.-Led Policy Complicating Situation Worldwide—Gorbachev." *Interfax*, July 27, 2007.

"Russia Cancels All Military Cooperation with NATO." *Aftenposten* (Norway), August 20, 2008.

"Russia Diversification Talk Hurts Dollar, Boosts Yen." *MarketWatch*, October 16, 2006.

"Russia Energy Deal Adds to Europe Fears." Associated Press, January 26, 2008.

"Russia, India to Join in Moon Mission; Increase Weapons, Energy Cooperation." *Forbes*, November 12, 2007.

"Russia, Kazakhstan and Turkmenistan Sign Caspian Gas Pipeline Deal." Associated Press, December 20, 2007.

"Russia May Dump Weakening U.S. Dollar in Its Energy Deals." *Pravda.Ru*, December 15, 2007.

"Russian Armed Forces More Mobile, Combat Ready—Putin." *RIA Novosti*, February 15, 2008.

"Russian Army Chief: We'll Use Nuclear Weapons Preemptively If Threatened." Associated Press, January 19, 2008.

"Russian Bombers in Venezuela amid Tension with U.S." *CNN*, September 11, 2008.

"Russian Bombers Patrol Caribbean." United Press International, September 16, 2008.

"Russia New Missile Base Response to U.S." *Press TV*, May 3, 2008.

"Russia Resurgent." *Economist*, August 14, 2008.

"Russian FM Warns Military Action on Iran 'Disastrous.'" *Agence France-Presse*, March 20, 2008.

"Russian Navy Boosts Combat Presence in Arctic." *Agence France-Presse*, July 14, 2008.

"Russian Navy Prioritizes Construction of Nuclear Submarines." *RIA Novosti*, July 25, 2008.

"Russia Promises Retaliation If Weapons Deployed in Space." *RIA Novosti*, September 27, 2007.

"Russia Says It Is Ahead in Race to Put Man on Mars." *Agence France-Presse*, January 8, 2007.

"Russia to Upgrade Nuclear Systems." *BBC News*, September 26, 2008.

"Russia's Gazprom to Halve Ukraine Supplies as Gas War Looms." *Agence France-Presse*, March 4, 2008.

"Russia's Medvedev Warns Kosovo's Independence Could Set Europe Ablaze." *International Herald Tribune*, February 27, 2008. www.iht.com/bin/printfriendly.php?id=10476844 (accessed March 1, 2008).

"Russia Successfully Tests New ICBM." Associated Press, December 25, 2007.

"Russia to Double Bushehr Personnel: Official." *Space War*, February 15, 2008. www.spacewar.com/2006/080215001003.ei53w7k8.html (accessed February 16, 2008).

"Russia to 'Neutralize' U.S. Missile Defense Threat: Report." *Agence France-Presse*, July 14, 2008.

"Russia to Rearrange Troops Due to U.S. Missile Shield." *RIA Novosti*, January 30, 2008.

"Russia Warns of Arms War in Space." Reuters, October 3, 2007.

"Russia Warns of U.S. Missile Shield Retaliation." *Agence France-Presse*, December 15, 2007.

"Russia Warns over US–Czech Shield." *BBC News*, July 8, 2008.

Saad, Lydia. "Americans See China Crowding Out U.S. as Economic Leader." Gallup Poll, February 21, 2008. www.gallup.com.

Sachs, Jeffrey D. "Are Malthus's Predicted 1798 Food Shortages Coming True?" *Scientific American*, August 25, 2008.

Sachs, Jeffrey D. "Land, Water and Conflict." *Newsweek*, June 28, 2008.

Saefong, Myra P. "Oil's Tense Trading Scene May Sway a Move to Dubai." *MarketWatch*, May 23, 2008.

Sale, Kirkpatrick. "Imperial Entropy: Collapse of the American Empire." *Energy Bulletin*, February 23, 2005. www.energybulletin.net/node/4474 (accessed May 4, 2006).

Saleri, Nansen G. "The World Has Plenty of Oil." *Wall Street Journal*, March 4, 2008.

Salkeld, Luke. "The Real Good Life: An Entire Village Turns Against Supermarkets and Grows Its Own Food." *Daily Mail* (UK), April 16, 2008.

Samuelson, Robert J. "The End of Free Trade." *Washington Post*, December 26, 2007.

Samuelson, Robert J. "Farewell to Pax Americana." *Washington Post*, December 14, 2006.

Sanderson, Henry. "Chinese Satellite Enters Orbit around Moon." *USA Today*, November 5, 2007.

"S&P 500 Historical Trailing 12-Month P/E Ratio." *Bespoke Investment Group*, May 14, 2008. http://bespokeinvest.typepad.com/bespoke/2008/05/sp-500-historic.html (accessed June 28, 2008).

Sands, Sarah. "We're All Doomed! 40 Years from Global Catastrophe—and There's NOTHING We Can Do About It, Says Climate Change Expert." *Daily Mail* (UK), March 22, 2008.

Sataline, Suzanne. "The Changing Faiths of America." *Wall Street Journal*, February 26, 2008.

"Saudis, Indonesia Buy Arms from Russia." *Naked Capitalism*, December 5, 2007. www.nakedcapitalism.com/2007/12/saudis-indonesia-buy-arms-from-russia.html (accessed December 6, 2007).

Schemm, Paul. "America's Opponents in the Mideast See Divine Retribution in US's Financial Meltdown." Associated Press, October 11, 2008.

Schifferes, Steve. "The End of the American Dream?" *BBC News*, September 4, 2006.

Schifferes, Steve. "World Poverty 'More Widespread.'" *BBC News*, August 27, 2008.

Schiller, Bill. "Pakistan in Grip of Chaos and Anarchy." *Toronto Star*, December 30, 2007.

Schmitt, Eric, and Mark Mazzetti. "Bush Said to Give Orders Allowing Raids in Pakistan." *New York Times*, September 11, 2008.

Schofield, Matthew. "Germany Considers Increased Spying on Muslims." *McClatchy Newspapers*, September 6, 2007.

Scholtes, Saskia. "Bank of China Flees Fannie-Freddie." *Financial Times*, August 28, 2008.

Scholtes, Saskia, and Gillian Tett. "'Shipwrecks and Casualties' Warning for Credit Markets." *Financial Times*, January 11, 2008.

Schor, Elana. "Democrats: White House Must Publish 'Chilling' Climate Change Document." *Guardian* (UK), July 25, 2008.

Schroeder, Robert. "House Panel Passes Bill to Look Closer at Foreign Investors." *Wall Street Journal*, June 15, 2006.

Schumacher, E. F. *Small Is Beautiful*. New York: Harper & Row, 1973.

Schumer, Charles, and Paul Craig Roberts. "Second Thoughts on Free Trade." *New York Times*, January 6, 2004.

Schwartz, Ariel. "BioTown, USA: Is Total Energy Self-Sufficiency Possible?" *EcoLocalizer*, June 19, 2008. http://ecolocalizer.com/2008/06/19/biotown-usa-is-total-energy-self-sufficency-possible/ (accessed June 20, 2008).

"Scientists Blame Global Warming for Antarctica Ice Shelf Collapse." *Earth Times*, March 26, 2008.

Scott, Mark. "In Europe, New Life for Nuclear." *BusinessWeek*, January 8, 2008.

Scott, Peter Dale. "Homeland Security Contracts for Vast New Detention Camps." *Pacific News Service*, February 8, 2006.

Scowcroft, Brent. "The Dispensable Nation?" *National Interest*, July 1, 2007. www.nationalinterest.org/Article.aspx?id=14778 (accessed March 1, 2008).

Seager, Ashley. "Development: U.S. Fails to Measure Up on 'Human Index.'" *Guardian* (UK), July 17, 2008.

Sekretarev, Ivan. "Russia, China Hold Joint War Games." Associated Press, August 17, 2007.

Sender, Henny. "China's Safe to Invest $2.5 Bn in TPG Fund." *Financial Times*, June 10, 2008.

Sender, Henny. "A Company's Road to Restructuring May Teem with Hedge-Fund Potholes." *Wall Street Journal*, March 30, 2006.

Sender, Henny. "Sovereign Funds Cut Exposure to Weak Dollar." *Financial Times*, July 17, 2008.

Sender, Henny, David Wighton, and Sundeep Tucker. "Saudis Plan Huge Sovereign Wealth Fund." *Financial Times*, December 21, 2007.

Sengupta, Somini. "In Fertile India, Growth Outstrips Agriculture." *New York Times*, June 22, 2008.

Sesit, Michael R. "Dollar Reserve Is Trade of Fading Glory." *Bloomberg*, May 2, 2008.

Sesit, Michael R. "Smithers Sees Earnings Worldwide Peaking, Undermining Stocks." *Bloomberg*, July 10, 2006.

Setser, Brad. "America's Achilles Heel?" *RGE Monitor; Brad Setser's Blog*, January 2, 2008. www.rgemonitor.com/blog/setser/235051 (accessed March 1, 2008).

Setser, Brad. "Are the Foreign Exchange Losses of Central Banks Real?" *RGE Monitor; Brad Setser's Blog*, February 1, 2008. www.rgemonitor.com/blog/setser/241669 (accessed February 2, 2008).

Setser, Brad. "Central Banks Still Buy Dollars When No One Else Wants To . . ." *Brad Setser's Blog*, July 1, 2008. http://blogs.cfr.org/setser/2008/07/01/central-banks-still-buy-dollars-when-no-one-else-wants-to/ (accessed July 1, 2008).

Setser, Brad. "The Changing Balance of Global Financial Power." *Brad Setser's Blog*, August 14, 2008. http://blogs.cfr.org/setser/2008/08/14/the-changing-balance-of-global-financial-power/ (accessed August 15, 2008).

Setser, Brad. "The December TIC Data Lifts the Curtain That Has Hidden How the U.S. Has Financed Its Deficit." *RGE Monitor; Brad Setser's Blog*, February 15, 2008. www.rgemonitor.com/blog/setser/244382 (accessed February 16, 2008).

Setser, Brad. "The End of the United States Exorbitant Privilege." *RGE Monitor; Brad Setser's Blog*, January 8, 2008. www.rgemonitor.com/blog/setser/234560 (accessed January 8, 2008).

Setser, Brad. "The Flight from Risky Assets." *Brad Setser's Blog*, September 16, 2008. http://blogs.cfr.org/setser/2008/09/16/the-flight-from-risky-us-assets-continues/ (accessed September 17, 2008).

Setser, Brad. "Maybe the CIC Isn't Motivated Entirely by Commercial Gain . . ." *Brad Setser's Blog*, June 15, 2008. http://blogs.cfr.org/setser/2008/06/15/maybe-the-cic-isn%E2%80%99t-motivated-entirely-by-commercial-gain-%E2%80%A6/ (accessed June 16, 2008).

Setser, Brad. "The New Financial Superpowers (Part 1)." *RGE Monitor; Brad Setser's Blog*, December 6, 2007. www.rgemonitor.com/blog/setser/230793 (accessed December 12, 2007).

Setser, Brad. "The New (Financial) World Order." *RGE Monitor; Brad Setser's Blog*, January 18, 2008. www.rgemonitor.com/blog/setser/238557 (accessed January 19, 2008).

Setser, Brad. "State-Led Globalization." *RGE Monitor; Brad Setser's Blog*, January 31, 2008. http://rs.rgemonitor.com/blog/setser/241125 (accessed February 2, 2008).

Setser, Brad. "There Is Now Little Doubt: The U.S. Relies on Central Banks and Sovereign Funds to Finance Its Deficit." *RGE Monitor; Brad Setser's Blog*, March 23, 2008. http://rs.rgemonitor.com/blog/setser/250370 (accessed March 24, 2008).

Setser, Brad. "Ut-oh! Is China Starting to Blame the U.S. for Its Currency Losses?" *Brad Setser's Blog*, April 22, 2008. http://blogs.cfr.org/setser/2008/04/22/

ut-oh-is-china-starting-to-blame-the-us-for-its-currency-losses/ (accessed April 23, 2008).

Sevastopulo, Demetri. "China Looks to Build Up Military, Says US." *Financial Times*, March 3, 2008.

Sevastopulo, Demetri. "Chinese Hacked into Pentagon." *Financial Times*, September 3, 2007.

Sevastopulo, Demetri. "U.S. to Impose Stricter Visa Rule." *Financial Times*, June 2, 2008.

Seyoon, Kim, and Kiko Ujikane. "Japan, S. Korea, China Mull $80 Billion Reserve Pool." *Bloomberg*, May 4, 2008.

Sezer, Seda. "Germany's Biggest Mosque Spurs Fear of 'Islamization' of Europe." *Bloomberg*, April 2, 2008.

Shah, Anup. "World Military Spending." *Global Issues*, February 25, 2007. www. globalissues.org/Geopolitics/ArmsTrade/Spending.asp (accessed February 18, 2008).

Shah, Saeed. "Pakistan 'Could Be Another Somalia,'" *Independent* (UK), January 1, 2008.

Shanker, Thom. "Missile Defense Future May Turn on Success of Mission to Destroy Satellite." *New York Times*, February 16, 2008.

Shanker, Thom. "Russia Is Striving to Modernize its Military." *New York Times*, October 20, 2008.

Shapiro, Debra. "The Condition of Education 2008: U.S. Science Literacy Scores Below International Average." *NSTA*, June 5, 2008. www.nsta.org/publications/news/story.aspx?id=54947 (accessed June 6, 2008).

"Shariah Investments Top $260 Bn." *Hedge Funds Review*, May 27, 2008.

Sharpe, Robert. "America's War on Drugs Fuels Crime." *Morning Call*, November 4, 2007.

Sharrock, David, and Philippe Naughton. "Ireland Votes No to Europe." *Times* (London), June 13, 2008.

Shedlock, Michael. "Currency Twilight Zone." *Mish's Global Economic Trend Analysis*, November 26, 2007. http://globaleconomicanalysis.blogspot.com/2007/11/currency-twilight-zone.html (accessed November 27, 2007).

Shedlock, Michael. "Monetary Shock Therapy." *Mish's Global Economic Trend Analysis*, December 21, 2006. http://globaleconomicanalysis.blogspot.com/2006/12/monetary-shock-therapy.html (accessed December 21, 2006).

Sheehan, Paul. "Why the West Is Riding for a Fall." *Sydney Morning Herald*, January 15, 2005.

Shelton, Judy. "The Weak-Dollar Threat to World Order." *Wall Street Journal*, June 9, 2008.

Shen, Pu. "The P/E Ratio and Stock Market Performance." *Economic Review*, Fourth Quarter, 2000. www.kc.frb.org.

Sherwell, Philip, and William Lowther. "Russia Threatens to Supply Iran with Top New Missile System as 'Cold War' Escalates." *Telegraph* (UK), August 31, 2008.

"The Shifting Power Equation: Economics." *Digitaleconomyinter*, January 25, 2007. http://digitaleconomyinter.blogspot.com/2007/01/economics.html (accessed January 26, 2007).

Shilling, A. Gary. "Sell Commodities." *Forbes*, March 10, 2008.

Shinkle, Kirk. "Q&A: Jim Rogers, Adventures in Chinese Capitalism." *U.S. News & World Report*, November 29, 2007.

Shlapentokh, Dmitry. "Wary of China, Russians Look West." *Asia Times Online*, July 24, 2008. www.atimes.com/atimes/Central_Asia/JG24Ag01.html (accessed July 27, 2008).

Shorrock, Tim. "Exposing Bush's Historic Abuse of Power." *Salon*, July 23, 2008.

Shulman, Robin. "Fed Up by Food Prices, Many Grow It Alone." *Washington Post*, August 3, 2008.

Sierra, Sandra. "Chavez Threatens U.S. Oil Cutoff." Associated Press, February 10, 2008.

"The Silent Tsunami." *Economist*, April 17, 2008.

Silverblatt, Howard. "America's Other Pension Problem." *BusinessWeek*, December 19, 2005.

Silverman, Rachel Emma. "A Fortress for Your Money: How to Guard against Lawsuits and Other Claims on Assets; The 'Equity Strip' Maneuver." *Wall Street Journal*, July 15, 2006.

Simmons, Matthew R. *Twilight in the Desert: The Coming Saudi Oil Shock and the World Economy*. New York: John Wiley & Sons, 2005.

"Simmons, Oil ... Just the Beginning." *Angry Bear*, January 8, 2008. http://angrybear.blogspot.com/2008/01/simmons-oiljust-beginning.html (accessed January 8, 2008).

Simons, Bright B., Evans Lartey, and Franklin Cudjoe. "Titans Make Africa Their Stomping Ground." *Asia Times Online*, May 13, 2007. www.atimes.com/atimes/printN.html (accessed July 1, 2008).

Slackman, Michael. "In Egypt, Muslim-Christian Divide Seems Wider." *International Herald Tribune*, August 2, 2008.

Slater, Joanna. "As Yen Slides, Fears Mount of a Shakeout." *Wall Street Journal*, January 31, 2007.

Slater, Joanna. "Investors Bet Persian Gulf Will Loosen Dollar Pegs." *Wall Street Journal*, May 27, 2008.

Slavin, Barbara. "Beijing Builds Ties with Latin Countries." *USA Today*, May 4, 2006.

Smith, Charles Hugh. "Generational War and Our Future Prosperity." *Of Two Minds*, March 20, 2008. http://charleshughsmith.blogspot.com/2008/03/generational-war-and-our-future.html (accessed March 21, 2008).

Smith, Charles Hugh. "Inflation/Deflation III: The Limits of Deflation." *Of Two Minds*, January 10, 2007. www.oftwominds.com/blog.html (accessed January 10, 2007).

Smith, Charles Hugh. "The U.S.A.: The Third World's First Superpower." *Of Two Minds*, April 16, 2008. www.oftwominds.com/blogapr08/USA-TW.html (accessed April 17, 2008).

Smith, Rebecca. "New Wave of Nuclear Plants Faces High Costs." *Wall Street Journal*, May 12, 2008.

Smith, Yves. "International Trade Seizing Up Due to Banking Crisis (Updated)." *Naked Capitalism*, October 10, 2008. www.nakedcapitalism.com/2008/10/international-trade-seizing-up-due-to.html (accessed October 10, 2008).

Smith, Yves. "Private Sector Cooling on the Dollar." *Naked Capitalism*, February 16, 2008. www.nakedcapitalism.com/2008/02/private-sector-cooling-on-dollar.html (accessed March 18, 2008).

Sniffen, Michael J. "FBI: Violent and Property Crime Dropped in 2007." Associated Press, June 9, 2008.

Solomon, Deborah, and Damian Paletta. "U.S. Drafts Sweeping Plan to Fight Crisis as Turmoil Worsens in Credit Markets." *Wall Street Journal*, September 19, 2008.

Solomon, Deborah, Damian Paletta, Jon Hilsenrath, and Aaron Lucchetti. "U.S. to Buy Stakes in Nation's Largest Banks." *Wall Street Journal*, October 14, 2008.

Solomon, Deborah, and David Enrich. "Devil Is in Bailout's Details." *Wall Street Journal*, October 15, 2008.

Solomon, Jay. "Bush's Waning Term Gives Adversaries Time to Maneuver." *Wall Street Journal*, August 11, 2008.

Solomon, Jay. "Pakistani May Have Delivered Advanced Nuclear Designs." *Wall Street Journal*, June 16, 2008.

Solomon, Jay, Neil King Jr., and Marc Champion. "Russia Agrees to Halt War." *Wall Street Journal*, August 13, 2008.

Solomon, Jay, and Cam Simpson. "U.S. Will Attempt to Bolster Lebanese Government." *Wall Street Journal*, May 14, 2008.

Solomon, Jay, Cam Simpson, and Farnaz Fassihi. "Mideast's Balance of Power Shifts Away from U.S." *Wall Street Journal*, July 21, 2008.

Solomon, Jay, and Peter Wonacott. "U.S.-India Nuclear Deal Faces Uncertain Future." *Wall Street Journal*, May 15, 2008.

Solomon, Jay, and Siobhan Gorman. "Financial Crisis May Diminish American Sway." *Wall Street Journal*, October 17, 2008.

"Soros: Market Turmoil Sign of Shifting Influence." *Bangkok Post*, January 23, 2008.

Sorrells, Niels C., and Andrew Peaple. "Germany Seeks EU Curbs on Some Foreign Takeovers." *Wall Street Journal*, July 19, 2007.

"South American Leaders Support Evo Morales Amid Boliva Crisis." Associated Press, September 17, 2008.

"South American Union Is Created." Associated Press, May 24, 2008.

"South Korean Companies Pull Out of China without Paying Salaries or Debts." *AsiaNews*, February 16, 2008. http://new.asianews.it/index.php?l=en&art=11539 (accessed February 19, 2008).

"Sovereign Impunity." *Wall Street Journal*, December 1, 2007.

"Sovereign Wealth Funds Grow to $3.3 Trillion—Report." *CNN Money*, March 31, 2008.

Spencer, Jane. "U.S. Joins Climate Change Pact Laying Out Emissions 'Road Map.'" *Wall Street Journal*, December 16, 2007.

Spencer, Richard. "North Korea Provokes U.S. with Missile Test." *Telegraph* (UK), March 29, 2008.

Spindle, Bill. "Desert Oasis: Boom in Investment Powers Mideast Growth." *Wall Street Journal*, June 19, 2007.

Spors, Kelly K. "Green Acres II: When Neighbors Become Farmers." *Wall Street Journal*, April 22, 2008.

Squatriglia, Chuck. "Plug-In Hybrid Leads Toyota's Drive Beyond Oil." *Wired*, June 11, 2008. http://blog.wired/cars/2008/06/plug-in-hybrid.html (accessed June 13, 2008).

Stack, Megan K., and Borzou Daragahi. "Nations with Vast Oil Wealth Gaining Clout." *Los Angeles Times*, July 17, 2008.

Stålenheim, Petter, Catalina Perdomo, and Elisabeth Sköns. "Military Expenditure." *SIPRI Yearbook 2007*, Chapter 8. Stockholm International Peace Research Institute, June 11, 2007. http://yearbook2007.sipri.org/chap8 (accessed March 1, 2008).

Stark, Betsy. "The Future of the Workplace: No Office, Headquarters in Cyberspace; Some Companies Don't Care Where Workers Are as Long as They Get the Job Done." *ABC News* (Australia), August 27, 2007.

"States in Armed Conflict." Uppsala University Department of Peace and Conflict Research, December 21, 2007. http://info.uu.se/press.nsf/pm/number.of.idF52.html (accessed December 22, 2007).

Stein, Jeff. "Can You Tell a Sunni from a Shiite?" *New York Times*, October 17, 2006.

Steingart, Gabor. "America and the Dollar Illusion." *Spiegel Online*, October 25, 2006. www.spiegel.de/international/0,1518,440054,00.html (accessed October 26, 2006).

Steingart, Gabor. "Is America Slouching Towards Protectionism?" *Spiegel Online*, January 8, 2008. www.spiegel.de/international/business/0,1518,druck-527289,00.html (accessed January 10, 2008).

Steinhaur, Jennifer. "Governor Declares Drought in California." *New York Times*, June 5, 2008.

Stephens, Philip. "Uncomfortable Truths for a New World of Them and Us." *Financial Times*, May 30, 2008.

Stewart, Gaither. "The Crowded Rightwing Life Rafts or the Great Social-Political Divide: Left or Right." *Crimes and Corruption of the New World Order News*, December 11, 2007. http://mparent7777-2.blogspot.com/2007/12/american-counter-revolution.html (accessed December 12, 2007).

Stewart, Heather. "U.S.-China Trade War Looms." *Observer* (UK), March 26, 2006.

Steyn, Mark. "It's the Demography, Stupid." *Wall Street Journal; Opinion Journal*, January 4, 2006.

Stiglitz, Joseph E. "Central Banks Need to Act Pre-Emptively, Not Reactively." *Gulf Times* (Qatar), February 3, 2008.

Stiglitz, Joseph E. "Falling Down." *New Republic*, September 10, 2008.

Stiglitz, Joseph E. "The End of Neo-Liberalism?" *Daily News Egypt*, July 7, 2008.

Stinson, Jeffrey. "Mosques Increasingly Not Welcome in Europe." *USA Today*, July 17, 2008.

Stobbe, Mike. "U.S. Expectancy Rate Rises." Associated Press, December 8, 2005.

Strahan, David. "Have We Reached the End of the Road for Oil?" *Telegraph* (UK), August 9, 2008.

Strahan, David. "Oil Is Expensive Because Oil Is Scarce." *Telegraph* (UK), May 3, 2008.

Strauss, Lawrence C. "Light-Years Ahead of the Crowd: Interview with James B. Rogers, Private Investor." *Barron's*, April 14, 2008.

Strohecker, Karin. "More Countries Could Develop Nuclear Bombs." Reuters, October 16, 2006.

Strohecker, Karin. "World Sea Levels Seen Rising 1.5 M by 2100." Reuters, April 15, 2008.

"The Struggle to Satisfy China and India's Hunger." *Spiegel Online*, April 28, 2008. www.spiegel.de/international/worl/0,1518,druck-550943,00.html (accessed May 2, 2008).

Subik, Jason. "Forum Sees Oil Peak as World Crisis." *Daily Gazette*, June 7, 2008.

"Suffolk Bird Flu Is H5N1 Strain." *BBC News*, November 13, 2007.

Summers, Lawrence H. "Different Money, Different Rules." *International Herald Tribune*, January 30, 2008.

Summers, Lawrence H. "The Global Consensus on Trade is Unraveling." *Financial Times*, August 24, 2008.

Sun, Yu-huay. "Taiwan's Ma May Scrap Fuel-Price Controls, Boost Nuclear Power." *Bloomberg*, March 20, 2008.

Surowiecki, James. "In Yuan We Trust." *New Yorker*, April 18, 2005.

Swann, Christopher, and Kevin Carmichael. "Dollar's Share of Currency Reserves Falls, IMF Says." *Bloomberg*, December 28, 2007.

"The Swedish Model." *Economist*, June 12, 2008.

"Syrian Official: We're Prepared for War." *Jerusalem Post*, April 8, 2008.

Tahmincioglu, Eve. "The Quiet Revolution: Telecommuting." *MSNBC*, August 23, 2007.

"Taiwan Says China Arms Buildup Having International Repercussions." *Asia Pacific News*, May 11, 2008.

Talton, Jon. "Anxiety Spreads over Decline in U.S. Job Quality." *Arizona Republic*, September 21, 2006.

Talvi, Silja J. A. "As the Violence Soars, Mexico Signals It's Had Enough of America's Stupid War on Drugs." *AlterNet*, October 14, 2008. www.alternet.org/drugreporter/102857/ (accessed October 14, 2008).

Tanzi, Alex. "U.S. First Quarter Assets Held by Foreign Investors." *Bloomberg*, June 5, 2008.

"Tarapore for Increasing Gold Component in Forex Reserves." *Financial Express* (India), November 28, 2006.

Taylor, Bryan. "Trade Also Serves the Cause of Peace." *Barron's*, October 22, 2007.

Taylor, Rob. "Canada Rated World's Soundest Bank System: Survey." Reuters, October 9, 2008.

"10 Year Window to Prepare for Water Shortages—Conference." Reuters, June 9, 2008.

"The Terrorism Index." Foreign Policy and the Center for American Progress, August 18, 2008. www.americanprogress.org/issues/2008/08/terrorism_index.html (accessed August 19, 2008).

Tett, Gillian. "The Era of Leverage Is Over." *Financial Times*, September 22, 2008.

Tett, Gillian. "Western Banks Face Backlash as They Hand Out Begging Bowl." *Financial Times*, February 8, 2008.

Tett, Gillian, and Paul J. Davies. "Out of the Shadows: How Banking's Secret System Broke Down." *Financial Times*, December 16, 2007.

Thirlwell, Mark. "Food and the Specter of Malthus." *Financial Times*, February 26, 2008.

Thoma, Mark. "Are We Headed for Collapse?" *Economist's View*, November 10, 2007. http://economistsview.typepad.com/economistsview/2007/11/are-we-headed-f.html (accessed November 11, 2007).

Thomas, Landon, Jr. "Cash-Rich, Publicity-Shy, Abu Dhabi Fund Draws Scrutiny." *New York Times*, February 28, 2008.

"Thomas Malthus." *Wikipedia*, March 9, 2008. http://en.wikipedia.org/wiki/Thomas_Malthus (accessed March 10, 2008).

Thompson, Christopher. "The Scramble for Africa's Oil." *New Statesman*, June 14, 2007. www.newstatesman.com.

Thornhill, John. "Poll Shows Wide Dislike of Wealth Gap." *Financial Times*, May 18, 2008.

Thornton, Emily, and Stanley Reed. "Who's Afraid of Mideast Money?" *BusinessWeek*, January 10, 2008.

Thornton, Philip. "IMF: Risk of Global Crash Is Increasing." *Independent* (UK), September 13, 2006.

"Thousands Demonstrate as Belgian Political Crisis Hits Pockets." *Agence France-Presse*, December 16, 2007.

Tickell, Oliver. "On a Planet 4C Hotter, All We Can Prepare for Is Extinction." *Guardian* (UK), August 11, 2008.

"'Time of Dominance of One Economy, One Currency Is Over.'" *Economic Times*, October 3, 2008.

Timmons, Heather. "Trouble at Fannie Mae and Freddie Mac Stirs Concern Abroad." *New York Times*, July 21, 2008.

Tiomkin, Avi. "The Demise of the Euro." *Forbes*, April 21, 2008.

Tisdall, Simon. "The Clock Is Ticking." *Guardian* (UK), May 14, 2007.

"Tomgram: Chalmers Johnson, How to Sink America." *TomDispatch.com*, January 22, 2008. www.tomdispatch.com/post/174884/chalmers_johnson_how_to_sink_america (accessed February 3, 2008).

"Tomgram: Chalmers Johnson, The Pentagon Bailout Fraud." *TomDispatch.com*, September 28, 2008. www.tomdispatch.com/post/174982 (accessed October 7, 2008).

"Tomgram: Living in the Ruins." *TomDispatch.com*, October 13, 2008. www.tomdispatch.com/post/174988/living_in_the_ruins (accessed October 14, 2008).

"Total Credit Market Debt as a % of GDP." Ned Davis Research, Inc. 2007. www.comstockfunds.com/files/NLPP00000%5C292.pdf (accessed March 15, 2008).

Traynor, Ian. "Blueprint for Nuclear Warhead Found on Smugglers' Computers." *Guardian* (UK), June 16, 2008.

Traynor, Ian. "Bush Orders Clampdown on Flights to U.S." *Guardian* (UK), February 11, 2008.

Traynor, Ian. "France Unveils Pact on EU-Wide Immigration." *Guardian* (UK), July 8, 2008.

Traynor, Ian. "Pre-Emptive Nuclear Strike a Key Option, NATO Told." *Guardian* (UK), January 22, 2008.

Trumbull, Mark. "Why Budget Fixes Can't Wait; Rising Longevity, Healthcare Costs, and Federal Obligations Will Force a Reckoning in the US, Experts Say." *Christian Science Monitor*, January 10, 2006.

Tsai, Ting-I. "U.S. Weapons Package for Taiwan Stalls as China Tensions Ease." *Wall Street Journal*, July 21, 2008.

Tschang, Chi-Chu. "China Looks to Coal Bed Methane." *BusinessWeek*, January 3, 2008.

"The Twilight Zone." *Wikipedia*, May 17, 2008. http://en.wikipedia.org/wiki/The_Twilight_Zone (accessed May 22, 2008).

"2007: Deadliest Year for U.S. in Iraq." Associated Press, December 31, 2007.

"Ukrainian Defense Minister Reaffirms Ambition to Join NATO Despite Domestic Tensions." Associated Press, February 7, 2008.

"Under Attack: America Is Being Blamed for the Impasse in Global Trade Talks." *Economist*, July 6, 2006.

"An Unlikely New Ally." *Newsweek*, December 12, 2007.

"UN Says 30 States Could Soon Make Nuclear Bomb." *Business Day*, October 17, 2006.

Uren, David. "Institutions Can't Cope with a Crisis." *Australian*, December 26, 2006.

"U.S. Air Force: Israel Has 400 Nukes, Building Naval Force." *World Tribune*, July 4, 2002.

"U.S. Arms Pacts to Counter Iran, Syria: Rice." *Agence France-Presse*, July 31, 2007.

"US, Czech Republic Sign Missile Shield Deal." *Agence France-Presse*, July 8, 2008.

"The U.S. Faces Serious Risks of Brownouts or Blackouts in 2009, Study Warns." NextGen Energy Council, October 1, 2008. www.nextgenenergy.org/nextgen+blackout+study.aspx (accessed October 7, 2008).

"U.S. Falls to 6th in World Competitiveness." *CNN Money*, September 26, 2006.

"U.S. Figures Show 25.6 Pct of Citizens Obese." Reuters, July 17, 2008.

"U.S. Military 'at Breaking Point.'" *BBC News*, January 26, 2006.

"The U.S. Military Index." *Foreign Policy*, March/April 2008.

"US, Russia, China in Fierce Battle to Sell Fighter Jets in Asia." *Agence France-Presse*, March 23, 2008.

"US Urged to Bolster Missile, Space Defenses against China: Paper." *Agence France-Presse*, October 1, 2008.

"U.S. Sovereign Ratings Could Be Undermined by L-T Age-Related Spending Trends, Says S&P Report." *PR Newswire*, June 6, 2006.

"U.S. Troops to Hold Exercises in Georgia, Ukraine." *Agence France-Presse*, July 14, 2008.

"US: Venezuela Purchases Four Times More Weapons Than It Needs." *El Universal*, February 27, 2008.

"U.S. War Spending 'Out of Control.'" *Agence France-Presse*, May 28, 2008.

Vause, John. "Chinese Hackers: No Site Is Safe." *CNN*, July 3, 2008.

"Venezuela Breaks Ties with Exxon." *BBC News*, February 13, 2008.

"Venezuela to Buy Chinese Combat Planes: Chavez." *Agence France-Presse*, September 21, 2008.

Vohra, Subhash. "U.S. Concerns over India-Iran Gas Pipeline." *VOA News*, June 18, 2008.

Waddington, Richard, and William Schomberg. "World Trade Talks Collapse." *Reuters*, July 24, 2006.

Walker, Richard W. "Infrastructure Security on GAO's High-Risk List." *Government Computer News*, January 31, 2007. www.gcn.com/online/vol1_ no1/43029-1.html (accessed January 31, 2007).

Walsh, Bryan. "Finding Energy All Around Us." *Time*, March 6, 2008.

Walsh, Mary Williams. "More Companies Ending Promises for Retirement." *New York Times*, January 9, 2006.

Walter, Matthew. "Chavez Goes Weapons Shopping in Russia amid Arms Race." *Bloomberg*, July 21, 2008.

Ward, Sandra. "Yes, $8,000 an Ounce." *Barron's*, May 29, 2006.

"War Fears Put British Troops on Standby as Kosovo Declares 'Freedom.'" *Daily Mail* (UK), February 17, 2008.

Wasik, Bill. "Military Thinkers Discuss the Unthinkable." *Harper's*, April 2006.

"Water in the Works in December 07." *Angry Bear*, January 7, 2008. http:// angrybear.blogspot.com/2008/01/water-in-works-in-december-07.html (accessed January 8, 2008).

Watson, Paul Joseph. "Popular CNN Host Attacks Bush Administration for 'Shameless' Destruction of Sovereignty." *Prison Planet*, March 7, 2008. www. prisonplanet.com/articles/march2008/030708_be_defeated.htm (accessed March 8, 2008).

Watts, William L. "South Korean Fund Said to Shun Treasurys." *MarketWatch*, March 27, 2008.

"Weapons of Mass Destruction in the Middle East." Center for Nonproliferation Studies at the Monterey Institute of International Studies, November 14, 2006. http://cns.miis.edu/research/wmdme/ (accessed February 17, 2008).

Webber, Jude. "Argentine Debt Surge Raises Specter of Default." *Financial Times*, June 13, 2008.

Webb-Vidal, Andy. "Bush Told to Plan for Chavez Oil Shock." *Financial Times*, July 24, 2006.

Wei, Tan. "China's CIC Likely to Diversify Away from Further U.S. Banking Sector Investments, Source Says." *Financial Times*, December 30, 2007.

Weinthal, Benjamin. "Switzerland to Sign Huge Iran Gas Deal." *Jerusalem Post*, March 16, 2008.

Weisman, Steven R. "Eased Rules on Tech Sales to China Questioned." *New York Times*, January 2, 2008.

Weisman, Steven R. "Trade Bills Now Face Tough Odds." *New York Times*, November 16, 2006.

Wessel, David. "Fishing Out Facts on the Wealth Gap." *Wall Street Journal*, February 15, 2007.

Wessel, David, and Bob Davis. "Pain from Free Trade Spurs Second Thoughts." *Wall Street Journal*, March 28, 2007.

Wessels, Vernon, and Nasreen Seria. "South African Immigrant Attacks Spread to Cape Town." *Bloomberg*, May 23, 2008.

"West Must Prepare for Chinese, Indian Dominance: Wolfensohn." *Agence France-Presse*, November 26, 2006.

Whalen, Jeanne, Alan Cullison, and Andrew Higgins. "For Putin, a Line in the Sand." *Wall Street Journal*, August 12, 2008.

"What Americans Don't Know (But Should) about the Middle East." *Palestine's Daily Voices*, September 27, 2007. http://desertpeace.blogspot.com/2007/09/what-americans-dont-know-but-should.html (accessed September 27, 2007).

"What Comes after Unipolarity?" *Financial Times*, April 15, 2008.

"What Does Iraq Cost? Even More Than You Think." *Washington Post*, November 18, 2007.

"What Is the Earth Worth?" *Automatic Earth*, May 27, 2008. http://theautomaticearth.blogspot.com/2008/05/what-is-earth-worth.html (accessed May 28, 2008).

"When World Powers Invest Like Hedge Funds." *News Journal*, December 24, 2007.

"Where to Live and Collapse Survival." *Survival Acres*, July 31, 2007. http://survivalacres.com/wordpress/?p=815 (accessed August 1, 2007).

White, Jeffrey. "Germany: Germans Sour on Capitalism amid Corporate Scandals." *CorpWatch*, March 25, 2008. www.corpwatch.org/article. php?id=14986&printsafe=1 (accessed March 25, 2008).

Whitehouse, Mark, and Jeanne Whalen. "Russia's Geopolitical Aims Trump Investors' Concerns." *Wall Street Journal*, August 11, 2008.

"Who Wants to Be a Trillionaire?" *Economist*, October 26, 2006.

"Why SWFs Will Not Fix the Western Financial Mess." *Financial Times*, December 16, 2007.

Wiggins, Jenny. "Nestle Chief Warns of Land Resources Clash." *Financial Times*, February 22, 2008.

Wilkinson, Isambard. "Pakistan Facing Bankruptcy." *Telegraph* (UK), October 6, 2008.

Williams, Alex. "Duck and Cover: It's the New Survivalism." *New York Times*, April 6, 2008.

Wills, Ken. "China's Shoreline Waters Seriously Polluted: Expert." Reuters, June 8, 2008.

Wilmot, Jonathan. "View of the Day: Lessons from Past Commodity Bubbles." *Financial Times*, March 18, 2008.

Wilson, Bee. "The Last Bite." *New Yorker*, May 19, 2008.

Wilson, Harry. "Sovereign Wealth Funds Start Flexing Their Financial Muscle." *Financial News*, January 7, 2008.

Windrem, Robert. "'Obliterate?' Israel Can Defend Itself." *MSNBC*, May 5, 2008.

Woellert, Lorraine. "WTO Online-Gambling Edict Prompts U.S. Resistance to Trade Rule." *Bloomberg*, December 16, 2007.

Wolf, Jim. "U.S. Shot Raises Tensions and Worries over Satellites." Reuters, February 21, 2008.

Wolf, Martin. "Challenge of Rescuing World Economy." *Financial Times*, September 11, 2007.

Wolf, Martin. "Challenges for the World's Divided Economy." *Financial Times*, January 8, 2008.

Wolf, Martin. "The Dangers of Living in a Zero-Sum World Economy." *Financial Times*, December 18, 2007.

Wolf, Martin. "Food Crisis Is a Chance to Reform Global Agriculture." *Financial Times*, April 29, 2008.

Wolf, Martin. "The Market Sets High Oil Prices to Tell Us What to Do." *Financial Times*, May 14, 2008.

Wolf, Martin. "The Rescue of Bear Stearns Marks Liberalization's Limit." *Financial Times*, March 25, 2008.

Wolf, Martin. "A Slowing U.S. Could Brake the World." *Financial Times*, September 26, 2006.

Wolf, Martin. "Welcome to a World of Runaway Energy Demand." *Financial Times*, November 13, 2007.

Wolf, Martin. "Why Banking Is an Accident Waiting to Happen." *Financial Times*, November 27, 2007.

Wolf, Martin. "Why Putin's Rule Threatens Both Russia and the West." *Financial Times*, February 12, 2008.

Wolf, Martin. "Why the Climate Change Wolf Is So Hard to Kill Off." *Financial Times*, December 4, 2007.

Wolf, Martin. "Why Washington's Rescue Cannot End Crisis Story." *Financial Times*, February 26, 2008.

Wolf, Naomi. "Fascist America, in 10 Easy Steps." *Guardian* (UK), April 24, 2007.

Wolfensberger, Marc. "Iran May Reduce Use of Dollar, Tehran Papers Say." *Bloomberg*, December 6, 2006.

Wolff, Max Fraad. "Bridging the Globalism-Nationalism Gap." *Asia Times Online*, July 20, 2007. www.atimes.com/atimes/Global_Economy/IG20Dj01.html (accessed July 20, 2007).

Wong, Edward. "Booming, China Faults U.S. Policy on the Economy." *New York Times*, June 17, 2008.

Woodall, Pam. "The Unfinished Recession." *Economist*, September 26, 2002.

Woods, Amanda. "The Plastic Killing Fields." *Sydney Morning Herald*, December 29, 2007.

"World Bank Study Says 12 Economies Account for More Than Two-Thirds of World's Output; Chinese Economy Cut by 40%; Ireland Is Fourth Most Expensive World Economy." *Finfacts*, December 19, 2007. www.finfacts.com/irishfinancenews/International_4/article_101258_printer.shtml (accessed March 17, 2008).

"World 1950–2050 by Region: Historic, Current and Future Population." *GeoHive*. N.d. www.xist.org/earth/his_proj_region.aspx (accessed January 7, 2008).

"World Poll Finds Global Leadership Vacuum." *World Public Opinion.org*, June 17, 2008. www.worldpublicopinion.org/incl/printable_version.php?pnt=488 (accessed June 17, 2008).

"World Population Ageing: 1950–2050." Population Division, Department of Economic and Social Affairs (DESA), United Nations, 2002. www.un.org/esa/population/publications/worldageing19502050/ (accessed December 16, 2007).

"World's Best Medical Care?" *New York Times*, August 12, 2007.

Wright, Robin, and Joby Warrick, "Purchases Linked N. Korean to Syria." *Washington Post*, May 11, 2008.

Wright, Tom. "Trade Focus Now Shifts to Regional Deals." *New York Times*, July 26, 2006.

Wright, Tom, and Steven R. Weisman. "Trade Talks Fail over an Impasse on Farm Tariffs." *New York Times*, July 25, 2006.

Wroughton, Lesley. "Higher Food Prices Here to Stay: World Bank." Reuters, April 9, 2008.

"WTO: Developing, Transition Economies Cushion Trade Slowdown." World Trade Organization, April 17, 2008. www.wto.org/english/news_e/pres08_e/pr520_e.htm (accessed April 18, 2008).

Wynn, Gerard. "Water Shapes Up as New Investment Class." Reuters, March 19, 2008.

Wynne-Jones, Jonathan. "Britain Has Become a 'Catholic Country.'" *Telegraph* (UK), December 23, 2007.

Wysocki, Bernard, Jr., and Aaron Lucchetti. "Global Exchanges Pose a Quandary for Securities Cops." *Wall Street Journal*, June 5, 2006.

Yao, Kevin, and Benjamin Kang Lim. "Senior Official Urges Cut in U.S. Debt Holding." Reuters, April 4, 2006.

Yardley, Jim. "Though Water Is Drying Up, a Chinese Metropolis Booms." *International Herald Tribune*, September 27, 2007.

Yidi, Zhao, and Kevin Hamlin. "China Shuns Paulson's Free Market Push as Meltdown Burns U.S." *Bloomberg*, September 23, 2008.

Ying, Wang. "China Shuts More Coal Power Plants; Warns on Shortage." *Bloomberg*, July 8, 2008.

Youngquist, Walter. "Alternative Energy Sources." *Minnesotans for Sustainability*, October 2000. www.mnforsustain.org/youngquist_w_alternative_energy_sources.htm (accessed June 21, 2008).

Yuan, Helen. "China to Introduce, Raise Steel, Iron Export Tariffs." *Bloomberg*, December 26, 2007.

Zakaria, Fareed. *The Post-American World*. New York: W.W. Norton, 2008.

Zakaria, Fareed. "The Rise of the Rest." *Newsweek*, May 3, 2008.

Zarakhovich, Yuri. "Why the Russia-Georgia Spat Could Become a U.S. Headache." *Time*, October 3, 2006.

Zaslow, Jeff. "Dealing with Hatred: How the Torrent of Anti-Americanism Affects Teenagers." *Wall Street Journal*, October 5, 2006.

"Zogby Poll: 67 Percent View Traditional Journalism as 'Out of Touch.'" Zogby International, February 27, 2008. www.zogby.com/news/ReadNews.dbm?ID=1454 (accessed March 1, 2008).

Zweig, Jason. "What History Tells Us About the Market." *Wall Street Journal*, October 11, 2008.

About the Author

Michael J. Panzner is a 25-year veteran of the global stock, bond, and currency markets who has worked in New York and London for such leading companies as HSBC, Soros Funds, ABN Amro, Dresdner Bank, and J.P. Morgan Chase.

He is the author of *Financial Armageddon: Protecting Your Future from Four Impending Catastrophes* and *The New Laws of the Stock Market Jungle: An Insider's Guide to Successful Investing in a Changing World,* and has been a columnist for TheStreet.com's RealMoney service and a contributor to BloggingStocks.com.

Panzner is also a New York Institute of Finance faculty member and a graduate of Columbia University.

Index